Sexual Abuse – The Child's Voice

of related interest

Boys: Sexual Abuse and Treatment
Anders Nyman and Börje Svensson
ISBN 1 85302 491 0

Play Therapy with Abused Children
Ann Cattanach
ISBN 1 85302 193 8

Good Practice in Child Protection
A Manual for Professionals
Edited by Hilary Owen and Jacki Pritchard
ISBN 1 85302 205 5

Child Welfare Services
Developments in Law, Policy, Practice and Research
Edited by Malcolm Hill and Jane Aldgate
ISBN 1 85302 316 7

Sexual Abuse – The Child's Voice
Poppies on the Rubbish Heap

Madge Bray

Edited and Introduced by Sarah Boyle

Jessica Kingsley Publishers
London and Bristol, Pennsylvania

First published in the United Kingdom in 1991 by
Canongate Press

This edition first published in 1997 by
Jessica Kingsley Publishers Ltd
116 Pentonville Road
London N1 9JB, England
and
1900 Frost Road, Suite 101
Bristol, PA 19007, U S A

Library of Congress Cataloguing in Publication Data
A CIP catalogue record for this book is available from the Library of Congress

British Library Cataloguing in Publication Data
A CIP catalogue record for this book is available from the British Library

ISBN 1 85302 487 2

Printed and bound in Great Britain by
Athenaeum Press, Gateshead, Tyne and Wear

ACKNOWLEDGEMENTS

Grateful thanks to my family, and especially to my parents who held my own childhood in their safe keeping. To my mother for her wisdom and patience, and for typing the manuscript. To Sarah, for her perseverance and love, during the times when the completion of this book seemed an impossibility. To Mary for the quality of our relationship and for the quiet balance she provides in the creation of our shared dream. To our remarkable staff team, at SACCS and now at Leaps and Bounds for their creativity, commitment and tolerance of my many foibles. Above all, however, I would like to acknowledge the small person, somewhere, dry mouthed and afraid, who, as I write, is preparing to face an abuser. To that child, I dedicate this book.

CONTENTS

INTRODUCTION

The world of the abused child is one which is unfamiliar and inherently shocking to most of us. The taboo, which has cloaked and concealed the whole issue of sexual abuse up until recently, still functions to keep the door closed on a realm of human experience which for many of us defies belief. Emotionally we want to shut it out – it doesn't happen in our world, in our families, or amongst our friends. Yet the subject doesn't go away. The unpalatable statistics, reports of appalling sexual attacks on children, and harrowing accounts from adult survivors all bear witness to the scale of the problem. Throughout the country those who work in the caring professions continue to encounter sexual abuse amongst their case loads with undiminished frequency. As a result the medical and social services are being acutely stressed by what is emerging to be a major child health problem in our society. Whether we like it or not we are being forced to recognise that child sexual abuse is widespread and is an issue which directly or indirectly will affect many of us.

It is an emotive subject. Deep down in our gut it provokes torrents of revulsion, shock, anger and disgust to a point where being reasonable about the issue seems impossible. We want to deny its existence because to encompass the truth is intolerable to the person who basically sees society as a good place, containing nice people who don't do those sort of things. We shun the problem and instead direct our venom at dirty old men in rain coats, sex perverts, beasts, and certain lower income problem families – in other words people who have nothing in common with us and who do not belong in our world. 'What sort of a person could do THAT?' is used to justify our dismissal of those who commit these kinds of offences and slams the lid on something we basically wish to know no more about. It's part of an old adage – if you don't speak about it, it'll go away.

We feel reassured every time an offender is put behind bars, but in reality these offences, the great majority of which take place in the privacy of the home, shrouded by secrecy and denial, are far from easy to detect. The conviction rate for sexual offences against children is low because of this. The nub of the matter is that it is extremely difficult to protect children because parents are placed in a position of enormous trust which endows them with a great deal of power. If parental trust is breached the child is uniquely powerless and isolated. This exploitation of children to gratify adult sexual needs is a phenomenon which takes place in all sections of society. This fact in itself challenges many of our preconceptions. The abuser cannot be distinguished by any particular characteristic, and by the same token, neither can the child recipients of abuse. What happens to these children? How can they be reached? How are they affected? What can we do to help them? These are important matters about which we are as a whole poorly informed, because this is a realm of experience which is beyond the reach of most of us.

In this context it is ironic that the public debate is more focused on what punishment should be meted out to abusers, rather than on the measures we need to adopt to protect children and safeguard their well-being. It is an area rife with contradictions. We have for example a high profile public campaign which tells children to say 'No' to strangers, while there is in contrast a complete absence of advice for the child who is being sexually exploited by a parent. How should unwelcome approaches by adults in the home, be they family member, friend, or babysitter be resisted? Our inability to address this issue reflects our continuing difficulty in accepting that many children are abused, not by strangers, but by those who are supposed to be responsible for their care.

Children attempting to tell their stories continue to be met with denial and disbelief. They are told that they have over-active imaginations or that they have been watching too many videos. Professionals grapple with the problem, often inadequately prepared by their training, stressed by expanding work loads and limited by structures and practices which are adult, rather than child centred. Their difficulties are compounded by being vulnerable to sudden swings in public opinion which may on the one hand berate them for failing in their duties to protect a child, on the other castigate them for removing a child without sufficient evidence and doing an injustice to parents. Even such an eminent professional as Freud was driven to deny his patients' stories of childhood sexual abuse, describing them instead as fantasies. While his lack of moral courage is understandable, particularly in a historical context, his failure to acknowledge the reality behind these stories unfortunately resulted in the whole issue becoming clouded with layers of theory and prejudice which have had a deep and long lasting effect. Meanwhile we can only wonder how many children are helplessly trapped in situations where they are having to endure ongoing abuse because of the inability of the adult world to see, hear, and act on what they are trying to tell us.

Given this situation with its backdrop of virulent public debate and the clamour of professionals crossing swords, it is hardly surprising that the voice and experience of the abused child is the most silenced voice of all. Yet it is ultimately from these children that we have most to learn. Only from them can we begin to understand and unravel a problem which is apparently deeply embedded in our social fabric. This book is about building a bridge of communication with such children. Madge Bray is a social work consultant who has developed a particular expertise in this area. She is a uniquely visionary and creative person who has evolved her own approach to communicating with children who have had abusive experiences. In addition to this she has, with an equally skilled colleague, Mary Walsh, established an independent agency SACCS – Sexual Abuse: Child Consultancy Service. The services offered through SACCS include individual work with children, support and preparation for fostering and adoptive parents, and training for different groups of professionals. They believe that it is largely through the medium of play that children communicate their thoughts and feelings to the world. If we as adults can cross the bridge into the child's world, we can share its journey.

Madge Bray has written about her own journey across this bridge and through the medium of stories, created from her personal experience of working with abused children, she offers us glimpses into their world. The impetus for this book has been based on her conviction that these children are in many senses our best teachers. Writing the book has not been easy because of the obvious dilemmas of confidentiality, and protecting identities, not to mention the pressures of the work itself and the shortage of time because of long hours spent seeing children and training. Despite the difficulty of the task a book seemed essential as a contribution towards bridging the gap in understanding between these children and the adult world. Assistance was required, and coming from a different professional background, but finding many similarities in approach, I stepped into the breach. Aware of my own previous ignorance of the experience of the child I was keen to see Madge Bray's unique contribution as a teacher in this area being made available and accessible to the many who I know will greatly appreciate the insights which she has to offer. It is not a textbook, because a textbook would suggest that this is a book aimed solely at professionals, rather than to a wider public which she is so anxious to reach – the parents, the carers, the fostering and adoptive families, the adult survivors and all those whose lives have in some way been touched by this problem. It is also hoped that professionals in many different spheres – social workers, doctors, the police, lawyers, politicians, teachers and policy makers – will read this book and will make use of the knowledge gained to enhance their present understanding and practice.

The essence of the approach which Madge Bray describes is simplicity. It is based on a willingness to receive, at the child's own pace, whatever it is that the child wishes to impart. As the adult she listens, responds and sets the boundaries. Creating warmth and trust comes before making any attempt to impose her own adult agenda onto the process. Showing a willingness to enter into the child's own world and interact with them at this level is the overriding characteristic of her work. She sits on the floor with a toybox and creates an environment where play is the natural medium of communication. Using toys and the simplified language of the child, she is able to introduce us to this world, so that we glimpse close up the confused and contorted experience that is inflicted by adults oblivious to, or uncaring of, the consequences.

My first experience of Madge Bray was at a training session which she ran at a centre called the Gateway Exchange in Edinburgh. This session was attended by a range of different individuals – ex-prisoners, recovering drug addicts, community workers, students and volunteers. It was an unusual sight, a circle of adults gazing intently as different toys were held up for our attention. Looking at what appeared to be a pretty commonplace collection of toys, we were then shown how an abused child might react to the monsters, snakes, spiders and other such beasties which are common items in most toy shops. Toys which had looked innocent to us before, suddenly assumed frightening and disturbing connotations. Fortunately the toybox also contained comforting characters such as the wise hedgehog and big Bertha Bear who swallowed tears. Also memorable were the plastic telephones which were often used for making contact – how obvious – yet how seldom we as adults have the sense to think of how we can use these commonplace toys for purposeful play! Finally, the anatomical dolls, which some of us didn't want to touch – but if sexual parts are dominating a child's experience what better way to explore the experience than with dolls equipped with adult organs? The uneasy feelings they generated were no doubt related to the disturbing image they represented, which was of childhood innocence contaminated by adult sex.

The reactions amongst the group to the graphic and disturbing accounts of sexual abuse of children with which we were suddenly confronted, were mixed. Some of us were enthralled, moved and inspired by what we heard; many however felt deeply uncomfortable. One survivor present found memories of her own past pain being re-awakened, but she was left with a sense that if only there had been someone who could have believed her and helped her as a child, the mental distress which in her case had culminated in adulthood with a series of suicide attempts and a mental breakdown, might not have been quite so severe.

I found myself connecting to what was being said at different levels. As a mother I felt shock, nausea, and a deep aversion to what I was hearing. At the same time, as a parent I knew that if my son or daughter were ever abused, I would hope for someone like Madge who could work sensitively with them to allow and encourage whatever expression they wished to give to the experience. As a doctor, currently working in the community but with previous psychiatric experience, my knowledge of sexual abuse was limited to having met adults who were able to disclose that this was something which had happened to them in their childhoods. I was well aware of the traumatic long-term consequences of abuse which I'd seen expressing itself in a number of different ways – in depression, repeated suicide attempts, drug addiction, alcoholism, promiscuity, damaged relationships, extreme self-loathing, fear of being touched, fears of harming their own children, nightmares and deeply rooted feelings of low self-worth, guilt and inwardly directed aggression. Living with the after effects of abuse was for many equivalent to serving a life sentence where the goal of freedom from symptoms seemed impossibly far away.

From this perspective the session provoked in me a sense of the importance of refining and developing our child protection services, as well as creating more services which can help children to begin to heal from these experiences. Far too many of the women and men I have seen never received any skilled help at all when they were young, their accounts if they had attempted to tell them had been disbelieved, and the signs and the symptoms of some kind of disturbance in their lives frequently misdiagnosed and misunderstood. This is scarcely surprising when professionals as a whole are poorly prepared to provide a more sympathetic service. Changes in the legal system and in the social services are beginning to take place, but training in the area of sexual abuse is even now still patchy and skills in communicating with children are not taught as a matter of routine.

Communicating with children who have been damaged – physically, mentally and emotionally – as a result of sexual abuse is a daunting task. What Madge Bray contributes, however, is something that I consider to be of fundamental importance. She has an intuitive ability to understand the logic of a child and with unique clarity she helps us to understand how we as adults often obstruct rather than assist the natural flow of communication. As adults we have often become distanced and estranged from the world of small children. Re-entering this world requires establishing a contact with our own inner child, and drawing on our creative and imaginative resources. Many of us have simply forgotten how to use these skills but they are present in us all, for we have all been children once. With our adult need to direct and control, however, we impose formal settings and structures on children, and expect them to enter our world and relate to us on our terms. We use a flow of words and don't understand when the child clams up and avoids our gaze. We raise our voices, plead, cajole, but recognise that this impedes communication even further. We feel flustered, stuck, awkward, embarrassed. An uncommunicative child is an absolute enigma, for even the most persistent adult.

Rather than expecting children to enter our world and being frustrated by their natural reluctance to do so, Madge Bray suggests that we consider turning the whole process about. My own image for this is that if we wish to make contact with a child, we must, like Alice, be prepared to shrink in size in order to enter into the world as they experience it. We must allow ourselves to interact at the child's level, rather than the level which we are accustomed to as adults. When we enter this world, we may find things which deeply disturb us. A child having sexual knowledge and experience clashes sharply with our belief in childhood innocence and our emotions are likely to be those of shock, horror and disgust. The discovery may make us want to beat a hasty retreat and slam the door shut. Madge Bray however is asking us to remain a little longer. She would like us to be willing to explore this world with the child and not let our own fears hold us back. What she is asking us to do, is not only to reappraise our approach to these particular children, but in a sense to all children, so that we become more ready to learn from what they have to tell us.

The essence of a skilled teacher is that they make obvious something which we already knew but have never seen quite so clearly before. Madge Bray has this gift. She has the potential to awaken in us our own childhood roots, and to show us the way forward. She is the channel through which these children speak and theirs is a story that must be told.

Out of an otherwise barren landscape, she resurrects these 'Poppies on the rubbish heap'. I am sure that people will be touched by the remarkable dignity and courage of these children. Individually and collectively it has been their lot to bear a burden of private confusion and pain more extreme than most of us are likely ever to experience. The dilemmas and conflicts remain, but for children as well as adults, the most important need is the need to be heard and understood. As adult members of society, our responsibility is to care enough to be willing to listen, so that children who have important things to tell us, can use their own words to break the silence.

Sarah Boyle

PREFACE

'It were them little ones that hurted, weren't it, Jess?' James ventured, matter-of-factly. 'You know, the ones you cut your nails with, with the pointey ends, weren't it, Jess?' He pressed his elder sister for confirmation. 'Them other ones what you sew with, the big ones with the jaggy bits…you know…round the sides, well, they never really cut much, did they, Jess? 'Cos there was no points on the end probably,' he added wisely.

Jessica sat, detached, twisting a blade of grass round her finger. With a sudden flourish she rose to her feet and began to pirouette round the lawn. James wrinkled his nose, exasperation in his voice. He cupped his face in his hands and sighed deeply. 'She knows, but she's not tellin'; I never had it as much as her. You can't make her talk sensible, can you, Madge? She's stupid!'

The scene was the foster carers' garden. I was collecting information for a court report. James, aged six, was explaining from the perspective of the consumer, the relative merits of pinking shears over nail scissors as instruments of anal penetration. It was becoming clear that the children's father had not limited himself to penile or digital penetration in his sexual assaults upon them.

On the face of it this case was by no means unusual. I had by this time been working in the field of child abuse for thirteen years and had dealt with many children under tragic and often chilling circumstances. As my understanding increased, so too did my ability to listen with an openness to what they had to say. Such events, it seemed, had been a matter of routine in James' life. I struggled to regain composure. In the meantime, James' mind had moved on to another subject.

'Have you seen my hamster? I'll get him…'

He ran off eagerly up the path towards the house.

Jessica continued her dance, stooping here and there to pull off a chrysanthemum head or two. She had an eerie, dramatic quality about her, reminiscent of Hamlet's Ophelia. I felt afraid, overwhelmed. The grossness of her abuse was almost unimaginable. How could a child like this possibly see the world? Locked inside her own tortured, distracted little mind, what *was* her reality? And what would it take to reach her? I felt profoundly moved and challenged by Jessica. Reaching her would surely demand every ounce of any skill I possessed, and more.

In the event, the process of making contact with Jessica was to demand of me an intimate acquaintance with aspects of human experience which my mind had hitherto preferred to restrict to abstract phrases such as 'sexual abuse allegations', 'digital penetration', or 'vaginal bleeding'. For me, Jessica was to represent the catalyst which heralded a deeper exploration of the world of the abused child.

The story which I wrote for her, 'Jessica's Story', grew into a book about such children. Children who share a common, yet uniquely individual experience of adult use of their bodies for sexual gratification. The book describes the development of an approach to communicating with such children, an approach through which we as adults may begin to reach out to them and make contact with the pain and confusion which dominate their young lives. It has been written partly as a contribution to assist those who are involved in meeting the challenge in whatever capacity, be it as parent, professional or volunteer, to enable them to survey the scene through the child's eyes, and through the child's perspective. If, by creating such a bridge to understanding, the child's predicament can be appreciated more fully and more accurately, then it will have served its purpose.

The subtitle of this book, *Poppies on the Rubbish Heap*, is taken from a poem which I first heard at the age of four years, on the radio programme *Listen with Mother*. For me, it provides a vivid metaphor for children like Jessica, children who have touched and moved me with their special courage and spirit. The writing of this book has also provoked a desire to trace some of the early influences in my own life which have a bearing on my present work. For the process of learning surely takes place throughout our lives, in often unexpected ways. A textbook account therefore would have lacked both context and depth.

I begin, therefore, with my own story, for within it lie the clues to the germination of forces in my life which both propelled, compelled and opened the way to my career as a social worker, therapist, educator and communicator. A life interspersed with moments of shared agony, of peace and beauty, and at times inspirational joy at the capacity of the human spirit to maintain its own dignity and integrity – sometimes against impossible odds.

The early chapters of the book trace the development of my career as a social worker, a career which became increasingly frustrated by a growing awareness of my failure to make any real connection as a human being with many of the children with whom I worked. Initial glimmerings of understanding led to the building and refining of a shared ethos and approach with a friend and colleague, Mary Walsh. This culminated in the establishment of an independent agency, SACCS (Sexual Abuse: Child Consultancy Service). In describing this personal and professional journey I have tried to share in a frank and honest way the difficulties, uncertainties and moral dilemmas inescapable in this field of work.

The second part of the book is a collection of short stories inspired by my own work with abused children. All of these children exist, although not necessarily in the context described. For obvious reasons, their identities have been protected. On the pages of the book they speak for themselves, and in doing so represent the many children in communities up and down the country whose daily experience continues in this way and whose voices are not heard. There may be people who find it difficult to believe these stories. I genuinely have no answer for them, but I do have a question – 'Why?' What lies within us that renders us so determinedly unwilling to hear? Indeed the same question 'Why?' remains a preoccupation for Jessica, too.

While some readers may feel daunted at the prospect of attempting to comprehend the experience of abuse if they have never been exposed to it personally, it should not be forgotten that abused children are only different from other children in that they have experienced disturbed and abusive adult behaviour. Every one of us shares at least one experience with these children, as we have all early on in our lives been small people in a big persons' world. Perhaps we can remember incidents when we felt belittled, ashamed, confused, hurt and yet were too afraid to speak.

To open our hearts and minds to these children will necessarily demand a re-acquaintance on the part of the reader with his or her own inner child. For some, this may be an uncomfortable and distressing process. Surely as adults, however, we have a responsibility to listen and learn as we expose this pain, so that we are able to offer these children the help that they need in order to begin the process of healing. Those of us who have attempted to respond to this enormous challenge know that we will be tested every inch of the way, but that ultimately the task is an essential one. For in these young people's lives lie the seeds of both our future and theirs.

PREFACE TO THIS EDITION

It is now November 1996 - five years since *Poppies on the Rubbish Heap* was written. As I write, the train leaves London, Euston. It has been nearly ten years since SACCS began, in January 1987. The intervening years have seen many changes.

In response to a clamour of public concern over reports of abuse of children, on a massive scale, in children's homes in Wales, a public inquiry has now been commenced. The Government is about to legislate to introduce a list of paedophiles. Paradoxically the conviction rate for sexual crimes against children has dropped. Faced with an ever increasing problem of disruptive pupils, the Education Secretary is advocating a return to corporal punishment in schools and, according to this weeks headlines, yet another child, Rikki Neave aged six, has sustained appalling cruelty at the hands of his drug addicted mother resulting in murder by persons unknown. And as the public bays for the blood of two unfortunate public servants who, the argument goes, have failed in their duty to prevent such heinousness, more children like Rikki suffer alone, with their voices unheard.

The early nineties saw an introduction to public awareness of the concept of organised or ritualised abuse. We were greatly comforted by the notion that this remains a fantasy, entertained by some social workers and health professionals and other such zealots. And, if the evidence exists, it remains locked in abused children's minds where it is destined to remain until those with the courage to do so help it to find expression. We looked on in incredulity as the sleepy town of Gloucester witnessed the gory unravelling of one of the most grotesque multiple child sex and murder scandals of the 20th Century. With remarkable courage the surviving children, now adults, told their stories. The nation received the edited version of events, for the reality contained no comfort. Almost too dangerous to know.

We enacted the Children Act, with its emphasis on family values and the maintenance of family responsibilities. We keep families together because we believe in families. As we move towards the next 1997 election 'family values' will be at the forefront of our Government policy. Rikki Neave was part of a family. The West children lived as part of a family too. It is unlikely that their perspectives on family life, and that of many children like them, will ever enter the debate.

Since the introduction of the Children Act in 1989, to act quickly to protect children is arguably more difficult, because the Children Act demands evidence in a shorter space of time. Sexual abuse continues to remain a syndrome of secrecy and denial. In the adult therapy world, the False Memory debate rages. Enabling pain, confusion, and terror to surface into conscious awareness and unravelling the distortion of decades, is a confused and confusing process – itself open to misinterpretation, further distortion and more polarised thinking. The law continues to operate on the basis that if bad things happen to children, they will be able to recount accurately the details of such events in court, in an adult focused decision-making forum. Trauma, and its effects, on the tiny developing human mind is beginning to become more clearly understood, but as yet this information has not found its way into many courtroom settings. Young children are often not enabled to testify (a bit unreliable – best left alone) and left alone they are to grow on and up, amidst such unresolved distress, potential blighted. An immeasurable loss to the future. And like a voyeuristic cohort we look on, perplexed, believing that a little bit of discipline would not do any harm, wondering why some children do not respond to a good caning or other form of institutionalised violence which never did any of us more law abiding souls any harm! Sadly, to a child who has never lived with respect, other people become commodities to be treated accordingly, and when you are a small person hurt, hurting and fearful, fighting for survival, fisticuffs poised, a little bit more corporal punishment inflicted upon you, be it measured and justified or otherwise, is of little consequence and even less effect.

In 1991 when *Poppies on the Rubbish Heap* was first published, we were about to establish the second Leaps & Bounds house. Mary Walsh and I now have 5 houses and 2 smaller units. We have 30 children all of whom are survivors of family life thus far, and live with the legacy of that survival. We have Georges, Traceys, Jessicas and Michaels. We have a skilled team of therapy staff who work with the children in the playrooms, and who teach other people how to help abused children heal through play. We have established a remarkable team of carers who care for the children as their own, with love, dedication and considerable good humour. Despite kicks, spits, sleepless nights and sexual propositions and all the other things desperate children need to do to find out whether they are worth loving and rebuild a faith in themselves, other human beings, and in life itself, they stay focused to the task.

Then we ask our children to make an enormous act of faith and move out again into the external world to live with a family again. Not the average perfect happy family who adorn the back of cornflake packets. But ordinary human beings who are capable of extraordinary things, who know about life and about love and having had their own share of suffering, have learned about the value of loving. People who have the guts to do something to complete a process, and thus change the course of a young person's life.

After two years of bureaucratic nightmares, tougher and infinitely more debilitating than any playroom interlude, we finally managed to establish a fostering/adoption service for our children which allows for the recruitment and training of families and single carers who want to dedicate their lives to completing the cycle.

When the child goes to live with them, we will continue to be part of their family's life until the child no longer needs us.

And me? Well there is still so much left to learn about the remarkable and infinitely creative ways in which very young children like Zoe use whatever resources they have, to make an order out of chaos, normality out of abnormality, sanity out of insanity. And through this learning I may yet refine skills in enabling such children regain an equilibrium.

As I am moved to discover more about that process, to honour and celebrate the remarkableness of each child's capacity for survival and healing, I will write more stories about the meaning of these discoveries. About fragmentation, integration and who knows, if and when greater awareness dawns, the deeper meaning of it all.

CHILDHOOD INFLUENCES

'Poppies on the Rubbish Heap' came into our kitchen one day during *Listen with Mother*. Our radio was a big brown bakelite, with gold knobs and a green and red line which moved when you twiddled them.

> *Poppies on the Rubbish Heap!*
>
> Some seeds, one day,
> Were thrown away,
> And there they lay
> On the rubbish heap.
>
> Now, to my delight,
> There's a lovely sight,
> POPPIES, red and white,
> On the rubbish heap!

The suspense was uncontainable. Perched on her knee I would stare at my mother's face, my mind begging answers. Just imagine! Poppies on a rubbish heap! Poppies growing on a pile of rubbish! How did they do it? How did they survive?

'Well, where did they come from, Mum? Did a man buy a packet of seeds and lose it? Did the bin man come and take it away by mistake? And how did they get out of the packet? Did it burst open in the bin lorry? Well, if it did was it only the white and red ones that got out? Do you know, Mum? Was it a packet?...'

And so it went on. Answers came in their time. But never the whole answer. Always there seemed to be part of the answer suspended somewhere in a glimmering haze just beyond reach, waiting in the shadows to be born.

My father knew about gardens. Trees were his job. He would surely know.

'Dad, can seeds grow if they're still in a packet?'

'No.'

Dad carried on mowing the lawn. Daisy heads flew everywhere.

'Well, what do they need to grow, then?'

'Flowers grow in the earth – they need earth to grow.'

'Well, can some of them grow in rubbish?'

'No.'

'Yes, they can'…then more urgently… 'Poppies can!'

'No, they can't.'

'Yes, they can! I know they can! If they fly away and land on rubbish they can grow.'

Purposeful and earnest interrogation of the bin man and trips to the local tip in the bin lorry did not reveal the answer either. But still the poppies remained, in my child's mind and in my dreams. Under the orange feather quilt in the twilight moments as sleep beckoned I would imagine them. Banks and banks of brilliant dancing poppies growing on top of old tin cans, dead sheep's heads and stinking mattresses. Like the picture of the dead lion on the front of the green syrup tin with the bees buzzing round its gaping stomach. 'Out of the strong came forth sweetness', it said on the syrup tin. If bees can make honey inside dead, rotting lions, I reasoned, then poppies can grow on rubbish heaps. Anyway it says so in the poem.

As an adult, over thirty years on, my thinking is less concrete, although arguably I am further away from the truth. I reason in a more sophisticated way. Yet poppies on the rubbish heap remains an important image for me. I know now that poppies can grow on rubbish heaps. I've seen them, touched them, watched them bend in the wind. And in a sense, other people's rubbish has become an integral part of my life. A life which is lent momentum by the conviction that deep in each and every one of us lie the poppies, delicate, colourful and exquisitely unique. Expeditions to the rubbish tip were then, as they are now, guided by an unshakeable knowledge that the poppies exist; they have to exist. Of course it must be possible! And the poppies as they reveal themselves to the world are more startling and beautiful against the backdrop of the decay and debris which make up their surroundings.

It was as a child that I learned, too, that it was not by any means plain sailing for seeds which fell on potentially more fertile soil. When I was seven, the family adapted to the birth of my youngest brother, who was born physically handicapped and severely deaf. As his big sisters and, close to him, I watched as he struggled daily to be heard and acknowledged. I saw, too, the increasing potential for social handicap as the effects of his disability threatened to leave him isolated, withdrawn and unable to take his place in the world. Intuitively I observed his clumsy attempts to make his needs known in an often ignorant and critical world. And when he learned to walk, tottering precariously, his quiet insistence demanded that we respected his need to stand, however shakily, on his own two feet. For it was clear that my offer of a steadying hand was not always welcome, and was of positive value only when he wanted it. Otherwise it was a hindrance. This was his life, his struggle, his journey, and shaky tottering was fundamental to it, as indeed it is for all children. Like any child, he resented being 'done unto'.

'Margery, can you come down to the front, please, and let me know what your brother wants?'

This was a daily occurrence at school. Sometimes I or my younger brother Chris sat beside him and helped him with his sums, listening to the incessant whistle of the National Health hearing aid strapped with pink tapes to our little brother's chest like a giant rosette. It had to be strapped on top of his pullover; clothing rubbing against it made a sound like gravel crushing in his ears.

'What do you want, Dave?'

I would look him in the eye and speak slowly and pointedly like we did at home.

'A cah chee ve bod.' He would look at me earnestly. 'A cah chee ve bod.'

'Miss, he can't see the board.'

'Why not?'

'Because your chair's in front of it, Miss.' Eyes averted, with great solemnity.

'Oh, thank you, Margery. Now go and sit down.'

I would return to my seat at the back of the class, where Primary Seven sat: Katrina Morrison, Angus MacLeod and me. Dave would set to work again, painstaking, and determined.

Spasmodic tremors would pulsate through his body, forcing his hands to go in the opposite direction to where his mind intended, but he got the answers right. Despite his difference, he had a quiet dignity about him. Although born physically handicapped and severely deaf, Dave had a determination that was not to be trifled with. His effect on other people was to draw the best from them, including me. The village children did not ridicule him; rather they respected his earnest attempts to communicate, however clumsily, in a hearing world.

I learned two important lessons from my brother. First, that whatever the nature of one's life experience, the need to be accepted, heard and understood is a fundamental human need. Second, the knowledge that despite major obstacles, communication must always be possible.

Early in my adolescence the family moved nearer to the east coast of Scotland. The sounds of the smooth Gaelic lilting voices of the west receded into the past to be replaced by guttural twangs, and crisper, more clipped tongues and people. Davie needed more specialist care, and this was more conveniently to hand in the north-east. As I grew older, new challenges, new obstacles gradually beckoned. Adolescence. Boyfriends. Music. A talent for public speaking. A love of English taught with verve and passion by an Englishman who spoke English 'properly'. The move to University seemed inevitable. We went with the tide. The expectation existed and so it was fulfilled. Most of the 'A' stream children went on to University or College. In a culture where education was traditionally held in high regard it would have taken a brave young woman to step out of line.

Once there at University a whole new world opened. I revelled in the stretching – the freedom of it. The exploration. Heated debates until the small hours on ethics, religion, politics. The University Folk Song Club, the Union Management Committee. Men. The gaudy excesses of student life at the end of the sixties. Studying psychology, sociology, moral philosophy. A major love affair; liaisons. A bridge to the future.

And after that, what then?

WHAT ABOUT SOCIAL WORK?

'What about social work?' suggested the careers adviser. 'You get on well with other people. You've done a bit of relevant work in the summer holidays, and the money's good.'

And so on to a two-year postgraduate social work qualification.

A child of the 1950s growing up in the 1960s. It was a wise choice. Youthful idealism dominated a fresh-faced, open approach to human beings. A love of life, and an enjoyment of people and an apparent empathy with their difficulties made the task an endlessly fascinating exploration. Cameos of human experience; the perversity of male/female relationships; the tragedy of society's inequalities and its effects on its weakest members; the ramifications of the mentally sick mind; the theatricals of the courtroom process; the suffering of abused children. All this carrying with it society's expectation – 'Well, you're a social worker now – do something about it all! That's what you're paid for. Fiddle around on the periphery – ease things a little here and there – do a bit of meddling. And find someone to marry! Don't go having babies yet – wait a while.'

Not a difficult task, in retrospect. Already in love, and about to inherit three stepchildren, idealism was tarnished not a whit. Self-willed and independent, attempting to be competent and efficient, there was a career ladder to be climbed. And in the climbing a twist of fate found an interest and specialism developing in child abuse. The dawning was a gradual one and came with tantalising glimpses into my individual past and aspects of a personal and individual journey through life so far. A life that was mine.

And before it, a veritable battleground of human suffering – an agony of cigarette burns, brain-damaged babies shaken half to death, broken limbs, torture; and a quiet, empty withdrawal. All flying in the face of a disbelieving public.

'Of course he went down the stairs on his scooter, Mrs Bray. Oh, the old bruising? Well, that must have happened at school. See him on his own? No. There's no need for that. I'll sit with you – he's my son!'

If I ever spoke to the child concerned, the conversation would be predictable. Sitting in the living room in the family home. Parents present.

'John, my name is Madge Bray – I'm a social worker.'

Silence.

'How are you? OK? How's school?'

Shrugged shoulders.

'John, how did you get those bruises on your face?'

Quick sideways glance.

'Fell over.'

'And what about the ones on the top of your arm and those on the bottom of your back. How did these happen?'

'Fell down the stairs on me scooter.'

'Sure?'

Emphatic nods all round.

'OK, John.'

Hardly worth persevering. Explanation consistent with injuries, the doctor says. Case closed.

These events reflected society's view. Children belong in families; it is the right and duty of parents to make decisions on behalf of their children. In reality it would take at least ten years before the pendulum was to swing slightly and society was to move towards a recognition that children are human beings with individual human rights, such as are taken for granted by adult members of society. Among these is the right to live free of constant fear of persecution and of physical and sexual assaults on their bodies. There would be times when by dint of their behaviour adults would have to forfeit the inherited institutionalised right of total power over their children. It was a hard lesson, for which some individual children – the Maria Colwells and Jasmine Beckfords[1] – were to pay the ultimate price.

---

1   Maria Colwell and Jasmine Beckford. In 1974 Maria Colwell was murdered by her stepfather, Mr Kepple. She had been returned to her mother's care by a juvenile court in Sussex after spending a number of her early years in the care of her aunt. Soon after her return home she was murdered. A public inquiry followed. Some ten years later in 1984, Jasmine Beckford, aged four years, finally died after a long

I found myself pondering the problem – what does the child make of it all? How does she feel? What does she think? Nobody knows. Nobody asks. It's all so upsetting. Don't want to upset her too much. So here we all are working very hard on her behalf. Scurrying around. Doing... And what's the consumer response? Don't know. Sorry. Haven't talked to her yet.

You know the little lad in Ward III – the little one who came in on Sunday. Dad sat him on the cooker because he wet the bed. How does he view these events?

Child? View? What do you mean? He's too young to understand. We don't want to upset him too much. The nurses seem to think he's calmer now. Apparently there's a history of bedwetting and soiling. Poor school attendance too, and he's been running away recently. Mum came to see him yesterday. Wouldn't look at her, apparently. Didn't cry when she left. It'll be weeks before the burns heal – he's likely to need skin grafts. He doesn't know his Dad's on remand, locked up. What does he feel? Sorry, don't know. Better ask the nurses. They might have noticed something.

Such a fascinating phenomenon. Countless children. Countless agonised units of human suffering. Nobody asking. Nobody talking. Eyes well averted. Detail obscured. The police took a statement, but he didn't tell them much. We'll never really know what happened. Why not? Because it would upset him to talk about it. How do you know? Did you ask him if he wanted to?... No, well...not really.

These were well-meaning people. Sensible professional people. They cared deeply. They worked overtime unpaid to get the job done, and to complete reports for Case Conferences. Maybe reassurance lay in paper and pens and the written word, which was one step removed. Decisions would be made. 'Upon discharge from hospital Jonathan will go to live with Mr and Mrs So-and-so until the matter comes to court.'

The doctors had done their job. They had diagnosed the problem, ascertained the cause and administered the appropriate treatment.

---

period of cruelty and suffering within her family. A public outcry followed and an inquiry was established. Many of the professional workers involved were publicly castigated. Jasmine's father was subsequently convicted of her killing. This case, like that of Maria Colwell, had a strong effect upon public opinion at the time. Child protection procedures and practice underwent close scrutiny.

Physically the child was healing. And what of the residue? The emotional wounds – what of them?

Well…it's not our job…we're not trained to do that. Mustn't meddle. Well, who is? Child psychiatrists…it's a job for a child psychiatrist. We could refer the family for therapy but Dad's in prison – he won't co-operate, so that would be difficult, and there's a waiting list for treatment. The consultant psychiatrist works on a family model so he wouldn't want to see Jonathan alone, and his mother probably won't keep the appointments. You see, we know he's been having problems for some time now. He's wetting the bed, running away. He's had terrible nightmares on the ward, and we know he's aggressive to other children.

What a dilemma! How confusing! How can you treat a problem if no-one has identified it? How can you treat a symptom if you've never isolated the cause? How can you make something better if you don't know what it is? So what's behind all this? Well, we don't know. We haven't asked. I mean, you wouldn't know what to say or how to broach it. And he wouldn't want to talk about it…

Yet men had walked on the moon! These were the days of black box flight recorders and computerised railway stations. We had devised ways of holding a conversation with people half way across the world. Communication was easy. Yet talking to an abused child about his experience was out of the question. Was it that he had nothing to say?

Maybe.

Or maybe he would be unable to put what he wanted to say into words?

Possibly.

Maybe he would have difficulty. And then he'd get upset. Maybe he would need to cry. Yes, well that could happen.

And you know how children make stories up…

So was it that we believed that children would be unable to express their experiences? Or was it that it would cause the listener too much pain to allow the child a voice? Or maybe one worked from the premise that children were fundamentally untrustworthy and that the safest approach was to disregard the child's account as a matter of principle lest one might feel duty bound to act upon it. A strange set of circumstances, all of which militated against allowing children in general a voice. But more particularly disadvantaged were abused children, whose life experience had taught them that the world, and powerful people in it, were not to be trusted. For often the only option they were left with was to speak with their eyes in withdrawal, their feet in running away, their bodies by wetting the bed, their hands by stealing.

Surely it must be possible to reach silenced children without a voice, and help them to speak. By enabling them to speak out and be listened to and respected, we could surely begin the first step in the process towards wholeness and healing. Albeit in another context I had witnessed my mother perform precisely that task in her communication with my brother. Throughout my childhood I had seen it happen every day and had learned as a matter of course. So without question it had to be possible; one simply had to learn how.

BREAKING THROUGH

In a world where we have been taught as adults to advise, control and direct children, we leave no room for a body of knowledge to develop on how to communicate with them and thus enable them to be part of their own decision-making. Traditionally within a culture where children have for centuries been 'seen and not heard' we have as a society developed neither the skills nor the inclination to hear what they have to say. We devise scenarios for children in which they feature merely as consumers of a service, being 'done unto'. Thus as professionals who deal with children either in a welfare context or in medical and other scenes we are not taught to listen to children. 'Communication skills' with children is a subject which is seldom taught in professional training courses. Within my own training, it had not featured. The message has been fairly clear: either it is a subject which bears so little relevance or importance that it can be ignored, or with luck avoided, or alternatively it can feature as something we can all do anyway because we have enough contact with children, don't we?

Hardly surprising, then, that so many adults in the 'caring professions' find themselves ill equipped for the task. The prospect is an uncomfortable one, carrying with it uncertainty and fear. What if I say the wrong thing? Maybe she'll be upset. Don't want to cause any more damage. Best leave things well alone – don't want to make things worse. I haven't been trained to do this – best left to a child psychiatrist. Do what? Talk with a child about her experiences at the hands of other adults? Dreadfully upsetting subject. Let's talk about something else. Don't want to get morbid. How about a trip to McDonald's? Make us all feel better.

In child abuse, communication difficulties are often compounded by the fact that the child has learned not to trust adults or indeed the world in general. The child may live in fear of the consequences of sharing information. The child may have no faith in the fact that she has a right to be understood in an alien adult world.

And thus it continues that abused children and those caring for them swill around in a mass of compressed pain, of studied avoidance and of great grief, anger and fear. Inside this emotional cauldron swirl eddies of disaffection, often born out of years of mistrust of the adult world, colliding with society's indifference; tempered now and again by dogged yet often frustrated attempts by 'caring' professionals to push through. Encounters with social workers, court officials, psychiatrists, psychologists, police officers. Conducting interviews, doing visits, holding clinical appointments. Looming overhead, like a predatory bird, is a constant veil of threat as these children risk withdrawal of love by the most powerful and precious people in their lives – those who abuse. Simply overwhelming.

By now I was a social worker specialising in child abuse. As part of my work I had responsibility for some children in children's homes.

I would arrive at three o'clock by appointment to see Shaun, a boy on my caseload. I wanted to make time to see children individually; that was important. Must remember to talk to him about school; the headmaster wants to suspend him because of his behaviour. Oh, yes – must let him know his Mum moved in to live with Clive again and mustn't forget to remind him to take his trainers when he goes to meet his new foster parents on Saturday.

'Hiya, Margaret – where's Shaun?'

'Oh, I think he's disappeared somewhere on his bike.'

'Knew I was coming, didn't he?'

'Yeah, but you know what he's like.'

Eventually Shaun would arrive from somewhere by which time I knew I had only half an hour left. He would follow me to the interview room. We would sit opposite one another on green plastic chairs.

'Hi, Shaun.'

'Allo.'

'How's things? All right?'

'Mmphm.'

'How's school?'

'OK.'

'Can't be OK, can it, Shaun. I mean, Mr Edwards wants to suspend you. He rang me up yesterday.'

Shrugged shoulders again; eyes fixed on the floor.

'What have you got to say about it, Shaun? I really want to help get this sorted out.'

Silence.

'Shaun.'

'Well, it's boring.'

'Is that all you have to say?'

Smirking grin; looks out the window.

'Shaun, it's not a laughing matter…'

'Never said it was.'

Silent. Fidgets. Taps fingers.

'Can I go now?'

'No, hang on a minute. I want to talk to you about your Mum. You know she's moved back in with Clive again?'

Sudden momentary flicker of interest.

'What do you feel about that?'

Plucks at piece of rubber band between fingers. Eyes lowered.

'Up to 'er, innit? Can I go now?'

I would drive home, sad, frustrated and angry. How come I get so many kids on my caseload anyway? I'm fed up with it all. Maybe it's me? Maybe I'm just not cut out for it. Maybe I should have the case transferred or ask for a psychiatric opinion. Not much point though, most kids can't stand psychiatrists either and anyway I don't want him labelled sick. He's not sick. He just won't open up. And I know he tells his mates 'Can't stand me effin social worker' – that hurts, that does. But then, most kids say that about their social workers, so maybe it isn't just me.

An awareness began to percolate through. Dimly at first. Maybe the stumbling block was about the *process* of communication between us. Maybe if I could change the way I worked and do it differently. Because right now the interaction was all one-way. How could we make it two-way? What would need to happen to encourage him to participate more fully? What about if we talked about some of the things he wanted to talk about? Maybe next time I saw Shaun I could give him a bit more space in the conversation. What would happen if I just let myself forget about what I had to do and the issues I wanted to talk about? It seemed worth a try.

I had to go off looking for Shaun the next time. I waited twenty minutes and he still had not come in. He was down by the stream on his bike.

'Hi,' I shouted.

Head turned towards me. No response. He had seen me coming. I sat down on the grass bank overlooking the stream and watched him. Backwards and forwards he sped 'doing wheelies', staving off the moment when I would demand he accompanied me back to the house for our talk. I stayed put, watching each wheelie in silence. Surreptitiously he glanced at me watching him.

'Cor, that was a good one.' I found myself grin with enthusiasm.

Another try, then another. Wheels skidding, trainers encrusted with mud.

'Watch this!'

I did as I was bid and witnessed the partial dismount and balance on one pedal.

'Good, eh?' He grinned triumphantly.

'Yeah.'

'What have you come for?'

'Oh, just to see you.'

'Well, haven't we got to go in or somethin'?'

'No – unless you want to.'

'Well, I don't.'

'OK.'

Another week passed. Another wheelie display.

'Do we have to go in now?'

'Not unless you want to.'

'Nope.' He shook his head.

On the third week he was waiting for me to arrive.

'Madge, you 'ave a go, then.'

'I can't.'

'Why not? Too fat, then?'

'Yeah.'

'Come on. I'll hold the bike.'

'But I can't get one leg over the bar.'

Giggles. 'Stupid! Now do a wheelie, like this.'

'I can't. I'm scared. God, Shaun...hold my arm... Don't let go.'

The bike's all over the place.

'Just like my sister, you are. Silly cow!'

Shaun and I were off – the barriers beginning to fall between us. And I was preoccupied with more important matters. God! I hope nobody's seen us. I mean, messing about with kids on bikes isn't real work. I should be writing up files or doing a proper interview. Better not tell anyone else.

I read everything I could lay my hands on. I reviewed the almost nonexistent literature on communication skills with abused children. I looked for inspiration amongst colleagues in my own profession and found little. I read books written by psychiatrists and therapists. Carl Rogers, Elizabeth Kubler Ross, and Virginia Axline on play therapy. I scoured the alternative therapies – Gestalt, transactional analysis, psychoanalysis, psychosynthesis, co-counselling. Ideas. Ideas. Ideas. The Social Services Department, my employer, offered no training. So on weekends and holidays I travelled and watched, writing to authors of books, inviting myself to watch them work.

I apprenticed myself to inspirational people and watched them work. Dr Rachel Pinney, an unorthodox psychotherapist living and working in London and a genius with children, who had written about her work, healing autistic children. I watched her, and learned. I watched holding therapy in York, and learned. Each set of revelations set new boundaries within which my own creativity and imagination found expression. I undertook personal therapy. It was an exciting and exhilarating time on one level. On another level, though, an impossible new set of dilemmas presented themselves, as the straight and narrow local authority perception of how the job should be done threatened to stifle the seed before it had had a chance to grow leaves, let alone bear fruit.

The challenge was to absorb some of these ideas into practice in a way which worked with children. As time went on, colleagues began to notice. Tiny results were beginning to happen.

'How come, Madge, that your little Shaun is doing so well now? How come he told you that? For goodness sake, imagine looking forward to going to work. Wish I did! What's the secret, Madge?'

Yes, what exactly was it that was different? What exactly was happening between myself and the child which had suddenly borne fruit? How was it that things were changing? What was different? Certain elements of the process were clear. Certainly I had stopped sitting children on chairs in interview rooms and talking at them. Instead I allowed the child to choose the medium where the communication could happen. And we were playing wheelies, space invader machines, dressing Barbie Dolls. So the medium was different – it was child centred as opposed to adult dominated. By enabling the child to choose, we were maximising the potential for true communication to take place. I was also watching the language I used, simplifying complicated adult concepts such as 'court hearings', and 'case conferences', and 'divorce', crystallising the process down to its simplest form so that it could be readily understood.

What began to happen, in addition, was that my own adult fear, the preoccupation with doing things right and getting things done, was diminishing. By switching off my need to understand, to control and direct children just for a little while, it was as if a receptacle could be held out to Shaun and children like him into which he could deposit his fears, anxieties, anger and hurt. There were no preconceived notions on my part. All I was doing was switching off my own need to grab information for my own purposes, to lecture about school or to advise about parents. For within Shaun lay the solution to his own dilemmas. Helping him to heal was not a 'doing unto' process. It was his journey – all I could do was walk alongside him for a part of it, and by hearing him clearly, help him find a direction, take charge of his own life and make decisions which were uniquely his. By not sitting children on chairs and questioning them, and by switching off my need to know, I would be given the knowledge I needed to have.

Through attempting to impose an adult centred medium upon children, I had unwittingly been minimising the potential for true communication to take place. As the adult who possessed the power in the interaction, I had made the rules which dominated our contact. Because sitting on chairs and using language to communicate came naturally to me, as it does to most adults, I imposed it on children without thinking. Yet, surely play was the child's first language, through which thoughts, feelings and dilemmas were communicated to the world. Maybe I needed to enter Shaun's world, anxious, uncomfortable, uncertain though it may be for me, rather than trying to drag him kicking and screaming into mine, demanding that he co-operate on my terms. I was beginning to understand that children are our greatest teachers and that they would guide me when we strayed off the path. What was necessary was that I had to take the risk: and risk only myself.

Of course there had to be boundaries. I had to make these clear. I can't let you hurt yourself or damage anything or do anything that isn't OK, but within that, you can do whatever you want to do, and I'll just be with you. There will be time for the things I need to know, but not now. You, the human being, you are the most important person here and now, and you are in control of what you put out. I am not here to snatch and you do not have to defend yourself from me. Whatever you give me will be your choice and what we do with it will be our decision. I may have to negotiate with you if we need to share it, but at the end of the day it's your life.

I bought a plastic box and put some toys in it and put it in the car boot. I asked my stepchildren for advice. I scrabbled around on my hands and knees on the floor. I read as much as I could and discussed themes and impressions with any social worker, psychiatrist or psychologist who would listen. Children waited excitedly for the toybox to arrive. Therapeutic processes were happening by themselves – not only were children able to be more open, but the continuous nightmares began to diminish, running away ceased, and they began to concentrate at school.

As the years went by I was given more responsibility and my work evolved into a management post chairing decision-making about children in residential care. Parents themselves would approach me asking for their problem children to be seen. The local Consultant Children's Psychiatrist was enthusiastic and kind, and I borrowed his playroom at weekends to see children.

Certain of them stood out – four-year-old Crispin, startlingly numerate, whose parents were worried about his constant displays of aggression towards his baby brother. Dartboards and scores became a preoccupation, whilst Crispin, a stickler for order, would add scores he had made on the dartboard with computer-like precision and accuracy, checking to see if I had caught up with him.

'You're not watching and you haven't counted, have you?' he would say matter-of-factly as my own slower mind laboured to catch up.

'You can't do it both, can you?'

'No, not very well.'

It was Crispin, too, who challenged my perceptions of the learning process and put into perspective what I had read of the work of educationalists such as A.S. Neill and R.F. MacKenzie. I now understood how it was that even well-motivated adults could actively impede the progress of children's learning by compulsively offering answers. One day Crispin picked up a handful of darts, two red, two blue, two yellow, six in all, and threw them in the air. They fell in a heap on the carpet. Four fell to lie horizontally on the floor. The two red darts, though, stood up vertically at right angles, embedded in the carpet.

'Red darts stand up when you throw them, don't they?'

I opened my mouth to advise him of the correct explanation: adults know these things – no, of course it wasn't because they were red that they had landed that way; it was simply an accident. Then I stopped myself. That was against the rules. So instead, I said, 'You're telling me it's because the darts are red that they stand up?'

Crispin nodded.

Then, deeply absorbed, he picked up the two red darts again and threw them into the air. This time they fell horizontally. He looked at me, a smile grimaced on the corner of his mouth.

'It's not cos they're red that they stand up, Madge. It's how you throw them, isn't it?'

'You reckon it's how you throw them?'

'Anyway' – with great certainty and solemnity – 'I *know* it's how you throw them.'

He had learned for himself.

At the request of others who wanted to understand what I was doing, I was beginning to be able to put these discoveries into words. I encapsulated the process in a paragraph within a booklet published in 1984 for a TV documentary on child abuse.

'When I work with a child in this way I see myself as providing the child with a board game – it has four clear edges within which it is safe to be. I say to the child, "Here is a board game – go ahead, play." The playroom is the square and the toys are the pieces. I give him the opportunity to create his own moves and sequences on the board. It is agonising to watch, because I want to lead him and show him where to go and caution him when he makes a wrong move. Because I am an adult and I think I know the rules.

'As he moves and glides with the unfolding of his fantasy he checks on many occasions to make sure the board is still there and the edges are still in the same place. He needs to know that the board is steady enough to take the strain of his discoveries and sometimes he tests it severely. When he learns that it will endure, he is, for a short time, in control of this part of his world and feels safe enough to travel on a journey into his fantasies, his sadnesses, anxieties and confusions. He plays out his life experience and, having encountered the strength and power of his own uniqueness, he can then take his strength out of the playroom into other parts of his life where he feels powerless.'

The potential for creativity in the free-flowing process of communication seemed endless, but within the Social Services Department there were administrative decisions to be made, forms to be completed, car mileage to be justified and no budget for toy purchase. Furthermore, in many quarters playing with children was not regarded as real work. By 1984, it was time to leave. But for what?

Maybe a few courses teaching communication skills; perhaps some court work. Post-Colwell, the climate and the law were changing. Children were to be given an independent voice in court processes affecting their lives. Beckford was yet to come. Whatever it was to be, there was no doubt that the decision had been taken. Now nothing else, including marriage, was more important than this growing determination to explore the area of communication with children more fully and more creatively. For within that process I was beginning to discover myself.

CARVING A WAY FORWARD

The transition was terrifying. The ranks of independent social workers were few. Doubting voices clamoured for dominance in a mind enlivened by the prospect of change. The climb up the conventional career ladder was well on its way. Why abandon it now? The work trickled in at first. Our income plummeted. Ends only just met.

But new avenues were opening. A part-time lecturing post on a social work training course, and the courts were beginning to ask for independent representation for children by appointing a Guardian ad Litem in welfare cases where the court was faced with the invidious task of deciding what a child's future should be. The enormity of the responsibility was huge and weighed heavily upon the shoulders of those whose task it became. The challenge was a daunting one. How could one adult or set of adults who had often never seen the child, the tragedy of whose life experience was beyond the scope of the imagination of many more fortunate, be put closely enough in touch with the child's unique circumstances to be able to make informed decisions about its future? How could the guardian, as officer of the court, empower and enable the child to take as full as possible a role in its own decision-making? The guardian had a duty to 'assess the child's wishes and feelings and make these known to the court'. The function demanded a child-focused contact with children.

Suddenly communicating with children was becoming a more legitimate occupation. Indeed within the space of five years it was to become an expectation.

My professional isolation began to erode. Like-minded people emerged with whom I began to exchange ideas and impressions. Precious colleagues, with a shared perception that abused children were unique and important in their own right and could with help say what they wanted to say. Mary Walsh's name emerged on a list of delegates at a relatively obscure conference run by a related organisation. She was a senior social worker, working with abused children, who lived not ten miles away! Suddenly, and almost miraculously, I was no longer alone. And as we fuelled one another's creativity, the development of ideas, the assimilation of new toys, and games, and approaches, became an exciting shared adventure. As it turned out, Mary's strength and wisdom were to provide a cornerstone to the evolution of my own work with children. And it was to be this synthesis which was eventually to provide the basis for the shared identity we created – SACCS. Other important people emerged. Tony Baker, a consultant psychiatrist who had seen one of my training courses advertised, wondered if we could do some training together. A television producer who rang up one day with the opening gambit, 'I understand you're doing exciting work with abused children...'

'Er...yes...well... I suppose I am.'

What had begun as a ragbag of strands, ideas, impressions, some leading nowhere, some changing colour and shape, had begun to weave themselves into a tapestry. My work with children had developed shape and form which could be grafted into daily experience as a social worker and communicator, officer of the court, therapist, trainer and enabler of others.

More and more children were being referred. Children with particular difficulties. Children who posed extreme challenges because of the terrible damage, mental and physical, which had been inflicted upon them at a time when their lives had hardly begun. Fragmented, shattered children. Catherine, aged six, 'has been in care six months but can't give eye contact and flinches when you touch her'; or 'Graham is eight. His sexual activity is indiscriminate and he molests younger children – last week he was caught with the dog.'

'What about the dog?'

'Well, er...'

'What was he doing with the dog?'

Embarrassed silence.

'We're not sure, exactly.'

Children were beginning to reveal stories about lives within their families which defied belief. One's imagination was stretched like chewing gum, never to regain its more comfortable restricted shape. Could these accounts be true? The same themes emerged again and again until one struggled to maintain a balance, a middle line. Sexual abuse of children. Children who were used for sexual gratification by the adults they loved. In their own families?! Incest existed, of course it existed in the odd case here and there. It's been around for centuries. But in these numbers? Surely not in these numbers! Not in Britain anyway.

Common themes emerged too; other professionals in other countries had begun to identify a shared phenomenon. Common features present in child after child to a mind-boggling degree. And with a new awareness came an explanation for the hitherto inexplicable. The adolescent drug abusers, the runaway children, self-mutilation, suicide, gross learning and behavioural difficulties in children, which had hitherto seemed to exist without clear cause. Many of these children were destined to complete the depressingly predictable cycle towards mental hospitals, prisons, and hostels for the homeless. And what of many adults currently languishing within such institutions? How many of them carried this legacy? The question, it seemed, had simply never been asked.

Here was the fundamental betrayal: parents, loved ones, relatives, in whom trust is total, abusing that trust for their own gratification. A threat to a child's very existence. How could anything ever truly make sense again? It was breathtaking. So this was the penalty for listening to children? Hearing the unhearable. Listening to the unlistenable. Thinking the unthinkable. Answering the unanswerable.

Painfully, falteringly at first, adults themselves abused in childhood afforded snippets and glimpses of their own experience. Men and women who had struggled all their lives under the heavy burden of an unwelcome legacy.

And what of those who perpetrated this horror?

'Committing sexual offences against children', or 'going a bit too far', 'loving too much' or 'giving vent to their perverted lusts', however one framed the behaviour. Who were they? Ordinary people. Ordinary men and women living in a semi-detached house in Rosamond Street, or in the vicarage, or by the post office. Women? Surely not! Adults who, in order to satisfy their sexual drive, lived their lives under constant threat from the revelation of a guilty secret and faced the daily risk of public disgrace from such a scandal. In a society where sex and sexuality are taboo subjects seldom fully discussed even in marriage relationships, how could such admissions be possible? Quite simply they were not. The message to adult abusers and their child victims was clear. 'Maintain the collusion or risk public humiliation. If threatened with exposure deny. Whatever it costs, deny.' For within a society where social attitudes remain confused, acceptance of responsibility will surely be worse. The family secret should never be placed at risk. Children disclose such information at their peril. If the story comes out, deny it. Use various strategies to ensure no further information comes to light. Under such pressure the child, whose information must surely be unreliable anyway, will retract. Pay vocal and committed mouthpieces to challenge the child's account through the courts until no one knows what to believe. Indeed the taking of a life, the very act of murder itself, carries far fewer social penalties. And in doing so, exploit a wave of sympathy from a disbelieving public. The prospect was outrageous anyway.

And even supposing the facts could be established to the satisfaction of the court, what then? What did we have to offer these children? Children who had suffered not only abuse, but more fundamental attacks from all quarters, on their individual perception of reality. Did this happen, or did it not? Surely the child must be mistaken. Penalised further by their lack of language to express an already confusing set of sexual experiences devoid of meaning. Denial carried with it a funda-mental attack on the child's reality. Ascertaining the truth was like wading through mud.

'I don't know if it happened, Madge,' said six-year-old Sandie with a gaping anus. 'The wiggly worm goes in the tunnel. I felt it go in, like, but me head was in the pillow. But me Grandad said it wasn't him.'

'Sandie, was anyone else there?'

'Nope, just me and him.'

'So how could your bottom have got to be bleeding...?'

'Dunno. Me Mam says it never bled anyway. She says the doctor never saw right.'

And then the courtroom scenario.

'The wiggly worm goes in the tunnel, Mrs Bray? This is what the child said to you, was it? Been grubbing in rabbit holes, has she? Playing in the garden, perhaps? Most children play in the garden, do they not?'

'Yes. That is not exactly what she said to me, though.'

'Then would you like to tell us the exact piece of childish mumbo jumbo you refer to?'

She said, 'The wiggly worm goes in the tunnel and the sticky glue drips down my legs.'

Because they were unable to express themselves in adult language, time and again I was forced to witness children's accounts diminished and discounted in adult arenas.

On a more personal level, what was called into question was not only the accuracy of the child's statement, and his or her status as a credible human being, but along with it, one's own. This was a new phenomenon for which, as child care professionals, we were poorly equipped and trained. There had been little ambiguity, post- the early 1970s and Maria Colwell, about society's message to us hitherto: 'Child abuse is a social evil which cannot be tolerated. Your duty is to winkle it out, bring it to our attention in order that our courts can protect children from it.' After the Jasmine Beckford case not one of us could have been unaware that the penalty which would be paid, should any of society's publicly accountable servants fail in that duty, would be public humiliation and dismissal.

My own experience over years of professional practice was that the courts wanted to hear about child abuse and in the main listened carefully and assiduously when presented with information pertaining to children's welfare. One could legitimately expect the content of such information to be challenged and tested as solicitors, representing parents, had quite properly subjected one's account to cross-examination in order to test its veracity. Suddenly, however, as if by some perverse twist of logic, these goalposts appeared to slip away. Suddenly professionals were on trial. Public denial gritted its teeth and dug itself in. The presentation of such children's accounts had become an impertinence, something to which blame and censure could be attached. For many who had been trained to see their role as mainly working with the courts in order to secure children's welfare, the courts were becoming arenas of dread to be avoided.

'He called the doctor a liar in there...' said a foster parent incredulously as we sat outside the court. 'I can't believe it. Imagine calling a consultant psychiatrist a liar!'

Dr Summers looked as though he could hardly believe it either as he emerged from the courtroom door, flushed and perspiring.

For me, cross-examination often carried with it personal attack and innuendo.

'I understand you make your living out of child abuse, do you, Mrs Bray?'

'Well…'

'Just answer the question, please.'

'Yes.'

'So you hear lots of children's little stories.'

'Yes.'

'Then would it not be true to say that you have at the very least a vested interest in finding abuse wherever you look?'

By 1986 the lessons were clear; in cases of alleged child sexual abuse where the welfare and safety of children may be at stake, existing standards previously held in the investigation of physical abuse could no longer apply. One had to be scrupulous and meticulous in one's approach to the child and collect information in a way that was compatible with its accurate presentation in court.

Days went by in a deluge of phone calls. Worried professionals who were dealing with their first case, or doctors, asking questions gently and carefully, unable to believe their ears. Teachers, chastened by a child who had sat in school for years unable to concentrate, finally disclosing the truth.

'I gather you're an expert on child sex abuse and communicating with children?'

'Well, no; not exactly. But I'll try to help if I can.'

'But I'm no expert. I don't feel like one. I mean, there's so much we don't know about all this, George,' I bleated, mulling it all over in the pub one day.

'Madge, what you need to know is that you are an expert if enough people give you that status. Hard luck, Madge. You just have to get on with being it, I'm afraid. Your professional reputation is very good – you know it is.'

'Is it?'

Police officers, for whom ordinary interview techniques proved woefully inadequate, who needed help to shift the focus of their skill, rang up for advice and to request training. These were committed, dedicated people. Lawyers representing their adult clients, whose instructions were that they had been falsely accused, and who were paid to protest their innocence, requested our help in order to prepare a case to discredit the child's account. We took a decision only to represent children, as opposed to other parties, in court. A social services department with five grossly abused little sisters from two to seven years requested individual therapeutic help for them, with a view to placing them for adoption.

'The judge says they should be adopted together. Where do we start? Where can we possibly find a family who is prepared to adopt five children?'

The list seemed endless, overwhelming. The temptation to work in a sweet shop beckoned urgently.

By the end of 1986 the decision had been taken. Mary Walsh would work with me. We would join forces and pool our skills. We would work in a highly professional way, creating our own style of practice based on non-directive play, sharing and imparting a commitment to child centred practice. We would consolidate, develop and nurture our existing skills to help such children find a voice and begin the journey towards their own healing. Play would provide the structure. The toybox the tools. The philosophy would be on one level a commitment to the belief that most adults within our society learn to take for granted – that every human being regardless of its size, age, race or creed should be afforded the right to live without victimisation and the constant fear of physical or sexual attacks on its body. And on the other, a fundamental belief in the power of love and the capacity of human beings to alter their behaviour.

It proved to be a step in the dark. We were determined to create a service with an identity of its own. We would call it SACCS, Sexual Abuse: Child Consultancy Service. By this time some social workers had left local authority employment and were working individually on a self-employed basis, as I myself had done, but coming together to create a specialist service in the field of child care was a new venture. In a sense it was an act of faith, viewed by some as foolhardy, by others with a mixture of envy and scepticism. There were yet others in whose eyes such problems were strictly the province of psychiatrists and psychologists and for whom we represented amateurish meddling. In reality, however, no branch of the helping professions, whatever its background, could claim a body of knowledge in this area of work. For in some professional circles its very existence was still the subject of debate. Many had not yet progressed to an understanding of how to recognise sexual abuse, far less how to deal with its effects.

Requests for our work came in two roughly discernible categories. Firstly there were requests for advice and consultation on individual children who needed help to talk about what had happened to them. What was imperative was that this information had to be collected in an evidentially sound way in order that its presentation would be acceptable in a court of law. This was what was to become known as 'disclosure work'. The truth was that, because it was new, no guidelines existed as to how precisely it should be done, save what appeared to be hastily constructed DHSS guidelines which advised 'believe the child' – advice, which, in retrospect, proved staggering in its naivete.

Another major component was to be requests for training. These came from many varied sources: local authority social services departments; the police, area health authorities; charities such as NSPCC, National Children's Homes. Over and above this, more broadly based groups: magistrates in training, doctors, solicitors, teachers, the Samaritans. Suddenly our service was in demand to an extent we had never imagined. We travelled the country, seldom in the same place for more than two days, seeing children, appearing in court, and training groups of professional staff. As our reputation grew, requests for training came in on a national basis and eventually the work extended abroad. The pace was frantic.

We used my home as a base and decided to employ a part-time secretary. From the day she arrived it was obvious that the task was going to take up her full-time attention.

Across the country the picture was one of siege proportions. Children were being referred in increasing numbers to be dealt with by grossly overstretched resources, understaffed, undertrained social services departments whose management structures were simply not attuned to the difficulties which the social workers on the coal face were experiencing. Staff training strategies were piecemeal. In some parts of the country training did not exist. As the size of the problem gained wider recognition, an unprecedented number of children came forward requiring services which hardly existed. Resources then had, of necessity, to be diverted from elsewhere.

There were some areas of the country where social workers found that the majority of their workloads were suddenly composed of children in this category. Some of these staff had received no further professional training and many had to find their own way. It was impossible to remain untouched by some of the horrors with which one was confronted. In conducting our training courses we learned that before any real learning could take place we had to help participants identify some personal reactions and responses and talk about them.

Revulsion: 'I had to stop in the layby and be sick. I didn't want to go in the house; I just felt dirty – I had to come home and have a bath.'

Vengefulness: 'I couldn't look at the bloke – I wanted to chop off his you-know-what.'

Incredulity: 'A few months ago we dealt with a bloke who was using a bicycle pump on his kids. I mean, I came home and looked at me own kids – I couldn't imagine it – I just can't see it. So I had to ask my wife to bath the kids and I went off to the pub.'

Protectiveness: 'All I wanted to do was pick her up and cuddle her.'

And the sensationalist, voyeuristic horror competition:

'You mean they put a live mouse up her vagina?'

These children's pain was devastating. Its effects on the lives of those who dealt with it was profoundly compelling, and to absorb it and continue life as normal was a difficult task. Its subtle effects pervaded one's life and affected personal relationships with children, partners, and friends. Talking to one's children, cuddles at bedtime, the very sex act itself carried perplexing and discomforting undertones.

For all of a sudden this was real. It had stepped out of the safely distant columns of the tabloid press. Social workers were meeting it in the psychiatric clinic waiting room this week, two weeks ago in the police station, and on Sunday night in Casualty when the baby with the torn rectum came in. You saw it, touched it, felt it. Undeniably it existed for those who dealt with it.

After what seemed a gargantuan battle, and the doubting voices in one's own mind were finally silenced, what then? How was one to find the courage to begin the task of dealing sensibly and rationally with everyone else's doubting voices? Those who haven't seen, haven't touched, haven't felt it; haven't seen the child's anxious, imploring glances in the interview room or had to intervene as she was shaken violently in the toilet and told to shut up. Trying to forge a middle line, managing not to appear extreme, gently cajoling, while inwardly boiling with frustration. Having to stand by to witness yet another human scenario where, amid the clamour, the child's faltering, half-whispered words were lost – sometimes forever.

So in this case the truth remains untold. Hard not to take it personally. Hard to pass it off. To rationalise. Whose failure was it? The child's account was open to interpretation anyway – it would never have stood up to cross-examination. Easier, by far, to say you're not convinced. There's not enough evidence to proceed. Far more acceptable. Living with oneself, and squaring things up with one's own conscience, was a different story. Even ventilating the problems at home wasn't easy.

'My husband says he's sick of hearing about sexual abuse.' And where else can such dilemmas be aired? Hardly dinner party conversation.

All in all a complex morass. And so it was on a broader level too. The situation was becoming critical.

The courts were beginning to face case after case of a similar nature, to an alarming degree. What were the courts to believe – that an alarming new epidemic was hitting the country? That the world had gone mad? Or that a handful of zealots were bent on creating chaos by blowing up a relatively marginal problem which had been in existence for centuries out of all proportion?

When the courts did come to a decision, in a sense that was only the beginning. For the aftermath of that decision there was little or no provision either. Indeed it seemed that over and over again once the problem had been identified, the legal process undergone and the child thereby protected, usually by its removal from home, then in administrative terms the job was done. Society's expectation was fulfilled. Place the children in alternative care and treat them normally. In a public sector starved of resources this was an understandably attractive philosophy, but potentially catastrophic in its short and long-term implications. Catastrophic because, without help, these children were usually quite unable to repair the inevitable damage which such exposure had caused, let alone make the adjustment to live within 'normal' families. So in case conferences, review meetings and courts one found professionals arguing a case for ongoing therapeutic help for children whose need for appropriate help was urgent. In reality, though, this help hardly existed.

Within six months the system had collapsed under the strain. Cleveland[1] had happened. The media's war of attrition had begun.

---

1   Cleveland. During a relatively short period between April and June 1987, in
    Cleveland in the north-east of England, a large number of children were diagnosed
    as victims of child sex abuse by two consultant paediatricians, Dr Geoffrey Wyatt
    and Dr Marietta Higgs. A public furore ensued out of which emerged a

'According to the *Daily Mail*, you've done a hundred disclosures in your back bedroom in a three-month period,' said our secretary Joanie, ashen-faced.

'You only ever see children on their own territory unless you borrow a school room, don't you. I mean, they've never come to us...it sounds really squalid, doesn't it? And...' her lip quivered, 'your neighbour says they've been trampling all over your crocuses to get a picture of the back bedroom! And the neighbours are getting a petition together to have us removed from our new office by the planning department. Seems the excuse is they don't like the parking.'

I rang Mary in Slough. We sat bewildered. Long silences. Staccato sobs. We discussed the newspaper coverage of our work.

'It's the bits about us interrogating children. It's the language I object to. I mean. Kafkaesque ordeals and all that. And that's from the quality press. Madge, that's the exact opposite of what we do, what we teach, what we're all about!'

'I know.'

'Madge, I gather that Stuart Bell, the Middlesbrough MP, has written to the DHSS to try to have us closed down.'

'What does he know about it?'

'Well, you know some of the Cleveland parents have gone to him?'

'But, Mary, we've always had excellent feedback from the courts up until now; from magistrates and from judges. Didn't the last High Court judge in his summing up say that the work you did with the five little girls was beyond his wildest dreams? I mean, these kids were in a dreadful state when they were referred to you and look at them now.'

'I know, Madge, but they won't report that.'

'No. Nor the hours of slog on the motorway every week.'

'Nope.'

'Mary, do you think we'll survive this?'

'God knows. Makes you realise what some of these children have to go through.'

---

government-backed Commission of Inquiry chaired by a High Court judge, Mre Elizabeth Butler-Sloss. The inquiry, which reported the following year, made many far-reaching recommendations, including the review of inter-agency joint working procedures. Media reports of these events did much to shape and influence both public and professional attitudes to the problem of child sexual abuse.

The parallels were obvious. Blame, distortion, rejection, and the humiliation of private and public censure.

Neither of us slept for three days.

Our relationship was rocked to its foundations as individually we grappled to find direction.

FINDING OUT ABOUT ABUSE

We began to understand how children who had been subjected to inappropriate sexual experiences by adults worked from the perspective that it was *their* responsibility, *their* rudeness, *their* naughtiness and therefore that they deserved punishment. They came from that perspective precisely because that was often the only conclusion they could reach as the adult typically denied complicity and placed responsibility elsewhere.

Those whose task it was to gain an understanding of what the child's experience may have been, worked from the premise that it was against the law to commit offences against children who were not of an age and understanding to give informed consent. Interviews were therefore geared towards obtaining a detailed account from the child of the nature of the activity involved, to determine, in conjunction with the rest of the information, whether there was enough evidence to satisfy a court of law. Often, from the perspective of the child, however, he or she was being asked to impart information which was self-incriminating, which confirmed personal badness, and which at the very least was likely to mean trouble – possibly a telling off. The result, with depressing consistency, was that professionals worked at cross-purposes, achieving very little, amid averted eyes and self-absorbed foot shuffling as the child determinedly used every strategy available to avert suspicion. Unable to proceed, cases were abandoned.

Nevertheless, across the country the doctors, police officers, and social workers were learning new skills. An awareness was growing within professional groups that, no matter how skilled the questioner, sitting children on chairs and asking them details of their sexual experience was likely to be even less successful than undergoing the same process with adults. For no matter what methods were adopted one was faced with the difficulty of having to create bridges. First a bridge between the child's experience and the adult world, so that the necessary information could be obtained. A second bridge was then needed with the courts, where an understanding was required of the process by which the information had been obtained, in order that an assessment could be made with regard to its validity. How open-mindedly were the questions asked? Had pressure been exerted on the child? Had inducements been used? Inevitably approaches which could have enabled the child, such as asking leading questions, could prove unacceptable in court and could lose the whole case. On the other hand in order to be effective some compromises had to be reached. Children were after all not adults. They possessed neither adult language nor experience. For the courts to demand the adoption of adult interview techniques was impracticable and self-defeating if the task was to be accomplished.

So how could it best be done? Great Ormond Street Children's Hospital in London had pioneered investigative work of this nature with abused children from a psychiatric interview perspective. From other sources, too, emerged interview structures and guidelines to be followed to elicit information in a way that was compatible with courtroom requirements, using dolls with anatomical parts. Valuable and important although this approach was in the development of a *modus operandi,* we found it incompatible with the flow of our own work. For many of the children with whom we dealt had experienced tension and constriction in their interactions with the world – if we were to get to the root of their difficulties rather than imposing more strictures, the process would surely only be successful if it could be one of opening out; of removing from one's interaction as much structure as possible and allowing the child true freedom of expression.

So rather than ask questions we reversed the process. We took the toybox out and sat on the floor. We deliberately switched off our need to advise, control and direct children. We said to the child, 'This can be some time for you. You can do whatever you want to with the toys. I'll make sure you don't hurt yourself or damage anything. And I'll just be with you.'

And tentatively the child would begin to explore. Within that exploration there would be familiarity, recognition and often a sense of safety and security at having been there before. This was because the box contained many and varied images which connected with their experience – sad toys, angry toys, tentative toys, destructive toys, tactile rubbing toys, monsters, aggressors, toys which popped out suddenly, toys which cut, toys which put their tongue out, places for concealment, toys which hid themselves from the world, toys which hurt and killed, vulnerable baby toys, naughty toys which made rude noises, ambiguous toys which hung on to each other's backs and jumped along, countless variations collected together from numerous toy shop forays, the vast majority being ordinary children's toys. In this context these toys varied from the norm only because they were *seen* from a different perspective.

So in our play sessions the toys were played with by children whose information told them that rubbing was something you did with wiggly worms to make them go hard and big. For children's play is dominated by their experience of the world, and for children who had suffered abuse many of these toys acted as visual stimuli – triggers which brought these experiences to the surface. Children would use this opportunity to make sense of the world.

So, watching me carefully, they would bury the toy with the tongue before I saw it, in case I might want to play the naughty lick lick game. That game could wait until they got to know me better and had worked out that they would not be told off for being rude. Then if I proved to be a 'nice lady' it could be used to play the 'messing lovey' game like Andrew and Grandad. The naughty 'lick lick' game could in other circumstances lie buried for ever only to become visible in a different form to adults perplexed by obsessive swallowing or constant vomiting in a child who could not bear the feel and texture of its own tongue and the memory of where it had been last night.

Once the connection had been made, and often it was made quite quickly, it was important to help them to make the bridge with reality. What, if anything, had happened? Did the naughty people have names? What precisely had happened that was so naughty? If anything had, where had it happened? Once these scenarios unravelled and the child gained in confidence, more detail came naturally. We would work together with the police, who might then be able to locate the tube of 'blue jelly stuff that smells like bathrooms' – precisely where the child said it would be – in the drawer by Grandad's bed.

Children operate differently, in numerous ways both conscious and unconscious, to draw attention to the problem. Some refer to it directly, using language, and mention it by name. Others use strategies to draw the adult gaze to focus on the problem. Through nuances of gesture or other subtle means they catch the adult eye and focus it on the general area in a silent but determined way. There are some who smilingly pretend 'it' doesn't hurt or even that 'it' does not exist, and others who, knowing the time is not right, conceal its existence. The very determination of their efforts to mask the truth often inadvertently draws attention to it, when yet again Karen has abdominal pains and can't do gym. Indeed the connection between sexual abuse and many physical illnesses, such as migraine, abdominal pain, gynaecological problems, asthma, soiling, enuresis and anorexia has slowly begun to become an area of medical exploration and research.

The adults charged with the task of investigation operate differently too, and approach the dilemma in a number of ways. Some self-assured adults who consider they know best, do unto. They produce a metaphorical scalpel, as if about to lance a boil, and amid fear, terror and anxiety, they proceed with the operation. 'Now, tell me, because I know what's good for you.' Others work differently. They lecture the child persuasively from their own store of wisdom – boils need dealing with; they can't be left, we know that this is the case. Meanwhile the child squirms anxiously, hiding the wound, fervently hoping it will disappear of its own accord – an unwilling participant. But the essence of effective healing lies in the communication of a shared understanding that somewhere between two human beings is the power to deal with the problem and make it better. In order to achieve it, one has to tune into the child's inner knowledge that, as a unique and self-determining individual, he has the power to help himself. In this way the adult links up with the child's own inner process and both parties work together to sort the problem out and ensure that the wound is dealt with in the most effective way possible.

For it is surely by the development of this bond of trust and shared knowledge that one truly communicates and achieves a working together in the child's interests towards a jointly understood goal, rather than imposing an adult need to have the task dealt with.

But what of the morality of it all? For those of us undertaking what became commonly known as 'disclosure work' self-doubt became a debilitating companion at times and at others lent a steadying hand. Was it right to be trying to tackle the problem at all? For were we not simply meddling in other people's lives? Undermining the nuclear family? Was it right to open a child up and thereby subject them to a future of uncertainty as the legal and bureaucratic processes ground forward in fits and starts, inexorably slowly without, it seemed, any regard for the child's real needs? Some children would willingly have chosen to stay at home and continue to be victimised rather than leave the family they loved. But laws are laws, children must be protected and offenders prosecuted, theoretically in any case. Although in the latter respect, practically all those who had to use the legal system shrugged their shoulders in pained resignation as yet another child victim was subjected to the barbaric ordeal of giving evidence in an adult court against someone they loved. What on earth were we all playing at? Far better to leave these children alone and let them be. The consequences of disclosure for some children could be unthinkable, with the whole fabric of their lives torn asunder. There were no guarantees of a better future. One shuddered at the prospect of it all.

On a good day, the arguments took another course: if we are to live in a civilised society, surely a measure of that society is the quality of life which it offers to all its members. The rule of law exists to protect the interests of those who cannot protect themselves. Freedom from persecution is a civil right which we purport to hold dear. Should not this right be extended to all? Does it not behove all of us who are in a position of power over others, whatever the nature of that power, to use our best endeavours to contribute to the eradication of such abuses? These children are our future. If we abuse them, we abuse our future too.

Over the last decade we have learned much about the complex and delicate problem of sexual abuse and of the devastation it wreaks, which serves to threaten the very fabric of society. We have choices. At present we either ignore the problem and leave it to fester on untreated, or continue to attack it with blunt instruments leaving in our wake a pile of shattered fragments. At SACCS we took a decision as a team that our stance would be to enhance our existing skills, and to forge an approach which was based on unequivocal respect for the child. With a combination of the two, we would teach by example. That way the confusions, although ever present, became more manageable.

MAKING IT BETTER

Amidst all the prevarications, misconceptions and public vitriol, what of the child? What resources existed for enabling the abused child and his or her family to come to terms with such profound and potentially life-changing dilemmas? Once such problems had been identified and dealt with by the courts, what then? Where were the resources to enable such children to re-assemble the wreckage of their lives? Where were the treatment facilities to help them therapeutically? Where were the foster and adoptive families willing to care for children eroticised, betrayed, soiling, running away, making indiscriminate sexual advances to all and sundry? Where was the specialist training and preparation they would need to accomplish the task of re-integration, creating wholeness and reshaping such distorted perceptions, and thereby easing such children into 'normal' life? In truth they hardly existed.

By this time in the evolution of our tiny agency two other social workers, Pauline and Judith, had joined us and we worked together, mulling over approaches to healing, reading textbooks, sharing small steps forward. The beginning of a body of knowledge was emerging and we devoured new treatment methods (mostly American) greedily. There was so much to learn. The children proved the most important teachers, closely followed in their contribution to our work by adults who told their own stories. Painfully, falteringly at first, adults, abused themselves in childhood, afforded snippets and glimpses of their own experience. Women who had struggled all their lives under the heavy burden of an unwelcome legacy. Constance Nightingale was one of these. Inspirational, ahead of her time, she was now directing her considerable energy into healing abusers.

A tiny, frail figure, half-blinded by male violence, and a survivor of devastating abuse which had hitherto served to cripple her life, she had confronted her own pain, worked hard at its resolution, undertaken professional training, and now devoted her life to her project 'Light in Darkness' which offered treatment to sex offenders in prison. Pauline met her at a survivors conference where she was being heckled and booed by women survivors understandably incredulous at what they perceived to be betrayal. We invited her to talk to us, and up until her death she was to act as consultant to SACCS. Her influence was both humbling and immeasurable, for her life was a testament to what could be achieved. The wisdom which she showed came from a position of wholeness, integration and strength. Many people held Constance in high regard but her most powerful message was the level of respect which she had gained for herself: a respect which came from within. Constance helped us to understand the position of the abuser more clearly.

'Until abusers have dealt with their own pain, Madge, they will continue to inflict it on others. They will continue to abuse children.' *See addendum page 193.*

For abusers in their own childhoods have often been frightened and in pain. Often themselves at the receiving end of abuse. Unless we can help them get to the root of their own pain and become whole, they will surely re-inflict some of the aftermath upon others. Society's focus on the problem is to scratch heads in a perplexed way and scrabble around setting up woefully inadequate treatment facilities for adults. Have we not missed the boat? Should we not be concentrating on children? For what we are seeing again and again are the effects of such abuse on the mind of the developing child. In terms of the effects upon the child of this form of abuse, the most seriously affected children were often not what one may have expected. Children subjected to violent sexual attack sometimes showed a remarkable capacity to come to terms with it, pick themselves up, dust themselves down and carry on. The healing·process could be hastened or undermined by the reaction and response of the important adults in their lives. In a sense there is an unambiguous clarity about an attack on another human being. The potential for confusion and conflict is less pronounced. Children are generally taught not to bully other people and do things to hurt them. So when a grown-up attacks a little girl in the street, we have a right to be angry: the offender must be dealt with. Outraged grown-ups demand retribution. The child's position is validated and the episode carries with it a logicality. Such happenings confirm what we already take for granted within a civilised society. Big people are not allowed to hurt smaller people. When they do they are punished.

But for a large number of children subjected to sexual abuse that is not how it happens. Their experience instead may be warm, loving, inviting, stimulating, enjoyable, exciting – and taboo. It may represent a natural part of living, such as cleaning one's teeth or the story at bedtime. It may even involve no physical touch. We came across children whose bodies became an anathema to them only after daddy, a voyeur, had drilled holes in the walls to watch them dress and shower. What conclusions could a child with daily experience of this nature reach about her identity, her body, and what the world expects of her?

We came across other children for whom the experience had brought with it pain and terror so intense that the mind boggled at the horror of it. Some of these children had distanced themselves from the intensity of physical pain to the extent of denying its very existence. They lived their lives in a state of fragile repressed denial. Unreality. If one forced oneself to contemplate the horror of it one could see that process in action – it began to make perfect sense. Parents and care-givers superimposed as vicious pain inflicters. This was a dream which simply could not be happening.

'Mummy puts cream on my bottom and then a screwdriver,' whispered a little girl with a genital bleeding whose mother was subsequently convicted of offences of indecency. 'Why does she do that to Jamie and me? But she doesn't really,' eyes searching my face, 'it's just pretend… We just have to say it's just pretend. Mummy says it is. Don't tell nobody, mind? You're naughty if you do and the policeman will come and take you away.'

Would that it could be just pretend.

Adults in that position, too, 'just pretend'. For what we had begun to discover was compulsive behaviour. These grown-ups needed to do this. Why? Perhaps some of the answers lay in their own childhood.

'Look! It never happened. Me ex-wife had 'er make it all up. Me? You got to be jokin', love. Child molesters – bloody hate them, I do!'

(Sam was serving five years for abusing his six-year-old daughter.)

Caught up in their own often compulsive behaviour, some offenders were unable to move past the 'just pretend' in their own lives, far less understand the child's impossible, inevitable turmoil. Even, it seemed, when the evidence was there and the adult was convicted, we continued with 'just pretend'.

'But I love my dad,' said Stefan, one day. 'He won't do it no more. He never hurt me or nothin. Can I go home? Oh, please. Me dad says it's a fuss about nothing – it's all forgot now...'

'Returning a child home to live with this man even under supervision would be akin to giving an alcoholic a drinks cabinet and expecting the cabinet to remain intact because you've taken away the crystal glasses,' said the consultant psychiatrist philosophically.

'But doesn't he need treatment?' said the health visitor. 'I mean... His wife says she'll ensure it doesn't happen again. It doesn't seem right to penalise the child like this just because his father has...well...been a bit over loving, so to speak...'

'This family will surely never settle back in Bilton Street now,' reminded the police sergeant wryly. 'They've already had the windows smashed in once... How on earth do you sort this lot out, eh?'

The focus of our work was now shifting into healing. Much of the work we were being asked to undertake was of this nature. Play remained the context, the toybox the vehicle. Within the boundaries of the play common themes emerged and were repeated again and again. One learned to recognise their importance as they were performed with vigour and determination and an initially baffling sense of purpose to an overall script which gradually unravelled itself from the recesses of the child's mind. The often 'just pretend' plots were characteristically of naughty people being rude, doing naughty things to little people, often with masterful stealth and guile. Then suddenly a hero would arrive to mete out justice. The naughty man would be banished forever, fried in the fire, locked in the dungeon. Maybe then the mummy would come and make it better or the doctor would be required to attend with his bag to discover the little girl's secret and take her to hospital. Typically too, the offending grown-up might be offered a second chance, 'He's nice now – are you sorry, man?' and comforted.

As time went on, the toybox evolved to contain specific toys which encapsulated symbolically some of the inherent confusions. Not any old play materials but toys which made a direct effective connection with such a child's experience. For these were sad children, sometimes overwhelmingly sad and withdrawn; they were afraid – at times to the point of terror; they were angry, boiling inwardly or exploding outwardly; they were depressed and self-preoccupied. These feelings overwhelmed their lives and could affect every area of their functioning, be it educationally, socially or in the context of health. They would be drawn to certain toys in the box which reflected and validated that inner experience. The toys took on a meaning of their own as successive children taught us about them.

The little girl doll with the sad face whose head revolved on an axis and who looked as though she would dissolve in to tears any minute, preoccupied Rosie.

'She's got so many muddles in her head it's going round and round and round,' she said one day, having stared at the doll solidly for a good three minutes.

'Maybe we could draw a picture of the muddles,' I offered tentatively. 'Maybe that would help a bit.'

With great purpose, Rosie rummaged through the magic pencils and drew a picture.

'The mummy's telling the daddy off, cos the little girl was naughty,' she said, pointing to the red and black figures.

'Oh, I see. The mummy's telling the daddy off…?'

'Mmm – she is.'

'Why do you think that is?'

Puzzled frowning face – heavy sigh.

'I don't know really. She just does. My Mum was shoutin…'

The little girl with the muddles in her mind became a feature of the toybox. It was as if each child in its own way left a piece of its personal map in the box. This image made a connection again and again. The battery operated trembling rabbit which sat and shook silently in the palm of the child's hand was also powerfully moving. Often she was loved and nurtured and removed from danger by solicitous little fingers who, seeing her vulnerability exposed, knew well her fear and in making things right for her reached personal conclusions which were theirs alone.

The angry punching man with the Rambo face who could operate his fists from a lever inside his tummy was either pounced upon or studiously avoided in the initial stages. For anger was not always an emotion which lay on the surface, overlaid as it was on many occasions by fear. But when it emerged it came in torrents. The punching man was made to demonstrate his fisticuff prowess, manipulated by small wrists now in control. Sometimes he begged for mercy in the game. Surprisingly often he was shown it. At other times he met his fate –

annihilation by the snake, or carried off by the heroic, wise hedgehog, whipped repeatedly and plunged into the dungeon.

Then the wise hedgehog, fresh from his role as policeman, would be lectured to in no uncertain terms: 'He never meaned it. He's a good Kevin really. Don't smack him, naughty policeman. You're a silly, naughty policeman and you go in the dungeon too. OK, Madge?'

Some other toys symbolised the tentativeness of the process between us. The little bear, designed originally as a pram toy, played a tune and sat inside its honey pot, popping up gradually and peeping over the rim of the pot only to slither down into hiding again almost as soon as he had seen the view outside. This toy was the epitome of fearful interest.

Previously preoccupied by it, eight-year-old Gordon marched into the playroom on the fourth session with me and picked up the bear. Thrusting him at me with a beaming smile, he said, 'He's out today.' Something important had happened. He stayed out for the whole of the session with the help of an elaborately constructed pulley system. And so did Gordon. For being 'in', he discovered, was not his natural state. He didn't want to pretend and hide any more.

The magic pens were used to draw secrets. You could only find out what was underneath by then drawing over the opaque white ink with another colour, but only with permission. I would gain access by sharing a secret of my own. The big ordinary felt tip pens were used to create 'mess' and 'dirty'. The plastic girl doll divested of clothes was meticulously drawn over, with numerous coloured felt tip pens, and before our eyes became a 'dirty pooey stink' by six-year-old Sherrie who after two years continued to soil herself and smear excreta over the walls of her foster home.

Once some of the confusions had surfaced and some space had been cleared information could be fed in which was of a less erroneous nature. The spider hand puppet helped set normal limits and boundaries. He became part of the process where, very tentatively at first, he would decide to go for a walk up Katie's arm. He only ever went up to the elbow. The overriding message that some children receive from abusers is 'You exist to be used' or 'You have no rights over your own body.' Gradually using the spider, she was able to learn to assert herself. 'Go away. Stop it. I don't like it.' Her voice grew from a whisper to an authoritative statement.

In many cases because children were small they did not possess the intellectual maturity to process what had happened to them. A large piece of the jigsaw was missing because they had received distorted information which itself held no meaning. How does a small child, for whom the genital organs are for 'pooing and weeing' with, make sense of a set of experiences with adults who want to do other things with them? Sometimes we found that expediency dictated that the child needed to be offered basic information on the facts of life which acted as a counterbalance to the distorted picture they had already experienced. Children devoured this information greedily, poring over it page by page, backwards and forwards through the pages, playing out the experiences with a set of dolls until the truth began to dawn. The little boy learned why not all adults wanted to rub his willy and why some people were shocked, nay, outraged when he would invite them to do so. We talked about how not all grown-ups wanted to rub children's willies and some thought it was certainly not a good thing to do, and yes, that was probably why Mrs Wallace got a red face and started coughing during story time. Of course he was still a nice boy, but we would have to work hard at showing him other better ways of letting people know what a lovely boy he was, which did not involve touching willies.

Yes, and that was why the policeman had been so angry with Daddy and Uncle Graham. Because grown-ups always know they shouldn't do that to children. And, yes, policemen and who else?

Teachers?

Yes, teachers and who else?

Doctors?

Yes, doctors, and anyone else?

Judges?

Yes, well done! Judges get very cross, don't they? Because grown-ups always know they shouldn't do that to children.

Why?

Because sex is for grown-up people who love each other and want to share their bodies.

Yes, and sometimes they make babies, like it shows you in the book.

But children's bodies are too small to make babies, aren't they?

They're too small.

How do we know they're too small?

Because we can show you, using the dolls.

(At this stage the anatomically complete dolls would come into play including the lady doll with the baby in her tummy. The little girl doll with the little tummy and little opening between her legs was laid down next to the big pregnant lady doll with the big tummy and the large opening between her legs, big enough for the baby to come out. It was patently clear that the opening between the little girl doll's legs was far too small for an adult penis to go in and for a baby to come out. So, yes, it hurts when grown-ups have sex with children's bodies.)

And so it went on…

Often the facts of life remained a preoccupation until it no longer had to be so. Things had begun to make sense.

There emerged, too, a theoretical framework within which these processes took place. These became easily discernible. At the beginning, blocking behaviour such as foot-tapping, hysterical giggling or averted eyes – the child would keep its dilemmas very close to its chest and would resist any adult attempts to make contact. I was reminded of how many of my earlier interactions with children had never proceeded past this point. Gradually, then we would move on until the child began to test the ground tentatively and trust began to develop, then would come the sharing part when we began to face the problem head on and share it, and I would learn for the first time precisely what it was and gain a measure of what the impact had been upon the child's life. Soon we would experience discharge when an outpouring would occur, often in the form of a torrent of words, anger and actions which led to confrontation. That was often the point where the persecutor would receive his or her come-uppance in no uncertain terms and other issues would be dealt with. The end of the process saw plateau, a calm resolution, a putting down of the baggage and moving on. Time and again we would move backwards and forward across this continuum as the child's own inner healing strength offered its own answers and dilemma after dilemma sought resolution.

For neither I nor anyone else held the answers. Deep within each child lay its own answers. I could only act as a catalyst. It was as if we made a journey together. I would come alongside and share part of the child's journey. Only the child would know the direction and it would struggle to find a route. Often once it had trusted me enough to accept a steadying arm we would stride forward together, sometimes at an awe-inspiring and exhausting pace.

With breath-taking courage, again and again children would explore the very depths of their anguish. Their often remarkable creativity fuelled one's own until it seemed there was no set of obstacles which could not be attempted, no goal too high to reach provided we had the humility to be guided on the route and the determination to reach the destination. When we arrived, and the bedwetting or the compulsive cleaning was over or the self-mutilation had ceased, adult onlookers, disbelieving and incredulous, would ask questions like 'How do you do it?' Or 'I wouldn't know where to start.' When I would answer in all honesty, 'I didn't really *do* anything,' some would mistake the answer for false modesty. So I learned to say 'The child did all the doing – I just made a place where it could happen, and let it be.'

Many times I would be reminded of the poppies. Poppies on the rubbish heap. Quite simply – you have to believe it's possible. And time and again I would see them, driving home in the early summer on a building site or a pile of rubble. Of course they would be there.

BACKGROUND TO STORIES

I have chosen to use short stories as a format for the presentation of this material. Each story is a cameo of an aspect of my work with individual children. These children have touched me deeply and my life is richer for their passing through it. The metaphor is their metaphor, the imagery is their imagery, and the power of the individual human experience, albeit once-removed, never fails, I find, to create an impact. In a search for meaning and understanding we have tended to create a structure top-heavy, laden with theoretical constraints, some of questionable relevance. Procedures and guidelines for agencies involved in child protection work are clearly essential, but if framed in a general context of denial the risk must surely be that they prove ineffective and inoperable.

I have never been a theoretician, but I believe firmly that we must underpin professional practice with a sound theoretical base. Although my work has evolved empirically, I now find the synthesis between practice and theory endures in a complementary fashion. Like many colleagues I have sought to find a way round problems as they occur and the human challenges which have been posed have been lent clarity by a never-ending search for causes, solutions and answers. This has in turn led myself and my colleagues into an exploration of areas such as the alternative therapies, branches of psychology, psychiatry, theology and the law. Out of this has come a style and approach which seem to work for many of the children with whom we deal at SACCS. A child centred approach which focuses on unconditional respect for the child, and is underpinned by the clear vision that the child's current behaviour often reflects an essentially sane response to an untenable set of life circumstances.

Others in the field have sought to learn from this working style, due perhaps to its very simplicity. It is important to acknowledge that any one of my colleagues might have written similar accounts from their own experience.

The six short stories which follow serve to open a window on the ways in which children experience abuse and on the effects which sexual exploitation has upon their lives.

The stories outline how we can work to help the child make sense of the hurt and confusion which almost invariably accompany the abuse. Therapeutic sessions can be fundamental in enabling children to leave such experiences behind and move on. They also illustrate, pointedly, how seldom ideal conditions exist for these children.

These children are our future – a unique and individual gift to life itself. The pain of their exploitation and betrayal belongs to them. Left alone and isolated with it as an unwelcome bedfellow, it has the potential to devastate not only an individual future, but our collective future too. What these stories illustrate is the resilience of the human spirit and its capacity to triumph over such crippling adversity. The capacity for healing is present even in the most damaged children. By showing a willingness to come alongside them and enable them to share their pain now when they are still very young, by helping them to make their own connections, create their own solutions and move on, we must surely be investing in our own future. That is why I work with children, and that is why I believe their stories have so much to teach us.

TRACEY

'Sir, can I introduce you to Madge Bray?'

The Superintendent rose to his feet. We shook hands. 'Superintendent Hackett.'

He smiled warmly.

'Sergeant Brown says you may be able to help us...'

'Yes...well.'

'Have you worked with the police before, Mrs Bray?'

'Yes.'

'How many cases?'

'Upwards of a hundred, probably.'

'Mmmm. And have you given evidence in criminal courts?'

'Yes.'

'Much experience?'

'A fair bit.'

'I gather your outfit lectures at the Police Training College?'

He had done his homework.

'Yes, well, my colleague Mary Walsh does.'

'This job's a difficult one. Sergeant Brown has made a number of enquiries and as a result we've isolated a suspect and there's a good deal of circumstantial evidence. Forensic looks as if it might come up with something. Seminal deposits on the child's nightdress and of course the medical evidence. Torn vagina and bruising to the hands and throat.'

I nodded. He continued.

'But this little one's not much more than a baby – only three and a half. Back with her mother now, but spent eight days in hospital.'

Puzzlement had obviously registered on my face.

'Seems like she was in an awful state for the first few days. Hysterical. Wouldn't let anyone anywhere near her. Screamed the place down.

Then withdrew into herself and retained urine for four days. They had to keep her in. She was like a zombie by all accounts.'

'I see.'

'So we couldn't get much sense out of her.'

'I'm not surprised. Poor little mite!'

'Yes, well…cut my staff up, I can tell you. We're bloomin determined to get this bloke if we can. We had a policewoman with her most of the time, but we didn't get much.'

'Didn't want to press too much in case we upset her more.' Sergeant Brown drew on his cigarette.

The Superintendent continued: 'Now she's recovered a bit and at home, and it's three weeks since the rape. But we need to get her to name the bloke who's done it…'

'I can see the problem.'

'And it's like this,' the Superintendent continued wearily, 'we really need something directly from her, otherwise the Crown Prosecution Service can't bring the case.'

'A difficult one, eh?'

'You're tellin' me! Do you think you can help?'

'Possibly…'

'Do you know about leading questions?'

'Yes, but I'm not perfect.'

'Who is? This will be for a criminal prosecution. You're aware of the rules of evidence?'

'Yes, of course.'

'Because it's a criminal prosecution we have to prove beyond all reasonable doubt that the suspect has committed the criminal acts in question.'

'Yes.'

'You'll be more used to the civil courts?'

'Yes.'

'Well, "balance of probabilities" is the yardstick there, isn't it?'

'Yes.'

'Have you had experience of such young children giving evidence in criminal courts?'

'Not directly, but I've heard of cases of it – in Scotland, mostly.'

'You're from there, aren't you?'

'Yes.'

'Thought I recognised some sort of accent…'

We were beginning to understand one another.

'We may be forced to produce this child to give evidence. He hasn't coughed yet. Admitted being drunk and not remembering. Can't account for his movements.'

'Mmm. So what do you want of me?'

'Well, could we set up for you to see her with your toybox? I don't know exactly how you work and I may get a bollockin' for calling you in at this stage in our enquiries. But we've come to a blank wall. We have to interview her; time's running out. We feel it's all locked in there, inside her head. But we don't want to do her any more harm. And it's been a while now. She's started behaving normally again. We don't want to set her back.'

'Why don't you ask a psychiatrist?'

'Well, we have asked around but we're up against it with them because most of them aren't keen on giving evidence and anyway they're not trained to interview in an evidentially sound way.'

'I see.'

'So will you give it a bash?'

'I'll try.'

'How soon? – This afternoon, OK?'

'Well...' At least he didn't mess about.

'We'll wire the room up and tape the session. The mother wants to be present and we're happy about that. We're quite satisfied she wasn't involved and she wants him dealt with. Only a kid herself. Can you also let me know what you think in terms of her giving evidence. Once you've seen her, like.'

'Mmm. Do you think you'll have to produce her?'

'Don't know. It depends how he pleads in the end – but we can't rule it out.'

'A bit barbaric, isn't it? I mean, she's a bit young, isn't she? Not a very civilised way of going about things.'

'Couldn't agree with you more, love, but it's like I say. We don't make the law, we only work within it.'

'That's why most of these cases are never brought. Makes you sick, doesn't it!' Sergeant Brown pushed his chair back.

'Makes you wonder what it's all about...'

'What resources can I have?'

'Whatever you need, and I mean that. You'll see to it, won't you, Brian?'

I was on my hands and knees when she came in, untangling one of the strings on the puppet. A diminutive little person with a business-like air and a pair of large wellington boots, which looked as if they were going to trip her up any moment. She waited patiently while her mother undid her coat and then walked purposefully towards the toybox.

'Hello,' I ventured.

No answer. No eye contact.

I picked up some of my toys and looked to find my telescope from underneath the pile.

Without a word she was reaching inside the brown box, pulling out each new toy as it came along. Soon she had a pile of snakes and wiggly worms and spiders. She carried them across to the sink and threw them all in. With great effort she turned the cold tap on until the water gushed out. By the time I walked across to her, her arm was soaking wet.

'Put the plug in,' she commanded.

I put the plug in. She looked at the plastic snakes and the furry worm and the frogs and the spiders.

'Them's drowning.'

I said, 'Wow, you're telling me these things are drowning?'

'Yep.'

With great effort she stood on a chair and leaned into the sink, pulling the plug out, watching the water drain away. She collected all the pieces and went across to a bin, and threw them in the bin.

'Them's in the toilet, them's flushed away! I'm fed up of 'im.'

'You're fed up of 'im?'

'I am.'

'Has that 'im got a name?'

'Nope.'

She went hack to the toybox and picked up the dolls, the mummy doll and the baby doll. She found a baby feeding bottle and fed the baby. I said, 'You're picking up the lady doll and now you're picking up the little baby and you're feeding the baby.'

She held the baby doll, rocked it to her and sang a little song. Suddenly she gestured towards me.

'Lie down,' she said.

I lay on the bean bag cushions at her request. She went back across to the bin and pulled out a snake. Soon she was back slowly and deliberately moving towards me – her eyes fixed on mine.

'Uuug.' She lunged over me with the snake. The snake went towards my mouth with quick stabbing movements and down towards my groin, again with the same movement. She stood well away from me.

'Ooh, what's happening now?'

'It's coming to get you,' she said.

'Oh, it's coming to get me.'

'Yeah, it's coming to get you. Scream now. Scream.'

I screamed.

'Say go away, go away.'

I shouted, 'Go away, go away.'

I said, 'Ooh, this thing's coming to get me, what's happening, what's happening?'

'It's 'im, he's coming to get you.'

'Has this person got a name?'

'Nope. Horrible!'

Again she repeated the stabbing movements. I lay sprawled on the beanbags as the snake came closer towards me with menacing intent.

'Cry, cry,' she commanded, breathless from her exertion.

I cried.

'Say stop, stop, stop, stop.'

I shouted, 'Stop, please stop, stop, stop, go away.'

She lunged and stabbed at my body with the snake, this time connecting with my shoulder. Then the spider appeared in her other hand and, contempt in her eyes, she came towards me. It was the spider's turn to do the terrorising. Shielding my face with my hand, I peered through between my fingers.

'Ooh, what's happening now?'

'He's coming to get yer.'

I said, 'Who's this coming to get me?'

'Nuffink.'

The policewoman in the corner of the room glanced quickly at the child's mother, a small gaunt young woman, no more than twenty.

When the terrorising had abated, I said, 'Can you tell me the name of that thing that's coming to get me?'

'No, nuffink.'

I knew I was moving in too fast. But the police were under pressure here. We had been close to it three times now and moved off again. She was not ready. Instinctively I knew it. And I knew, too, that there would have to be another way through. Far better to use this time to relax her, to take the pressure off her. I knew she knew what we wanted and she was quite simply insisting that she reserved her right to silence. I looked at the policewoman and shook my head. For another fifty minutes we played together with the doll's house. Every potential menacing image from male puppets to spiders, monster masks and even the big furry friendly bear was flushed down the toilet or put in the dustbin as we took care of the babies and fed them, changed their nappies and put them to bed. All the children were made safe. When the time came for her to leave, she turned to me.

'Keep them in the house here, OK?'

'You want them to stay home?'

'Mm. Come back another day. You play?'

After she had gone I sat down on the cushions. The two policemen left the sound control box. We found a cup of coffee in the machine in the hospital corridor.

'Not ideal conditions these, Madge, but we heard every word.'

'Sorry I didn't get far with her.'

'Crikey, Madge, that was great. Never seen her so relaxed, and she announced she was coming back!'

'I think she knows. I do. Knows exactly what we're after, doesn't she?'

'Looks that way.'

'You got real close in there. I reckon three times you were on the point of it, then she backed off. Damn good things, these toys. Beats interviewing kids with question and answer statements any day – but we have to use that, see. If you can get her to open up then we could get a statement no bother, I reckon.'

There were times when I so enjoyed working with the police – they were enthused and animated.

'Try again tomorrow, Madge? Tony's on days off and I'm on back shift, but we'll come in anyway.'

'But I'm training a group of staff tomorrow up north.'

'Sunday, then?'

'OK, Sunday it is.'

In the fast lane on the motorway I pondered the problem. Mirror, indicator out, pull in. Mind on automatic pilot, movements mechanical. By the time I reached Humberside, I had begun to formulate an idea. In essence what we had to deal with was a little girl who clearly had major difficulties feeling safe enough to describe in words what had happened to her. My guess was that her abuser had used his or her power over the child to instil fear and ensure her lips remained sealed. But if we could by some means subvert that negative power with a stronger, more benign power...? Children of her age, after all, thought in concrete terms, so somehow we had to let her see it happen. I used my phonecard at the motorway services.

'Brian Brown, please.' The switchboard hesitated. I shifted position uncomfortably – why wasn't he just there when I wanted him? I left a message at his office in the end. No time to hang about until he was located. I was already late. I told the woman at the other end my name and that Brian and I would work together on Sunday.

'Can you ask him, please, to provide the following – a panda car with a blue light on and a nice big kind-looking policeman with a kind face and a big hat and a baton and handcuffs and a black book – one who's not tight and brittle – know what I mean...one who likes kids.'

The woman at the other end had a sense of humour.

'You don't want a Maid Marian, do you, as well, love? I mean...or I could come as Little Red Riding Hood.'

I met them in the hospital car park.

'Bloomin' heck, Madge! What you up to, girl?' The police were enjoying themselves. 'Will Ray do? We've dressed him up for the part: baton, cuffs, leathers – the lot. He's a good un, he is. Loves a bit o play actin'! What's he got to do, then?'

'Play it by ear.'

They helped me lug the toybox into the room. I had made a mental note of how things had been left. I rearranged them carefully.

'Oh, come on, Madge. You got to come clean. What are we playin' at, then.'

'Look, Brian – just trust me. I don't know what's going to happen, but I'll feed him the lines if we get that far.'

'Hell, I'm nervous. It's like meetin' me mother-in-law for the first time, this!'

We heard her feet running up the corridor. She opened the door with a flourish, black ponytail swinging behind her. This time she wore shoes and a blue and yellow cardigan with the remains of her dinner down the front. Immediately she located the family of dolls and rummaged through them. I knelt opposite her, absorbed in the play. Suddenly she looked up, and stuffed her baby under the buttons on her cardigan, absent-mindedly pushing back a strand of hair from her forehead. With great solemnity, she sighed deeply. 'It's a hard life!'

'You reckon it's a hard life?'

'Yep. It's a hard life.'

In all seriousness I could only agree.

I nodded solemnly, trying to keep a straight face. She picked up the baby doll and looked at its nappy.

'Ooh, you little bugger, you've weed again.'

I said, 'The baby doll's weed?'

'Yep,' and crooning softly to the doll, she sang another song. Holding it to her, rocking the baby. Silence. I stroked the wise hedgehog puppet. The moment was beginning to present itself.

'You've got a little baby in your house, haven't you?'

'Yep.'

'Can you tell me your little baby's name?'

'Emma Jane.'

I turned towards the child's mother and directed my comments to her.

'Mummy. Can you remember, Mummy, the night of the fireworks?'

'I can.'

'Can you remember when you got back to your house?'

'Yes.'

'And can you remember you went upstairs and you heard your little girl crying?'

'I did.'

'And what was the matter with her. Was she very sad?'

'Yes, she was.'

'And was she crying?'

'Yes, she was crying very loud and sobbing and screaming. I didn't know what was wrong with her. I didn't.'

'Mummy, will you just try to answer as simply as possible?'

Mum nodded. We were beginning to get close.

'Was your little girl sore and hurting?'

'Yes, she was.'

'Where was she hurting – was it in her private parts?'

'Down below in her privates.'

'Oh dear, and were you very worried about your little girl? Did you think, my goodness me I wonder what's happened to my little girl, maybe somebody's hurt her.'

'Yes, I did.'

'So what did you do?'

'Well, I rang for the ambulance.'

The little girl sat feeding the baby doll, still singing softly to herself. But she did not attempt to silence me. We were making progress.

'Mummy, do you think that some naughty person maybe had hurt your little girl?'

'Yes, I think so.'

'Now, if you thought that, would you be cross with that person and angry?'

'I would – very angry!'

'But not cross with the little girl?'

'No, of course not.'

'Well, goodness me, do you think we'd better try and find that person?'

The little girl froze. She got up, dropped the baby doll and ran urgently to the toilet and the sink and the dustbin. The monster images were arranged largely as she had left them. Just checking. She ran round behind me and pushed my back with her fist. Grinning, she stood back to see what would develop. She was not in distress. If she became distressed I would back off.

'What do you think, Mummy. How do you think we could catch that person? Do you think we might ask the police people to help us? A very big, very strong policeman?'

'Oh, I think so.'

'Shall we do that?'

'Yes.'

I picked out the toy telephone from the toybox and rang a number. The little girl watched in silence, crooning over her baby doll, rocking the baby, singing a little song to herself, watching and listening.

'Hello, brrr, brrr, brrr, brrr, hello, hello, is that the police people; is that the police station? Yes? Oh, right, well do you think you could help us, are you very nice to little children? Yes, you are, I see. Well, I think you might be able to help us, because some naughty person has hurt a little girl and we wondered if you could help us. Do you think you could come and maybe help us to catch that naughty person? – Yes, OK, bye.'

The little girl looked up. She was losing interest.

'Play this game,' and threw me another baby doll, and we played that game for a little while, feeding the babies and burping them. Suddenly I got up and walked to the door and opened it. A very large figure stood in the doorway.

'Oh, my goodness me, are you a very, very big policeman?'

'I am.'

'Are you the biggest policeman in the whole world?'

'I think so.'

'Are you very strong?'

'Yes, I am.'

A very large policeman entered the playroom, grinning from ear to ear.

'Hello everybody. Hello, little girl, and what's your name?'

'Tracey.' She stared wide-eyed, transfixed to the spot – then scuttled off to the safety of her mother's lap.

'Have you come to help us, then, because we rang down to the police station for some help a minute ago?'

'I have. I certainly have.'

'Do you catch people who hurt children?'

'I certainly do,' he said with a flourish. 'I certainly do!'

'Well, are you very strong? Are you very, very strong?'

'Yes, I am.'

'How strong are you? Can you show us?'

'Yes, I can.'

'Can you lift that?'

The large policeman with the red, rosy, kind face picked up a table and lifted it high into the air. Face gleeful, but concentrating hard. He was doing well.

'Oh, my goodness, you must be strong, and can you lift this?'

He picked up a chair and lifted it even higher. The little girl gasped in amazement.

'Look, Mummy, look!' She giggled under her breath.

'Well, I think you must be a very strong policeman. Can you lift that?' and he proceeded to lift the rocking horse in the corner of the room.

I continued, 'Are you very, very strong?'

'Yes, I am.' The rocking horse stayed above his head.

'And do you catch naughty people who hurt children?'

'Yes, I do.' He winked at me, animated. I could read his thoughts: 'Not the usual run of police jobs, this. Damn sight easier nicking villains!'

'And when you catch them, do you get very, very cross?'

'Yes, I do.'

'And what do you do when you get very cross? Do you shout?'

'Yes.'

'And do you shout very loud?'

'Yes, I do.'

'Can you show us? Shout something.'

'What?'

'"Go away!" – Shout "Go away!"'

The policeman shouted, 'Go away!' in a very loud voice.

The little girl leapt up and down on her Mummy's knee.

'Shout louder, shout louder!' she cried. 'Shout louder!'

He said, 'Go away!'

She said, 'Shout go away, naughty man.'

'Go away, naughty man,' the policeman boomed.

Momentary silence. I picked the threads up again.

'Do you like little girls?'

'I do.'

'Are you very kind to little girls?'

'Yes, I am.'

'Well, do you think perhaps you could help us; would you like to help us?'

'Yes, I will. I'll try very hard to help you.'

'Oh, good, because we've got a smashin' little girl here and we think maybe some naughty person has done something to her private parts and hurt her a lot.'

'Oh, dear, that's terrible.'

'And do you think that maybe you could help us to help her and maybe you could go and find this naughty person who's hurt her?'

'I certainly will try.'

'Oh, good; well, what will you have to do? Will you have to get your book out and write this person's name down?'

'Yes, I will,' and he produced his book from his pocket.

'Well, and what will you do when you catch this person?'

'I'll get very cross.'

'How cross will you get?'

Brandishing his handcuffs, he banged his baton on to the hand covered with his leather glove. A dull thud reverberated round the room.

'Well, I think you are probably strong enough to help us. Can you go and catch that person, then?'

'Yes, I'll go off now and pick that person up. OK?'

'Oh, hang on a minute. You don't know that person's name.'

The policeman had reached the door.

'No, I'll have to get the name right, won't I? I'll have to catch the right person.'

The little girl sat, shaking her head violently.

'Well, who knows the name? We'd better ask the little girl.'

'Nope, nuffink.' Hair covering her face; kicking her legs offhand-edly.

'Oh dear,' I said, 'the little girl says "nope nuffink". Do you think that's the person's name? Do you know anybody called "nope nuffink"?'

'No,' said the policeman, 'I don't.'

Desperation was beginning to well in my stomach.

'Well, do you know what, Mr Policeman, do you know sometimes naughty people who hurt children, they say to children that they've got to keep it a secret and not tell anybody. Did you know that?'

'Yes, I did,' said the policeman.

'Well, little girls haven't done anything wrong, have they, but sometimes these grown-ups say to children that if they tell the secret they will get into a lot of trouble.'

'Do they?' he said.

I said, 'Yes, they do. And maybe some person's told this little girl that she mustn't say anything about it and she has to keep it a secret. But if you were to manage to get down on your hands and knees and put your ear very close to this little girl's mouth, then maybe she could whisper the secret name of the person into your ear, because you see, we could all turn round and pretend that we're not here, because we wouldn't hear the secret. Do you think you could maybe do that?'

The little girl peered very carefully at the policeman's face. She grinned. The policeman got down on his hands and knees and put his ear very close to the little girl's mouth. She whispered a man's name into his ear. As soon as she had whispered his name, like a bung out of a barrel information tumbled out of her mouth. Corroboration, detail, names. Who was talking in the kitchen. And the name of the man who took her upstairs. The brother of her mother's boyfriend.

'Well, goodness me, Mr Policeman, what a lot this little girl's been able to tell you. This little girl's been such a help to you. Do you think you could go and catch this naughty person now?'

'I certainly could.'

'OK, will we come and see you off?'

'Yes, I'll go right now and catch this naughty person.'

'Will you be very cross?'

'Be cross! Be cross! Shout loud and smash 'im!', the little girl squirmed excitedly on her mother's knee.

'I will. I'll shout very, very loud and be very angry with him!'

'Oh, OK.'

The policeman went out of the playroom and pressed the button on his black box. Everyone followed. Very soon a large blue car with a flashing light came round the corner very fast. The policeman ran down to the car and leapt into the passenger seat. We followed him to the doorstep. The little girl jumped up and down, waving and gesticulating. Her mother, overcome, danced with her on the concrete steps. From the soundbox came whoops of glee. A porter with a trolley wondered what was going on.

'He's going now, he's going, he's going to catch him, he's going to catch him.' She bounced up and down, burying her head in her mother's neck.

'Yes', I said, 'he's going to catch him.'

The mother found it hard to contain her pleasure and smiled and hugged her jubilant child.

'Clever girl, Tracey', she said. 'What a clever girl!'

We went to the canteen and had some chips for lunch. The police insisted on paying the bill. Chips and green jelly. Euphoria.

'Madge, we got it all on sound, clear as a bell.'

'Fantastic. I thought you were going to tell me after all this that the equipment wasn't working.'

'No, we'll have to transcribe it all – the original gets packed up immediately. Then we have to take a statement from you.'

After lunch I said to the little girl, 'Hey, listen. You know what, shall we go and have a look and see if we can see where the police people are going to put this naughty man?'

We returned to the police station soon after. I knocked on the door and walked in with her clutching a large teddy.

'Excuse me.'

'Yes?' said the policeman at the desk. Suddenly two other policemen arrived too, and leaned over the desk. Tracey stood her ground, peering upwards into a row of faces.

'Excuse me, is this the police place?' I asked.

'Yes, it is.'

'Are you very strong?'

'Yes, we are,' and each one of them showed his muscles like Popeye.

'Oh, you must be very strong. Do you like little girls?'

'Yes, we do.'

'Do you look after them?'

'Yes, we do.'

'And do you catch naughty people who hurt children?'

'Yes, we do.'

'Well, do you think you could help us, please, because another big very strong policeman has gone off to catch the naughty man who hurt this little girl.'

'An' her name's Tracey,' the child interrupted, grinning from ear to ear.

I continued, 'We wondered if you could show us where you will put this naughty man.'

'Oh, certainly we will. Please follow us.'

Down to the cells went the policemen with a big bunch of keys. The little girl followed, and the police lady, her mother and me. The policeman unlocked a big, creaking door and the little girl walked purposefully into the cell. She sat down, swung her legs, kicked the floor; one of her shoes fell off. Grinning sheepishly, she made her way round the cell feeling and patting all the parts of it, the bald wooden seat, the little toilet off the cell. Carefully she scanned each part of it, fingers running around the walls, testing the seating. She had a very good look, then turned to me.

'Will he be crying?'

'I expect he will be crying,' I said. The policewoman nodded in agreement.

Suddenly Tracey said emphatically, 'Lock me in.'

Quick eye contact between the grown-ups to check the position. It seemed the right thing to do. Simultaneously we left the cell and the policeman locked her in. The sound of bangs and scuffles emerged from inside the cell. After a little while she banged on the door.

'Let me out now.'

We opened the door. She stood, a tiny form in the doorway.

'He can't get out,' she said triumphantly.

'No,' I said, 'he can't get out. You had a look to see, and he can't get out.'

'Nope.'

With that, she walked determinedly up the steps and back into the police station. We reached the desk. She sat now, perched in her mother's arms.

'Better now?' I asked.

'Yep.'

'Can you show me what's better?'

She pointed to between her legs. I nodded.

'Yes, better down there now. Anything else better?'

She pointed to her hands, which had been badly bruised during the rape, and smiled.

I said, 'Yes, your hands are better now. Good. That's great.'

She studied me very carefully.

'Better now. Better now... Tracey better now.'

Afterword

To my knowledge, Tracey received no ongoing psychological help. I remember her as a forthright little girl – a life survivor. In common with many others in her predicament she had, it appeared, dealt with the brutal ordeal of her rape by determinedly closing her mind to its existence. As is often the case, when the context was created for these memories to find safe expression, they tumbled out in a torrent, and with them the information the police needed for prosecution. In circumstances such as these, in my experience, 'disclosure' takes place quickly.

It seems likely that one of the healing elements of what occurred was that she was able to 'replay' parts of what had happened to her, this time as a victor, with the full backing of some very strong people including a Mummy who was very, very cross with the naughty man. In my view, joint investigations undertaken with the police in an atmosphere of mutual respect, with shared objectives which include a desire to achieve the best possible outcome for the child, although fraught with difficulty, often offer the greatest chance of all-round success.

In this case the offender received a prison sentence and Sergeant Brown (not his real name) has since been promoted. As for Tracey, I had no further role in her life and have no up-to-date information on her save that I believe she is in the care of her mother.

MICHAEL

'Goosey Goosey Gander, whither shall I wander…'

A cacophony of excited young voices echoed through the cheap hardboard partition wall of the day nursery. I sat in the matron's office waiting for the social worker to arrive. Shifting my position I was able to peer through the small perspex window into the main hall. The children sat in two straight rows, nursery helpers at each end. A large pink-overalled woman was leading the nursery rhyme session. With great gusto and amid outbursts of chaotic giggling, she brought the rhyme to its climax, the children miming her movements:

'There I met an old man who wouldn't say his prayers,'

She rose slowly to her feet.

'So I took him by the left leg…'

Holding her position she raised her arms above her head with fervour, as if to wield a pick axe, peering intently at the rows of eager young faces. Some of the stragglers had not yet caught up:

'So I took him by the left leg – and – and *threw* him down the stairs.'

She cast her arms down in a theatrical gesture. Fifty small pairs of arms descended rapidly in ragged unison towards the floor. The room bubbled.

The door to the office opened slowly and Mrs Rafferty entered, pushing the door to, a tray of coffee mugs balanced in one hand.

'Yes, yours is the pink piggy mug. We're short-staffed today. Usually we take them out at this time, but today we have to wait till Claire comes on duty before we can let them out into the garden area. Some of our children need close supervision, else they'd either be getting hurt or doing the hurting themselves.

'Yes, we have a number of children here on the at risk register.'

Through the perspex window came the strains of 'Three blind mice'. The children were poised to cut off their tails with imaginary carving knives...

A sudden urgent scream rose above the hubbub. A little girl in a pink cardigan struggled fiercely with her assailant.

'Jason Mulrooney! Jason! Let go of Emma's hair this minute. Jason! What did I tell you?' Another lady in a pink overall moved forward and swiftly clamped her hand round the offending child's wrist. The children were duly separated, not without a struggle.

'Jason Mulrooney – now go and sit on the naughty chair. You've been a very naughty boy.' The grinning child was propelled across the room by the force of an adult hand firmly clamped on his wrist. 'Now sit there until you can behave.'

The matron shook her head, a smile played on her lips.

'He's the fourth Mulrooney we've had here. Jason was very backward, his speech was very poor when we had him first. Mind you, they were all the same, all grossly developmentally delayed. Kevin wasn't so bad, he was the second one I think, must be about seven now, Kevin. Jason can be really vicious – well they all could really.'

There was a knock on the door – a young girl with mauve painted lips popped her head round.

'I've just had a message from Karen Gordon's office – she's been delayed but she's on her way. She's bringing her team leader with her.'

Joyce Rafferty stood up.

'If you come and stand in the corner I'll point Michael out to you. See, over there, three along from the end, beside Melanie in the blue stripey dress.'

I peered along the row.

'You can't see him easily behind Melanie. See – now he's pulling at his shoe. Can you see him? He's the little one with the blond hair.'

My eyes came to rest finally. Wedged neatly between a blue stripey dress on the one side and a pair of denim dungarees on the other, I could make out only the back of a head of wispy blond hair and a small fine-boned arm.

'You mean the little blond-haired one?'

'Yes, that's right – he's very small for his age. Mind if I leave you for a bit? No point in starting our meeting yet, is there, until they arrive. I have some things to do in the kitchen – we're so short-staffed. Can I get you another coffee?'

'Thanks, that would be lovely.'

'Would you like a sandwich or something? I always offer social workers a sandwich – half of them don't seem to get lunch.'

I nodded gratefully, 'That would be lovely...'

'Corned beef OK?'

'Yes, anything, thanks.'

Left alone in the room I looked around me for the first time. The room was painted yellow. An array of Mister Man pictures and Staff Duty Rosters littered the wall. A poster of an adult stooping over a little girl was pinned on the inside of the door: 'Say No to Strangers' the caption read, as though saying yes to anyone who wasn't a stranger was the thing to do.

Through the window the hubbub continued, thin, watery high-frequency noises. A little girl with a plastic spade in her hand was crying. Jason Mulrooney had taken off with the naughty chair and had propelled it with his feet from a sitting position half way across the room. An adult marched across to him and lifted him bodily, chair and all, back into the corner. Jason kicked her.

At the top of the room the staff were arranging the camp-beds, crochet blankets on each, for sleep time.

'Now, let's have some hush, children. Quiet.'

The non-sleepers were ushered into another room.

My sandwich arrived; I munched it greedily, far too quickly. The tummy twinges would start soon.

I could just make out a blond mop of hair on one of the corner beds. I thought it must be Michael.

I retrieved the referral letter from my bag. It did not contain much information. I was invited to a meeting to discuss the case of Michael. Second child in a family of four. Young, immature mother, twenty-two years, separated from Michael's father whose whereabouts were apparently unknown. Couple had moved into the area two and a half years ago and had separated soon after. Mother now living with another man in his early thirties. She had two children by him, the youngest, Daniel, only a month old. This man was local. His family well known to social services and to the police. Convictions for drunk and disorderly behaviour... Baits badgers in his spare time. Twin brother serving four-year sentence currently for grievous bodily harm...

There were footsteps in the corridor and the sound of voices. The social workers had arrived.

'Sorry you had to wait, Madge. We had a team meeting this morning which went on a bit, then the traffic by the Randway roundabout was awful. Road works again.'

She turned to introduce me to her team leader – a jovial-looking grey-haired man in his late forties.

'Madge, this is Colin Martin.'

He shook my hand warmly.

More coffee, then down to the task.

'How much do you know, Madge?'

'Well, just what's in the referral letter.'

Leafing through the file, Karen began the story:

'The Department has known this family for over two years now. Mother first presented herself with financial difficulties. That must have been, let's see, about a month after her first husband left. The case was allocated to Collette Sargent then. For about four months Collette visited and we helped out with coal, and DHSS arrears. Kerry Ann, the eldest child, has a heart defect and chronic bronchitis, so Mum needed help with hospital appointments and extra heating allowance and the like. I spoke to Collette last week – she's moved over to the night duty team. Collette reckons that for a while she got on fine with Mum – Annette, her name is. Kids always scrupulously clean. Mum does love her kids – feeds them junk food and that, and they often go without breakfast, but you could say that about most of the kids up Garner Avenue... Collette had no trouble getting in, and she wasn't worried about the children – Mum seemed to want the contact. I think we even arranged for her to join a Mum & Toddler group...and that was when Michael got his nursery place. Then she met Michael's stepfather at a CB Radio do, "eyeball" I think they call them, don't they?' She picked up her coffee cup and giggled.

'He moved in after a few weeks. Been married before. Seemed quite reasonable at first. It was around that time that the case was handed over to me. I met him a couple of times. One time I went to pick Annette up to take her to see Kerry Ann in hospital he wanted me to talk to the Electricity Board because they'd been disconnected. I said I couldn't immediately, but I'd do it tomorrow. Then he gave me a mouthful of abuse and he said he didn't want any more bloody snoopers in his house. Slammed the door on me. Poor old Annette doesn't have the courage to stand up to him. Then, let's see what happened after that...' consulting her notes.

'Then, yes, that's right, then there was the golf club incident with Kerry Ann. They'd been down at Annette's family in south Wales for a few days at Christmas and Kerry Ann ended up in hospital again with acute bronchitis. When they examined her they found bruising around the bottom and on the inside of the anus were slight tears. The consultant couldn't make up his mind whether it could be non-accidental. Stephen, the stepdad, went up the wall when they were asked about it. Eventually the whole thing was explained away. Apparently the kids had been messing about with a set of golf clubs – sitting on them or something.'

I looked at her quizzically.

Sensing my scepticism she nodded. 'I know – sounds a bit far-fetched, doesn't it? Anyway the paediatrician wasn't certain. Said it could possibly have happened like that.'

'Mmm.' I shifted in my seat.

The team leader interjected, 'We've had great problems since Cleveland getting doctors to commit themselves one way or the other, Madge. Have you found that elsewhere?'

'Yes, I think it's happening everywhere…'

He lit a cigarette – 'Mind if I smoke?' – inhaling slowly – 'Lots of 'em weren't keen on the courts before… It was a dickens of a job to get them to be specific before, but now…well…'

'I'm sure courtroom skills aren't often taught at medical school…'

'That's probably why some of 'em make such bloody awful witnesses. They're just not used to having their opinions questioned and being called liars.'

'No, who needs it, really?'

I smiled at him. His face was grey and gaunt. Smoked too much for a start. But a seasoned campaigner, nevertheless.

'Yeah, but my social workers have to put up with it; it's what you have to go through in child protection these days. We've swung the pendulum back, haven't we, full circle. Come the new Children's Act it looks as if it's going to be even more difficult. I mean, all this emphasis on working in partnership with parents – how the hell are we supposed to do it with a man like this? What do they think social workers are – miracle workers? Bloody ludicrous, that's what I say…'

The social worker had lost her place – she scrabbled through the papers to find the relevant entry.

'We're two down on my team at the moment,' she said apologetically. 'That's why we were late, wasn't it, Colin? We had a nasty referral from a GP this morning and no one able to do it, so the hospital staff had to hold things until Kate comes back from court at four to do it...'

'That's 'cos all my bloomin able staff are either off sick or have gone off to work on an elderly team.' Colin coughed on his cigarette.

'Looks like you'll be well taken care of, then, in your old age,' I ventured. At least he had a sense of humour.

Joke over. We settled down again. Back to Michael.

'Next thing that happened was that they wouldn't let me in again. I went just after Christmas. He opened the door and told me to get lost – threatened to set the alsatian on me. Annette was standing behind him looking really frightened – looked as if she'd been crying. I didn't know anything about the golf club incident at that time – in fact it wasn't picked up until Kerry's GP got her medical notes. Annette was pregnant again by that time. He lets the health visitor in, so I arrange to see Annette when she comes to the clinic. Sometimes she comes. Sometimes she doesn't. I know she's scared stiff of him. Kerry's at Infield Infants now. Michael comes here to the nursery – when he turns up, which isn't regularly by any means.'

'What have you noticed about Michael here?' I turned towards the nursery matron. She sat behind the desk twisting a finger anxiously through her hair, poring over her record sheet.

'He's been with us – let's see – seventeen months now, though he's not a regular attender. He's very small for his age indeed – below the third centile looks like, in both height and weight. Hardly anything of him. And he hasn't put anything on, weightwise, to speak of. We feed him up well, breakfast as he comes in, big lunch, Weetabix whenever he'll take it – but as yet no significant weight gain.'

'What about his eating pattern?'

'Well, he doesn't eat well. It varies. Sometimes he takes a mouthful then sits with it inside his mouth, like a hamster, hardly swallows anything. Then on other days he sicks it all up.'

'Any medical problems?'

'Nothing to account for it. He's had a regular three-monthly medical, hasn't he, Joyce? Then when he sicks it up,' she continued, 'he plays around with it – the vomit – on his plate. Presses it with his finger as though he's trying to examine it. Very odd. The medicals are another problem. Can't bear to be examined or for anyone to take his clothes off, ever. Insists on going to the toilet himself. Won't have a nursery nurse in with him. It was really embarrassing the last time Dr Roberts saw him. Screamed the place down, he did. Hysterical. Took him a while to calm down. Most of the time he's no problem. Don't know we have him really. Sits quietly looking very serious. He doesn't seem an unintelligent little boy, though. He's quick to understand the requests you make of him. Oh, yes, and he doesn't like men much. Won't have anything to do with Charlie the caretaker, and the taxi man who brings him here says he's rigid to pick up.'

The social worker blew her nose. 'He's always well turned out and clean and when I've seen him with his mother...'

Suddenly the door burst open. One of the pink-overalled women appeared, breathless: 'Excuse me for bursting in. Joyce, can you come a moment? Kelly's cut her leg open on the climbing frame.'

'I'll have to go – do carry on.'

Joyce Rafferty left the room.

I probed further. The incident which had led to the request for my help had occurred at the nursery some weeks previously. The young Youth Opportunities girl who had been on placement at the nursery had been pushing Michael on the swing. She had been standing in front of him, pushing his knees. All of a sudden the child had become hysterical, grasping himself between his legs with both hands and, losing his balance, had toppled off the swing. He had refused to be picked up. Curling into a ball he had screamed in obvious terror. Someone had made a note of his words, which sounded like 'Naughty man. Rude. Don't do it. No.' Again it had taken some time to console him and he had not welcomed physical touch. He had bruised his head on the side of the swing. Eventually he was calm, but had reiterated his fear: 'No touch Michael. No...dirty boy.'

Later that afternoon a member of staff had accompanied him home to talk to the parents about what had happened. When Mum opened the door Michael had clung to her in hysteria. She had been alone in the house. Stephen was out working at the market. Annette had confided to the nursery nurse that Michael was scared of his Dad because he had to sit on the settee and not move and do as he was told 'for hours'. Stephen treated the younger two children – his own – very differently, it seemed.

The following day Annette had paid a surreptitious visit to the social worker's office.

'She begged me not to come near the house; said Stephen had come home drunk and beat her up again. She didn't tell him about the nursery staff visit. She popped in to warn me that she was frightened he would hurt me if I came round and brought up the subject of Michael and the nursery. He was already threatening to stop his nursery attendance altogether.'

Colin shook his head.

'I'd have to send two staff in if we were to make a visit in any case: the County's policy on violence to staff. So, you see, Madge, we were at a loss really about what to do. Here are the minutes of the case conference. We met last Friday. We thought it was too delicate just to rush in on, so we want you to get through to him and see if there's anything. Annette has given her consent for someone to work with Michael provided Stephen doesn't know. Says she's scared he's having a go at the kids but wouldn't elaborate. We don't have to inform him. The police want to work with you – they haven't got enough to go on yet. Not even enough to interview anyone. Plenty of suspicion of sexual abuse but we need something concrete before we can act. Legal department says we might have enough to warrant a Place of Safety Order, to remove the children temporarily, but even that's dicey in this climate. Then of course, the case would be contested immediately, and we'd surely lose. We just don't have the evidence at the moment. None of the medicals he's had have come up with anything. Mind you, he's been too upset to settle during the medical and because there was no suspicion of sexual abuse before this, the doctor wouldn't have paid much attention to his genitals.'

Joyce had now returned. The children were putting their coats on.

'Joyce, have you noted anything untoward about Michael's genitals here?'

She thought for a moment.

'We don't look too closely. You can't without forcing the issue with him. One of the girls did report reddening, but then lots of our kids have nappy rash.'

Colin continued: 'You see, Madge, we may only get one stab at it, so it has to be the best possible interview we can get done. Stephen goes to market on a Friday, so that would be the best day. Annette says she can make sure Michael comes on that day and you could work here, no problem. The thing she's worried about is if Michael doesn't keep his mouth shut: says Stephen would kill her if he knew, and she can't leave him.'

I mulled it over: ideas entered my head and left again.

'OK. I need to think about it.'

I excused myself and went to the toilet. I wanted to think this one over carefully, in peace and quiet.

I played devil's advocate with myself, measuring argument against counter argument. My heart went out to Michael. To use the jargon, his 'family situation' was precarious to say the least. He was fearful, withdrawn, underweight and fiercely protective of his private parts. Bizarre eating patterns too. I had seen these before in children who were forced to swallow semen. He was under acute pressure at home, probably victim of emotional abuse at the very least. Then there were the anal injuries to his sister and the fearful implication of a naughty man. The social workers were rightly very worried. Mother was unlikely to be able to protect him, whatever happened, it seemed. My gut reaction told me something was far from right. The question was whether I could free him up enough in one session to elaborate on what if anything was happening to him at home. If I was to see him I would have to act quickly before mother withdrew her co-operation. We would be completely dependent upon mother's co-operation.

And what of the courtroom process? What was that likely to hold? I could bank on Stephen knowing his way around the law. He was likely to instruct a good solicitor or at the very least push Annette to do so. The court would want to establish that the investigation had been approached in the correct manner. One could never assume in these situations. And Stephen's legal representative was likely to argue that he was pure as the driven snow. Gone were the 1970s when, after Maria Colwell, child protection workers were given a sympathetic hearing in the courts. As long as we continued to have an adversarial system in children's welfare cases, the quality of legal representation would be of paramount importance. Over the last few months children had been returned home by the courts only to suffer continued abuse. We all knew it. In the current climate, wronged parents were the order of the day. Social workers, in the form of 'over-zealous' lunatics, could be shot at dawn.

My mind worked overtime. What would my worst fantasy be? That Stephen would find out and burst in on the session? Beat me up? Maybe. Or perhaps that I would mess it up? Maybe. No: far more likely that Stephen would find out, Annette would deny that she had consented, and the whole issue in court would revolve around whether or not I had acted unprofessionally. That way, the lawyer would divert the court's attention from the real issues. 'Where did you learn your techniques, Mrs Bray. In the Gestapo?' Stephen might even go to his MP. So I would have to decide whether to see Michael or not. What it boiled down to was courage. In a way the Department of Social Services, demoralised and understaffed, were prepared to pay me to fight these battles for them...

By the time I reached the office door I had made my decision. I would undertake the task on condition that the local authority instructed a lawyer who knew what he or she was doing. I told them my decision. I was not prepared to compromise on the legal representation. The last time I had worked in their area I had found myself working with a young lawyer, very green, whose interests clearly lay in planning and whose advocacy skills hardly existed. I knew I was in a position to bargain. It would have to be agreed.

'But that's quite irregular, Madge!'

Colin looked anxiously at me. I felt for him.

'I'll have to get the Director's approval. I know we do instruct outside lawyers sometimes, but...'

'Colin, if this comes to court it's going to be hard enough going. I want the best representation we can have, OK? I'll need that agreed before I start the work. I'm quite prepared to stand by everything I do and say, but I absolutely refuse to have the case lost, and maybe my reputation with it, because some wally doesn't know what he's doing!'

'Called "being assertive", is it, Madge?' Colin started to laugh. 'That's what private enterprise does for you, is it?'

'Mmm.'

Self-preservation, more like!

I met Karen in the foyer of the nursery.

'God, I hope we get enough, Madge. I hope he tells us what's going on. I mean, the thought of him going home to that man, and us not being able to do anything, ties my insides up in knots.'

I shrugged my shoulders.

'I hope so, too. Where's the police?'

'Oh, sorry, Madge. They rang up about five minutes before I left. They don't have anyone to send. Mind you, it was Sergeant Caley – he's back in the dark ages as far as child abuse is concerned.'

Under normal circumstances I would have refused to proceed. If any information was to be forthcoming in the session, Michael would only have to repeat it again to the police. But these were not 'normal circumstances'. For many obvious reasons there might not be another opportunity. The decision to proceed was one for which I alone would have to take responsibility.

We went upstairs into the playroom.

The social worker sat in the corner of the room, writing pad and pen on her lap. She would take meticulous notes of what occurred as it occurred. My toybox sat in the middle of the room. Other nursery toys lay around the edges of the room – a bicycle, rocking horse, and a lot of wooden blocks.

'Don't you get nervous, Madge?' She searched my eyes.

'Mmm, sometimes. Karen,' I turned to face her. 'It's…it's really important we keep an open mind about this. I mean, it's possible that nothing's happening to Michael.'

'For God's sake, Madge, it doesn't take much to work it out…'

'But, Karen, I can't tell you how important it is that we consider other possibilities. The court will want to be clear about that.'

'Well, what the hell do they want, then? Blood? I mean, it's clear something's going on… I know we're not supposed to lead him…put words in his mouth. But you won't anyway, will you?'

'Hope not…'

'It's difficult, though, isn't it, when you just want to help him say it. You know bloomin well they've got it to say, but you can't get them to say it in a way that the court can understand.'

'Mmmm.'

Karen's anxiety was beginning to be infectious. I had no spare capacity to cater for it in addition to my own.

I got up from my hands and knees and went to the door. I could hear voices at the bottom of the stair. I left the room and stood on the landing. He was working his way up the steep wooden stairs, clutching a toy lorry. A nursery nurse held his hand. I knelt down to greet him, struggling, teeth gritted, up the steep incline each ledge half the size of him. A diminutive little boy in a pair of faded red shorts. I edged my way backwards through the door, and sat down cross-legged by the toybox.

Edgily he stood in the doorway, eyes darting everywhere. Pale, translucent skin, fragile and delicate, stretched over gaunt little cheekbones and grey shadowed eyes.

'Hello, Michael,' my voice lowered to a whisper. 'Shall we spend some time together today playing with the toys?'

He fixed his eyes on me. I smiled at him, my own hesitation and anxiety diminishing. The nursery nurse withdrew her hand without resistance.

'My name's Madge.' I picked up some of the toys and fiddled with them. He watched me very carefully. The nursery nurse turned to go. He let it happen.

I continued to play with the toys myself, but made no direct attempt to engage him or offer him a toy to play with. I talked to him, lifting my eyes for split seconds only and returned them to the task of untangling the cockerel's legs. Too much eye contact at this stage could scare him off.

'Michael, you can do what you want to with the toys and I'll just be with you.'

He stood and sized up the scene, foot shifting slightly. One of the toys played a tune; it broke the silence. Still he stood. I fiddled with the toys…silently at first. Then, taking each toy out I put it down in a circle round me: rabbit, face, police car, sheep. Some emerged tangled or stuck to one another. For the first time I gave him full eye contact. He was watching me intently. I smiled. He looked swiftly towards the ground. Slowly I continued: Little Red Riding Hood and the big fluffy dog; and I hummed a tune to myself, beginning to relax. Intuitively I knew he had begun to get the message. Nobody would pressurise him here. I looked up again. Our eyes met. Slowly, very slowly he held out his hand which contained the blue plastic lorry.

'You're showing me the lorry. Oh' – he moved across to me – 'you're giving me the lorry. Oh, thank you very much.'

I held out my arms towards him, cupping the palms of my hand. He dropped the blue lorry into my hand. Without a glance he moved across to the police car and pushed it along the ground.

'Now you've picked up the police car and it's moving towards the pencil box.'

Our interview had begun for real.

The white spindly legs were scurfy and chafed by the December frost. He discovered the bicycle and sat on it and pedalled his way around the room. I smiled at him.

'Now you're riding the bike round and round faster. Driving it to the box. Crash!'

I grinned openly now. 'Crash against the box!'

He lifted his eyes to meet mine — more confident now. I kept my voice level. Soft and level. A tiny smile played on his lips.

'Now you're riding round faster...round and round. And...bang! You've hit the wall.'

He had begun to relax...slightly. Determination played on his face as he pedalled full steam ahead towards the window.

'Crash. You've hit the wall with the bike!'

He laughed, aggression mounting in his movements. I watched his knuckles whiten as he gripped the bike. Suddenly he dismounted and walked nonchalantly across to the dolls' house and bendy play people. I lay down, sprawled on my tummy. Behind me the social worker scribbled furiously. He registered her, for the first time.

'Now you're looking at Karen writing. She's just going to sit there and write.'

Probably should have told him earlier, but the right moment had now presented itself.

He paid her no more attention, and kneeling down beside the dolls' house, he picked up the lady play person, then the little girl, the little boy and the baby, pressing the tummy of the baby, balancing its tiny shape between his index finger and thumb.

'Now you're picking up the people beside the house and you're putting them in the room downstairs.'

Michael was whispering to himself. I strained to hear but the murmurs remained out of reach, under his breath. He lay now, well absorbed, placing the figures around the table, pressing them into the chairs. He placed a brown play chair behind the door. Lifting the little boy doll, he whispered to it. I watched the scene develop. He found the small model television and lifting it out of the dolls' house, pressed carefully along the bottom of the set, replacing it in the corner of the room. A cosy domestic scene.

'Now you've pressed the button on the television.' I tailed off. It was almost an intrusion. Enough to be with him in the play. Just to be present and with him.

With a purposeful twist of his body he went off in search of something, rummaging through the toys in the box, tipping toys hither and thither. I wanted to help him, to advise him, to ask him what he wanted and find it for him, but this was his game, his exploration – not mine, and not my place to interrupt the flow. I could only hope that he found what it was that he sought so earnestly and bear witness to his silent forage.

Eagerly he pounced, extracted the figure he sought from underneath the Doctor's Kit and strode back towards the house. He lay down again beside the house to continue the play. Clutching the tiny male doll he walked it carefully and deliberately towards the front door of the dolls' house. The door was punched open. Suddenly the man was in the living room, manipulated by the three-year-old fist. Chairs flew willy-nilly. Figures so meticulously positioned on toy chairs were hurled against the wall. The baby landed under the table and the little boy face down in the corner. The male figure rampaged, kicking, hurling. Sounds came from Michael's mouth. 'Caa Sssy Uch Pow.' The living room scene, so carefully set up, now looked as though it had been hit by an earthquake. The man left the house and sat propped up against the toybox. The scene was rebuilt. The same figures, in the same positions, seemingly powerless to influence their fate. Imminent destruction. Time after time the male figure wreaked his havoc, left again, and sat outside surveying the scene. Whisper, whisper, whisper.

I could only hope that the social worker had been able to note his movements, but I knew she would be unable to see properly as they happened, unless she moved her seat.

'The man's been wrecking the living room. Lots of whispers. And now you're getting up.'

Michael stood surveying the scene, expressionless.

Then he stooped and picked up the tiny male doll. Pulling its legs apart he hurled it from him. With furious energy he retrieved it and kicked it across the room. The man came to a halt face down under the radiator. He ran to it, picked it up, hurled it with all his might against the wall. Retrieving it, he clutched it tightly in his fist and threw it again. It hit the window pane and bounced off, landing straddled across the wise hedgehog puppet.

The anatomical dolls lay among the other toys in the box. He pulled at one of them determinedly – the toys tumbled in a heap against the wall. He staggered backwards with the impact of the tug, the large male

doll this time unwieldy in his bony arms. Holding it at arm's length he punched the doll in the stomach again and again. Lost completely in the frenzy of his rage he ripped the jacket off and stamped on its face.

Frantic, running, face contorted, he made noises. More noises. 'Ha Schycch Cch.' He leapt on the bicycle and rode it round the room then paused, steeled himself, and rode the bicycle at the prostrate man. The pedal jolted the doll out of the way. Quick turn round, and another assault, this time more precisely grinding the neck of the doll under the wheels of the bike.

Dismounting to inspect the damage, then off again for another assault on the defenceless doll. His eyes shone. Colour in his cheeks.

Now the doll was being swung backwards and forwards round and round by the arm, and battered against the wall. The waistband of the trousers was undone, leaving the genital area exposed.

Michael stopped in his tracks, gasping from his exertions, pausing a moment for breath. Totally involved. He pulled the penis hard and twisted, jamming the now naked doll in between the radiator and the wall. He ran forward, picked up the yellow plastic sword and thrust it deep into the man's groin. He cut and twisted and pummelled at the genital area, twisting the penis round and round with furious grunting noises. The doll fell to the ground.

I knelt down beside him. Silently he paused for breath, staring at the devastated spectacle on the floor. He looked at me. Glassily. Eyes empty. Mind elsewhere.

'Now you're standing getting your breath back,' I murmured to him softly.

Time had gone by. Here we were. Michael and me. We had reached a point somewhere on his road. It was time to rest. To measure. To take stock.

For some time Michael considered my face. From the frenzied odyssey a victor was emerging. The whispering began again. He stood across from me, still measuring my face. He reached out towards me and, still whispering, placed a small grubby finger on my lips. I felt his exhaustion. The familiar tiny smile played about his mouth. Words seemed superfluous. The doll lay sprawled face downwards on the ground, limbs splayed, like some grotesque murder scene cadaver.

Our eyes met. Michael rubbed his nose. He bent over slowly and pulled up the doll by the hair, dangling him feet down.

I wanted to ask him questions. Who were the people in this play? Did this man have a name? What had he done to deserve such punishment? Superfluous questions. Questions which would get in the way. Questions which I knew from experience the child would disregard, brush aside with the contempt they deserved. But what would any court make of this? All I would be able to do would be to recount as accurately as possible what had happened today and let them reach their own conclusions. My concentration diverted momentarily, pondering imponderables.

Michael had not yet spoken a word. In his world, speech was superfluous. His language was the language of play. Michael was introducing me to his explosive and precarious world. Violent – jagged-edged. His soul rose up to challenge it head-on with courage which was unyielding, breathtaking. Michael was quite simply not having it! I marvelled at him.

He pulled my arm and, male doll in one hand, beckoned me towards the window. I held the doll for him. With great effort he dragged a chair twice his size halfway across the room and climbed on top of it. He took the doll from my arms and pushed at the window.

'You open,' he said.

My heart leapt. What was happening now?

I had to take responsibility here.

'Michael, if we open the window I shall have to hold on to you. We're too high up and I can't let you fall.'

He nodded. Sensible decision. It appeared he had already taken it into account. I opened the window and held on to him tightly, my hands around his tiny waist. He leaned out, inspecting the drop. We were on the third floor. It was a long way down.

He had stopped whispering and was singing softly to himself. Then with great ceremony he raised his arms. The cloth doll balanced momentarily above his head and then fell, hurled downwards towards the ground far below.

Michael leaned out of the window as far as he could. I held on to him tightly. We surveyed the speck on the concrete below.

'Man dead,' he said, his face wreathed in smiles. 'Man dead. Naughty man dead,' he repeated.

'Michael, has the man got a name?'

Michael shook his head.

'What has he done, Michael?'

No reply.

He jumped up and down on the chair, hands raised above his head. Victorious.

'Da da da da; da da da,' he sang.

I recognised the theme from *The A Team*.

'The little boy's thrown the naughty man out the window.'

Michael nodded. I felt like a co-conspirator. He jumped down off the chair and took my hand, pulling me towards the door...

'See now...'

Down the steps we went and into the yard. Michael picked him up, whispering again, to inspect the damage.

'Deaded,' he said slowly. 'Deaded now.'

'You're telling me he's deaded now?'

'Yep. Deaded. Naughty man deaded.'

'Mmm. I see.'

The December wind blew chill in the yard. I shivered.

We made our way back upstairs, the doll pulled along behind Michael, bump, bump, bump upstairs. I knew I had to ask some questions. The time was wrong. But there might not be another time. It was far too soon. But time was moving on. We had already been together one and a half hours and I knew that we would be open to criticism in court for prolonging the interview. I could hear the cross-examination line: 'Mrs Bray, how long did you subject this child to "disclosure interview" – two hours?' In reality my problem was often to encourage children to leave the playroom. Invariably they wanted to stay.

I tried again.

'Michael, can you tell me, where does this man live?'

Michael shook his head. I could feel him withdrawing from me. Things were becoming unsafe. We both knew it.

Now he would retreat to safety within himself, and close the door.

Much against my better judgement, I persisted.

'Michael, does somebody hurt the little boy?'

Panic flooded his face. He stood before me, eyes moving everywhere. His hands reached automatically to cover his penis. He backed away from me.

'Michael... Michael. It's OK!'

It was unbearable.

A knock at the door – matron popped her head round. The minibus would arrive soon to take the children home.

Michael walked towards the door.

Matron looked at me – at Michael.

'Time to go now, Michael. Say bye bye to Madge.'

He turned to face me again. Face more open this time. The fear had subsided a little.

I knelt before him.

'Michael!' I raised my arms above my head, fists clenched.

'Da da da da; da da da,' I hummed the tune from *The A Team*.

His face broke into a grin. We understood one another again.

'Bye, sweetie.'

No answer, as with gritted teeth he clambered mechanically down the stairs and disappeared from view.

The social worker had written pages of notes. We would have to go through them very carefully to ensure she had recorded the salient points in detail.

'How long do you think it'll be before he can put all that into words?'

'I reckon three or four more sessions.'

'Do you think he'll be able to?'

'Yes, but not yet.'

'It's too scary yet, eh?'

'Mmm.'

'But, Madge, we might not get any more sessions.'

'I know…'

'But it was wrong to push, wasn't it, even though you want to?'

'Mmm.'

'We need more evidence than that, don't we?'

'Yes. All I can do is report that to the court as it happened.'

'Well, what could they say about it? I mean, it looked pretty obvious to me.'

'Could have watched Rambo on the telly…'

'Mmm… I see what you mean.'

'No, *The A Team*, wouldn't it be? They'd make out it was *The A Team*, and he was just playing out what he had seen on the telly.'

'Yes, possibly.'

'Shall we try another session next week?'

'Of course.'

We had begun. The facts would come, given time.

There was another aspect to all of this too. Michael was learning what his life experience was teaching him. To offer him a chance for the expression of his confusion was fine as far as it went. But how was he to learn that what he was being trained to expect of the male species was unacceptable and that he must not inflict it on others in real life when he grew up? I made a mental note to argue strongly for therapeutic help for him if and when the case was resolved to the satisfaction of the court.

The social worker rang me at home late in the evening.

'Bad news, I'm afraid, Madge. He's stopped Michael going to the nursery altogether now. Annette's closed ranks. Hell, I guess she just can't bear the consequences of us finding out anything. God, Madge, it's awful!'

'Where does that leave your department, then?'

'Well, we talked to Colin and our legal department. They say there isn't enough to proceed. Can't take a place of safety order and expect to get through a contested interim hearing. The evidence just isn't there, according to the solicitor. It would be too big a gamble. We'd probably lose. A couple of years ago we might have been able to convince a court that something was far wrong, but you know how it is now. After Cleveland they're all dead pro parents...'

'Pity none of his offences are Schedule I offences against children. Then we could move. Otherwise, we'll just have to monitor the older child carefully and try to get access to the little ones at the clinic – if she brings them, that is. I went round to see her as I arranged and she'd really changed her tune. I don't understand fully why, but she's far less co-operative than she was.'

I could see it would have to be a waiting game. If I had been on more solid ground I would have attended the case conference myself and argued tooth and nail for an attempt to be made at least, to approach the court to protect the children. But suspicion wasn't enough. It was pointless continuing the conversation.

I put some music on and curled up on the sofa. Michael. Michael. His memory was imprinted on my brain. Chafed little legs, blond hair, spidery hands, frail translucent skin stretched over a pinched face. Rambo, Superman, James Bond – eat your hearts out! Courage?! You don't know the meaning of the word. Meet a *real* hero! He'll show you how it is.

I neither saw nor heard about Michael again. But he is often in my thoughts.

Afterword

The interactions with Michael are described as they happened and the broad outline of his family circumstances has also been represented here. The context in which the communication took place has been transposed into a nursery setting to protect details of his identity. I think often of Michael and other children like him. It would be a relief to be able to report that our perceptions were wrong and that Michael now lives his life free from abuse. But this is probably not the case.

Legislation, in the form of the 1989 Children Act, is currently being introduced. One of its effects will be to strengthen considerably parents' rights of access and appeal in child abuse cases. In the meantime morale among those working in child protection ebbs lower than ever. The fact that fewer and fewer people want to do the job is reflected in major recruitment difficulties within child protection agencies.

GEORGE

'I'm ever so glad you've come. I don't know what we're going to do if this carries on, I really don't.'

George's foster mother stooped, holding on tightly to the dog's collar. She looked anxious.

'Come in. He's not here at the moment. Out on his bike. He doesn't know you're coming. I haven't told him or else he would have been off out of it and I'd never have been able to track him down. Hang on till I put the dog in the other room.'

I stood, paused in the hall for a few moments, breathless, toybox perched on one hip.

'Bring that in here, love. Cup of tea?'

We sat in the kitchen, dog scratching at the door into the hall. Mrs Elridge lit up a cigarette.

'Don't smoke, do you love? Now where do I start? Well, I had him on, let's see, the 29th January I think it was. I'm on me own here, see, apart from me own lads; they're grown up and married now. I have fostered before – had two little girls before. Shut up, Trixie!! Excuse me. Now Trixie, you'll go in your box. Quiet now!' Exasperation in her voice.

'Anyway...where was I? Yes, well they came and asked if I would have him straight from the hospital... Regional Psychiatric Unit he was in. Been there six months. You see, I don't have no little ones here – I'm on me own, see, as I said and anyway, they said "We don't want him bein' with no little ones on account of the things he does", see...you know, the touching them up and that. So I said I would give it a try... Seven, he was, eight in September. Lovely little lad, bless 'im. Came in here, asked me where his room was and started to unpack his two poly bags. Couldn't believe it, I couldn't. It was as if he done it all before. Don't know how many places he'd been in before. Just a bed to sleep in till he moved on again it seemed like.

'His social worker didn't tell me much. I had to discover it all for meself. Some of them's like that, aren't they…don't tell you much. I knew he was in for the two things, you know, the touching up them little ones – he's been doing that for years apparently – and the rages, tantrums, like.

'What kind of problems am I having with him at the moment? Is that what you said, dear? Oh, you want me to say from when he came, do you? The problems from when he came to me first? Sorry, I'll talk a bit slower, so you can write.

'Well…good, he was, for the first couple of days. Didn't know I had 'im, so to speak, and then,' pausing thoughtfully, 'then…oh, yes, the first thing was when I was doing his bed…the thievin'. He thieves all the time. I found all these wrappers…underneath the mattress, they were…chocolate and crisps packets and Instant Custard and, you know that Angel… Angel Delight. All them empty packets stuffed under there they were – I never saw anything like it. Then I checked in the cupboard – they weren't all from here – only the custard was, see.

'So I 'ad 'im for that. When he came in – on a Sunday, it was – I 'ad 'im. I said "George, I've been upstairs and look at all these things I've found in your bed. You're in trouble now, lad," I said. "Where on earth did all these come from?"

'Well, you've never seen anything like it. His knuckles went white and he started to grunt. I could see the sweat and the colour in his face. Went for me, he did. Picked up a butter knife lying on the table. Head down and went for me. Trixie went mad. So I grabbed him, I did. Got the knife out of his hand. And he was kicking and shouting mouthfuls. You've never heard the language – effin this and cuntin that. God, it's a wonder Bet next door didn't come round, but she had the automatic on, see and you can't hear through the wall so well when it's on.

'Well, I grabbed him, I did, and held on. He was out of control, shaking he was. Biting and screaming. Hold on, I did. Thank God I'm a bit bigger than he is, that's all I say. After a long time he was quiet. I said "Look, lad, nobody's going to beat hell out of you here. Now, where did all these papers come from?"

…But he never answered. Never cried neither. I've never seen him cry. Never said nothing once he was calmer. And I never pushed it

either. I kept him in after. He never said no more. Then he wanted to
go out.

'I said "Where are you going?"

'I'm going to commit suicide,' he said. Clear as you like. Have you
ever heard anything like it? Seven years old committing suicide. And
he's tried it since, he has. Riding his bike down off the side road up
the hill there – straight into the traffic, eyes closed. God preserve us!
Where on earth has he heard that, I wonder? I think he wants to,
though. He really does. Such a sad little mite. And all that thinkin' he
does! He sits here of an evening staring at the telly and you know he's
not watching it. Just deep in thought, he is. Deep in thought like a little
old man.

'Oh, the violence bit? You were asking. He has do's like that often
– about three times a week, I'd say – doesn't care who he hurts. Well,
turns out one of his mother's boyfriends was violent. Locked up now,
he is, I imagine. Thought he would toughen George up and learn him
how to be tough. Broke his arm and both his legs. That's when he came
into care first, back when he was four, I think. I'm not exactly sure.
Then his mother couldn't cope with him after…she had all these other
little ones to manage. Not a bad lass, his mother. George lives for his
Mum, he does. Worships the ground she walks on. Only sees her at
Christmas and Easter. Shame. Poor lad.

'The touchin' up? Yes, there's the touchin' up he does. That's what
you've come here about, isn't it? That's the worst problem, that is. I
think if we could just sort that out he would be much happier. None
of my neighbours will let their kids play with him on account of it,
see. Call him a rapist they do. I suppose he is, really. I suppose that's
what he is when it boils down to it. And I can't keep me eyes on him
all the time, can I? I mean, you can't lock him up, can you?

'When it started off? He'd been here about three weeks then, yes,
three weeks it was, and I heard from my mate Betty that Carol up the
road – she wouldn't let her little boy out when George was around.
Scared stiff, he was. So I went to see her.

'"Carol," I said, "what's been going on? What's the matter with
George?"

'She just went scarlet. Bright scarlet, she went. She was too embarrassed to tell me straight off. Then she said her little lad had come in
one day with blood in his mouth, crying. Said George had hurt him in
the mouth. Not with his hand, though, with his willie. He'd been

putting his willie in their little lad's mouth – only four, he was – and telling him to suck it or he'd bash his head in. Terrified, he was, the little lad, and George had broke that little bit of skin – you know, the bit where your top lip joins on to your jaw? The bit that hangs down there? Well, that bit.

'So I had him for that. Walloped him, I did. Said it was disgusting and he was never, ever to do it again. He never cried, and he never had a violent fit either, come to think of it. But you know what he said? I'll never forget it. He just shrugged his shoulders and said "I'm like that, aren't I?"

'We've had a lot of them since that time. Any kid he plays with you can bet eventually he's threatened them, in the bushes usually. If they tell he says he'll bash their heads in. And he's had it everywhere. In their mouths, up their bottoms and in their front ends too – boys and girls. I think he likes it, meself. He must do, mustn't he... You can hardly believe it, can you? So none of the kids round here will play with him. None of their parents'll let them, come to that. They won't talk about it, see, but he knows. Can't blame them, can you? I shout at him. I threaten him. I take his pocket money away. And all he says is "Well, it's cos I'm like that." Every time, he says it. I think when he was in hospital they put him away in a separate room and not on the ward with the other kids, but I can't lock him away, can I, love?

'Hang on. Shut up, Trixie... Oh, that must be George back now. He'll wonder who you are. I'll leave it to you to explain, shall I? He'll have seen the car anyway.'

Seizing its chance, the black labrador pup bounded through the half open door, leapt over the toybox and, paws on my knees, wagged its tail furiously, narrowly missing the teacups on the pine kitchen table.

'Trixie! Come here!'

George stood in the doorway. He cast a sideways glance at me.

'Auntie Irene...is my laser gun back? Has Joe brought it back mended?'

'No, son, I'm sorry. Here, this is Madge.'

No eye contact.

'Hello, George.'

No answer.

'George, say Hello. Be polite now.'

Faint muttering.

'I'll bet you're wondering what I'm doing here?'

No acknowledgement. Then: 'Hey, what's them? Can I see them?'
(Pointing to the box of toys.)

'Yes, of course you can. Auntie Irene, can we go through to the living
room and let George look at some of the toys? Would that be OK?'

A small, fine-boned little boy he was, with rough crinkly reddish-
brown hair which stood up from his head like a scouring pad. His blue
eyes were alert and wary, skating over the surface of the toys. His
movements rapid and unselfconscious. Without a word he moved his
body this way and that, stretching over to unearth a particular toy which
caught his eye. Careful now, Madge...take it easy...wait for him to
come to you...no questions yet...not for a long time yet. I sat
cross-legged watching him play, echoing his movements, sometimes
feeding back his words when they came.

'What's that?'

'You want to know what that is.'

'Yep. I had one of these. Is it a carriage? I think it is. You know my
cousin, John his name is, he had one but me Mam threw it out cos he
smashed it under the fridge.'

Pauses, head on one side, trawling his memory.

'No, I think it was the stove,' shaking his head. 'Brrrrrrmmmmmm
Wyaaaaaaw Psssching... Ha... Crash...Smithereens!'

The police car with the blue light flew across the floor, nose wedged
under the settee.

'Ha-Ha! Filth bastards. Bang!'

Quickly he moved through the toys, picking one up, then another,
experiencing each momentarily. Investing in none. His eyes fell on the
anatomically complete dolls. He picked up the male doll; put it down
again. Then the female doll; pulled down her pants, glanced speedily
at her private parts. Momentarily our eyes met, then he threw her down
beside the man and opened the box of magic pencils which tumbled
out on the floor.

'You got some paper?' he asked, rubbing his nose on the back of his
shirt sleeve.

'No, not with me,' I said. 'I'll bring some next time.'

Slowly he nodded and, pausing, studied my face closely for the first
time.

'You always been fat?' he said.

'Yep. Ever since I was little. I've never been thin.'

'Neither has my Mum.'

The door was opening a fraction... I inched my way slowly...

'Shall I tell you what I'm doing here... Why I've brought the toys?'

'Nope.'

'Don't want to know?...that's OK.'

'Nope.'

Move out again, woman. You're going in too fast.

'I have to go soon. Next time I come I'll remember to bring the paper.

No resistance.

'I'll put them back now, then...'

And he watched as I tidied the toys back into the box.

The next time I saw George he was waiting patiently by the living room door, holding a plastic racing car.

'Hi,' I said. 'Where are we today? Back in the living room again?'

Silence. He gestured with his eyes in eager anticipation. I followed his gaze through the open door where he had erected his racing track.

'Wow! Pretty neat, eh?'

Without a word he handed me the other car.

'Want a game, then? OK.'

And we were off, skidding round the racetrack crashing and shunting and falling off backwards as the battery-driven cars sped round and round the room.

'What's them?' he said, noting a small box tied up with a pair of woollen tights.

'These are my jigsaws.'

'Can I have a look?'

Without waiting for an answer he was examining them closely.

'Can I tip them out?'

'This one? Well...watch...'

Before I could warn him the jigsaw lay in a pile on the floor. Wincing inwardly, I could see it was the most difficult one to complete – a double-layered animal scene it was, hopelessly complicated.

He lay on his tummy and surveyed the task. In a careful and considered way he matched the pieces, studying each piece, trying it for size, measuring it in his mind. His application was total. I lay on the carpet alongside him, sometimes handing him possible pieces, other times watching the meticulous child at work.

'George, you're very, very good at that, you know. I can't do that one. I'm hopeless.'

He smiled.

'Piece of cake!' he said slowly. 'Piece of cake!'

Gradually the scene was coming together. Together we watched as the deft hands gave meaning to the fragmented pieces on the carpet.

'George. You know that lady – your social worker – who comes to see you sometimes. I think her name's Helen, isn't it?'

'Yep.'

'Well, you know what? She knows I spend a lot of time with children and she knows too that I'm not bad at getting to the bottom of muddles and helping to sort them out...'

'Mmm.'

Still concentrating, eyes firmly fixed on the jigsaw. 'Well, she rang me up, you know, and she said, "Madge... I go to see a boy called George and he has lots of muddles, mostly hurting and touching muddles, I think. Would you go and see George, Madge? Will you take your toybox with you, and will you see if you can help George sort them out?"'

George looked up. 'And what did you say?'

'I said "OK". George, do you know what she means by touching muddles?'

'Mmmmm.'

'You know when you do touching to children in places they don't like...in parts of their bodies they don't want to be touched...'

'Yep...like on their cunts?' Giggling.

'Yes, like on their cunts. George, has anyone ever touched you on your body like that?'

'Yep... Elaine, I think. I can't remember her name. Have you got them pencils again and that papers you was going to bring? I'll draw you a picture.'

And so George drew me a picture of his 'nicest day'.

'That's the bed, see,' he said carefully, 'and that's me; bottom bunk bed it was and I'm lying on top of her see. I'm feeling her bits and then my willy goes in her bottom.'

Bit by bit the story emerged. When he was about three a young female babysitter had taken the child upstairs and involved him in sex acts, with anal and vaginal intercourse. This was to continue regularly until he left home finally when he was six. Secrecy was assured. If the child talked she wouldn't be able to come again and it would be his fault.

'Nobody knows. I've not told no one. You won't tell no one, will you?'

God...this would be difficult! I chose my words carefully.

'George, there are some secrets that are really too hard to keep. It would be wrong of me to keep that kind of secret.'

'Oh, God!' Fear rose in his voice. 'Oh, God! Don't tell. I don't want you to tell! I'll fuckin kill you, I will, like this, look.' (Kung fu-like chop aimed at my throat.)

'Don't tell 'er through there, then,' he conceded gesturing towards the kitchen. 'She'll go mad. And she'll shout. You won't tell, will you? Well, I'd prefer it. I'd just prefer it,' he said with great maturity.

The urge to comply was great. Much easier all round. But how would that help him? What would that teach him? That it is right to enter into secrets with adults about sexual abuse? That adults molest children and we keep it a secret? No. And what about the fact that serious offences have been alleged here?... So...

'I'll tell you what, George.' I pause. 'I won't tell her yet, OK? Next time I come back, though, we'll tell her together. I have books all about touching muddles (lots of children have them, you know) and I'll bring them with me next time.'

'Know them dolls with the bibs and bobs on?'

'Yes.'

'Well, will you bring them too?'

'Of course I will. That's a deal, then, is it?'

'Yep.'

In the circumstances it seemed important to gain a picture of George's home context. In any event his mother, I was told, wanted to talk to me.

George's natural mother was a small, stoutly built woman, slightly bloated, with bulbous eyes and bleached blonde hair. The house seemed to be full of children. Two small grubby faces peered at me from the recesses of the kitchen.

'Tracey! Take him, and will yer just take him out. Now you've had one ice lolly. Now, scat. Take one for Tom, mind and just disappear till I talk to the lady. Go on now.'

'But, Mum...'

'Look, I've had enough today...'

With a sudden deliberate flourish she propelled herself to her feet and quickly towards the open fridge. The children fled.

'Bloody kids. Who'd 'ave 'em, eh?' She grinned, closing the fridge door and sitting down again beside me on the settee.

'Well, I've been married before. I've two lads older than George. None o' this bother with them, though. Me ex-husband has 'em now, like.

'I reckon it started when he was about, well, nearly three, I think. Made me sick it did. I mean, he would just...well...letch at me...like a grown man does, like. He'd want to suck my breasts and he'd put my hand between his legs and rub his...you know...against me. Dirty little bugger! And he would play with himself all the time. Sit on the edge of the settee, like, and play with himself. Looked like I'd bred a sex maniac or somethin'. Made me ill, it did. I would belt him for it, I would, 'specially when he had a go at Tracey. I mean she would only just have started to walk, like. I remember one time, the babysitter came, she did, and he dropped his trousers and ran after her like – big erection and all that, like. I picked 'im up, I did. I gave him a good wallopin', I did. "You disgustin' little bugger," I said, "don't you ever do that again." Ever so embarrassed she was. Ran out of the room, she did.

'That was the worst of 'im, like. I mean, all the rest I could stand, all his stealin and that, like. But made me ill, he did I mean, it got so I couldn't stand the sight of him, couldn't bear to touch him or anything, like. I didn't want to cuddle 'im at all, I didn't. Couldn't even pick 'im up. I mean, I want to 'ave 'im, like. He's my son, but I couldn't have him back now. Too much water's gone under the bridge, like...'

The fact that George had begun to describe possible sexual offences committed against him now made this a matter which required discussions with the police.

The Detective-Inspector sighed.

'We'll give it a run, love, but don't hold out much hope about getting far. Most of these, we never get anywhere. I mean this one, it's old now. Three years at least, isn't it, and there's likely to be no medical evidence, even if it was fresh...there's not likely to be any medical evidence.'

We both knew the score. A tiny proportion of such cases ever got to court. The chance of a successful prosecution in such a case was minimal.

'Her word against his at the end of the day, isn't it, love? I mean, she ain't exactly gonna have set herself up with an audience, is she? There ain't likely to have been any witnesses...'

He was right. Absolutely right and we both knew it. What self-respecting child molester would publicly engage in sexual activity with a child?

'Need to have a few screws loose for that, love, wouldn't she? Probably married with a kid of 'er own now. Bloomin heck, eh? Christ knows what she's doing to that one, eh?'

We mulled the case over, this way and that. The task in hand was a very delicate one. One wrong move and the child was likely to clam up and deny everything. Regardless of the prosecution aspects of the case, my own duty was clear. How could I help to achieve the best possible outcome for George? To make things better for him now rather than worse would surely demand the very best of whatever skill I possessed. God, what if I got it wrong?

'Yes, I appreciate the position, love. I'll send one of my girls down. Sandra Carr. She's on back shift today, but she could do something tomorrow afternoon.'

The Inspector's words brought me back to the room.

'I can see the point, though. Might be wrong to introduce a new face at this stage. Maybe best see him again yourself once. Delicate business, this, eh? Best of luck with it, love.'

I drove back to see George the next day. He was lying in the gravel outside the front gate scoring lines between the stones with a piece of stick. I was five minutes early.

'Hi-ya, George. Been waiting long?'

'Ages,' he sighed, pulling himself up off the ground. 'I thought you wasn't coming... 'Ave you got them books an' that?' Moving round towards the car boot.

Silently we unloaded the boot, books, bag of dolls. George piled them up in his arms and carried them towards the house. Auntie Irene held the door open.

'Locked Trixie upstairs this time,' she said. 'She's a real nuisance sometimes, isn't she, George?'

Silence. He ducked under her arm.

'Glad you managed to catch 'im, Madge. He's been threatening to run away all mornin', he has. Haven't you, son?... Cup of tea?'

'Yes, please.'

'Irene.' Choose the words carefully. 'Irene. I wondered if you could come and read with us today. You see, I've brought some books and these are books that grown-ups and children read together – books about some of the things that sometimes happen to children. I thought it would be an idea if we read some of them together?'

George stood, transfixed to the spot, eyes searching, fearful, pleading.

'Oh…er… Auntie Irene… I read these books with lots of grown-ups and children together. Sometimes, you know, children get very worried because they think they might be in trouble and grown-ups might start shouting at them and being angry. But George isn't in trouble today, is he?'

'Oh, no. He's not in trouble today.' Auntie Irene looked surprised.

'So he doesn't have to worry about you being cross with him when we read our books together?'

'Well, no…'

By the time the tea arrived George was already well absorbed in the task. Perched beside me on the arm of the soft brown armchair studiously poring through the pages for clues. Puzzling. Puzzling.

We went back to the beginning. Auntie Irene sipping her tea, another copy of the Touching Book on her lap. We looked at 'good touching', when people held on to other people's arms to make sure they don't fall over, good touching, touching which feels nice, like when Trixie licks George's face when he comes home from school.

'Doesn't she, Auntie Irene.' He giggled excitedly. 'And she sleeps on my bed!'

Together we heard about bad touching – touching that isn't good to give to other people, and certainly isn't good to get – like punching and biting and shoving people out of the way.

'An' like this… Look, Madge, like Kung Fu,' and George was off across the floor. 'Look, like this!' Fast and deliberate his arms moved in an circular motion, then 'Pow!' dust flew as he drove his fist home on to the cushion on the settee.

'Yes, George. Well, that would be bad touching if you used it to hurt someone or damage something.'

Secret touching next. After defining the word 'secret', the book went on to describe 'secret touching', how that was something some adults did with children, when they made them promise not to tell about touching secrets… George nodded and looked at me, tension mounting in his expression, but determined to turn the page…

'Guess what, Auntie Irene. I bet you probably didn't know, but George and I reckon maybe that someone, some grown-up, might have done some of that secret touching with him, you know.'

'Is that right?' Auntie Irene looked at me, bracing herself, but staying with me, staying in tune. Dangerous ground here...

George edged closer to me, knuckles stiffening.

'Auntie Irene. Now, if you were to find out that some big grown-up had done some secret touching with George, would you be cross?'

'Yes, I would. I certainly would,' she murmured slowly.

'But who would you be cross with?'

'Well, I'd be cross with the grown-up, wouldn't I?'

'Well, would you be cross with the little boy?'

'No, I wouldn't be cross with him.'

'Why not, then...'

George was relaxing slightly, doodling on the page with his finger. Not interrupting. All ears.

'Well, because, well...it wouldn't be his fault, would it? I mean he's only a little boy.'

'It's not his fault, then, Irene. So it would be OK for George to tell us if someone had done secret touching with him, wouldn't it, because you wouldn't get cross with him?'

'Course not, bless 'im! He's a good lad, really. Aren't you, son?'

'Can you remember what you drew for me the last time I came, George?'

An' this is what she done...see... Where's them dolls with the bibs and bobs on?... I'll show yer what she did.'

George was off. An invisible suit of chain mail, dissolving as he spoke. Anatomical dolls in hand...

'See, it was like this. I had to put this bit – see this bit in 'ere – that's the fanny bit and I was lying on her jellies...like...'

'Jellies?'

'Well, 'em; boobs; an' that was how it was. Doin' sex, we was. An' then I had to put my willie there and she...'

More detail this time. Description of time, place, events, what happened after, where Mum was at the time (down the Red Lion pub usually), with Colin. It was when she was with Colin.

Irene sat, mouth vaguely open, the implications of what she was hearing gradually dawning. Poor woman.

'Now, Irene. What do you think about this lady and what has happened to George? Are you angry with her?'

'Angry! Angry? I could...well I could throttle her!' she said, closing the book emphatically. 'Poor little lad...him only a babby, like. Only a babby when this was all happening. You wouldn't credit it. Well, I'd never have believed it. I mean I've never heard anything like it. I mean you hear it goes on, but...'

Suddenly George was on his feet. Wham! Ker pow! The lady doll flew through the air and landed face down by the ashtray. Bang! Picked up again.

'I'll Kung Fu 'er. Fuckin bitch...!' Punching, pummelling at the female doll.

'Give it 'er, lad. That's right. Give it 'er!' Irene's instinct had taken over. 'Give 'er what for. She should never have done that to you – bad woman!'

Oblivious to her words, George was still locked in a reverie of his own. Banging, twisting, pummelling the female doll. Silently sawing at her neck with the side of his hand...

In the pit of my stomach the knot was beginning to unravel itself. The tension was breaking. Breathing deeply from the force of his anger, George lay back on to me, face open and receptive.

'You know, George, I feel quite cross with that lady too because, you know, children's bodies are for them, not for ladies to use like that when they feel like it...and adults know very well that they mustn't do secret things like that. That's usually why they make children keep it a secret, because they know that Mummies and police and teachers and other people would be very very angry if they got to hear about it. And the police have to go and see them and sort it out...'

'You know Sam...you know, where I was before at the other house? I think it was that house, the one in the Radbarn Estate, well, you know Sam...'

'Mmm...'

'He does them things...well, not like that but...you know that white stuff...like eggs before it's cooked...where the wee wee comes out of the willie...well, he used to rub my willie like and rub that stuff on my arms an' that...when it came out of his...'

'Who's Sam?'

'He's, you know him that was in the place before.'

I turned towards Irene for clarification. Irene sat rooted to the chair...crimson faced...there were tears in the corners of her eyes...her voice was trembling. Slowly she said, 'Well, George has talked about him. I think he was an older lad, about seventeen he was, I think. In the children's home wasn't it, George?'

George nodded.

'Well, you know,' I said lamely. 'Sam shouldn't have done it either.'

Irene got up and went out into the kitchen. George sat relaxed, poring through another book on *The Facts of Life*. I followed her through to the kitchen. Irene moved around the room distractedly, lighting a cigarette, hand shaking.

'Poor little blighter! Poor little blighter!'

Furious rush of water into the kettle.

'When I think... Oh God, Madge...can't bear to think about it, can you?' She bit back tears.

'Irene, you were smashing – just right. You were lovely with him.'

'But, Madge, well. I've just had an ordinary life. I mean you don't think, do you? All the things I've said to him an' all. Breaks my heart, it does. I mean I haven't had no special training or nothing... I've made it worse for 'im, haven't I? I have, haven't I?' Burying her head on her arms on the formica work surface.

'Irene... Irene...you were great! There's more to do, though, and I think today's the right time.'

I moved across to her.

'Irene, you're a very lovely lady and you've given him a great deal.'

'But it's not enough, Madge. It's not enough!'

She wept openly now, sobbing on to my neck. Moments passed.

'Irene, I'm going to go back in now. When you feel ready, come in too; but if you can't...it's OK.'

George looked up when I returned. Our eyes met... I winked at him and grinned. A spontaneous wink. He was re-reading the *Facts of Life* book. Disjointed, half-understood glimmerings began to be given meaning. It was beginning to make sense.

'What are you winkin' for?' He grinned.

'Don't know... I suppose it's because I think you were very brave today.'

'Do you like Auntie Irene?' he said...out of the blue.

'Yes, I think she's great.'

'So do I.'

'I bet she's a bit different from your Mum. I mean I bet she's great too.'

'Different great.'

'Yes. Different great.'

I explained to George that Irene was sad. Very sad. She was sad because she was shocked that so many things had happened to him when he was such a little boy. And she was sad because she was thinking about all the times she had shouted at him and been cross with him when she hadn't really understood why he was doing the things he was doing.

'But I liked them things. When I think of them things like sex things and that, me willie goes all hard and I rub it like Sam done.'

'I know. George. It is nice. Most people have nice feelings when they rub their private parts. Grown-ups and children do.'

'Does Mrs Archer?'

'Who's Mrs Archer?'

'My teacher.'

'I expect Mrs Archer does too, but,' hastily, 'that's not the sort of thing Mrs Archer would like to talk about, I think. We need to talk about how you can still rub your privates, but by yourself, not with little children. Now, can you listen, George, because I'm going to try and explain it to you. Then I think we should write a story about it so that I can be sure you really truly understand. Because all of this is a very big muddle and it sure is making life difficult, isn't it? Can we sit down, you, me and Auntie Irene, and write a story about it together?'

George's Story

The things George needs to remember.

Lots of grown-ups like *Tom, Birt, Helen Socal Warkr* are fond of George. They like him because they think he is a *nise little boy*. There are many good parts inside him. He is a *fast runner, cinned to animels, good at helping Tom in his ched.* Some grown-ups and some children don't like George. That's because he *tels lyies, pinch bykkes and hurts therr bottem.*

It's OK to give and to get good touches like *pat a dog in the bed*, and, *hold a hand cros the rode and scrub hand with sope.*

It's not OK to give and to get bad touches like *bitein Peter* or *hurt bottem an' Kungfu wiv rola skaets on an hurt Sayera.*

Sex happens when a grown-up mummy and daddy love each other and sometimes they want to make babies. Some grown-ups are very silly. They do secret touching, like sex, with children and tell them to keep it a *secrit*. But we never keep secrets about secret touching with a grown-up and George knows that now.

Secret touching puts muddles into little children's minds and gets them into *bad think an trubel* when they do it to other children smaller than themselves. So when George hurts other little children's *botems an mouth* with his willie what he's doing is putting muddles in their minds too, just like *Elan and Sam* did to him. But now George knows what he's doing. He knows now why adults like *Anti Irin* get so cross when he does *sekrit touching*.

What George needs to do now is to *stop sekrit touching an' bad trubel*.

If he wants to rub his own *wily*, he can do it…*in baf or in toylet* but he must stop touching other people's private parts. Now, there may still be some little muddles about touching left over and George might *forgot*. If he does forget and do a little bit more secret touching with another little child, then grown-ups like… *Anti Irin, Plice, Mrs Arche*…may get very cross indeed.

Auntie Irene may *showt lowed, say no pokit muney or stey in bed room*.

And now George knows why.

We wrote it in triplicate. A copy for each one of us to keep. We wondered if anyone else might be interested in reading George's story. Who else might like to hear about the silly lady in particular, and maybe the silly big boy, too, who might have done secret touching to George?

Mrs Archer? Yes, she might want to know. Well, yes. What about the police?

'Will they shout at 'er an' put 'er in prison?'

Sudden panic crossed his face…

'Oops, I think I've forgot 'er name.'

We pondered for a moment…

'Can we phone from here, Irene? Would that be OK?'

George stood up.

'No, I want to. I want to tell 'em. Can I, Auntie Irene? Oh, please, can I?'

He ran eagerly to the phone.

'Shall I ring first and find the right person and then you can speak to her. I think it'll be a lady…'

He dialled the number himself and handed me the receiver.

'Is that Detective Constable Carr?'

'Yes.'

'Well, my name's Madge Bray and I have a little boy called George here. We've written a story together and he wants to tell it to you. Yes, well… He's here now. Yes. You'll want to ask him questions?'

'George, she needs to ask you questions.'

He nodded importantly.

'Yep… I'll tell 'er. Ask me…one, two, three, four, five. Gimme the phone.'

'See, I've 'ad them muddles about touching, little kids an' that, but I ain't got 'em now. I ain't gonna do that no more and I ain't gonna forget,' he added slowly. 'I'm gonna stop, and rub me willy in the bathroom…'

Silence at the other end whilst DC Carr regained her composure.

'Right – fine. OK, George. I'll be down as soon as I can with my writing pad and a pen,' the policewoman's voice quavered.

'OK. I'll ask me foster auntie, me mam you know, to get the kettle on. And, oh, yeah. Will you bring some of them handcuffs, so I can see them…and come in a filth car an' all.'

He thrust the receiver at me and stalked back into the living room to await her arrival, closing the door behind him.

Afterword

I remember George as a street-wise, self-sufficient little boy. I was asked by his social worker to help with the sexually aggressive behaviour he displayed, which dominated his life. Although attempts were made, no legal action could be taken against either of his alleged abusers. I understand that for a significant period after these events George's behaviour improved considerably, but I have no current knowledge of him.

The dilemmas in treating a child who is both victim and victimiser are often overwhelming. Much research remains to be undertaken into the evolutionary factors which create adults who molest children. Our understanding of how to arrest such patterns in children already behaving in this way, is in its infancy.

We are about to embark on a research project, funded largely by public donation, which it is hoped will further our knowledge into this and other aspects of child sex abuse.

ZOE

The package from the court arrived on my desk one Thursday before Christmas. A sheaf of papers almost an inch thick. Social services reports, probation report, police statement and a psychiatric report on the person who appeared to be the father in the case, and affidavits from both the father and mother.

Pinned to the front of the package was the Court Order which contained the words 'It is ordered that Margery Evelyn Bray be appointed Guardian ad Litem to the child Zoe...' in what was clearly a divorce matter. The judge was being asked to make decisions with regard to custody and access and had made what he considered to be an appropriate interim step in appointing an independent person to represent the child's interests. I knew this was a normal course of action in cases where proceedings were being taken against the parents by the social services department concerned about the care of a child, but it was unusual in a divorce case. Perplexing, really.

I spoke to the Clerk of the Court on Monday morning. It was not a course of action I was familiar with, and I had never worked in that town before.

The judge had been particularly concerned about the details of the evidence so far. He had adjourned the case and given direction that I should be appointed, and could if I wished appoint a solicitor to act for the child. He wanted me to conduct whatever number of interviews I considered appropriate with the child, and to see any other party or parties necessary in the course of my duties. I was to return to the court for directions should the need arise, and the specific focus of my task was to ascertain the nature of this child's experience, if any, with regard to the question of child abuse, paying particular regard to the question of sexual abuse.

Apologies for the papers containing my home address in error. Yes, it would mean that both parties would have been notified of that address.

Yes, of course, it could place me in a compromising position because everyone involved would know where I lived. The Clerk would check to make sure it didn't happen again.

It was part of my function as Guardian ad Litem to appoint a solicitor. I made contact with Joanna Hornby, a solicitor I knew in the area, and asked her to take instructions on behalf of the child. We would need to work closely together. This was a complex High Court case: an acrimonious divorce. We discussed briefly the facts of the case:

The parents had been together for seven years. Zoe aged five was the only child of the marriage although mother had a child by a previous marriage – Rupert, aged 15 – of whom she had custody. Father, aged 45, a merchant banker, apparently had moved back to London and now had access to Zoe every fourth weekend.

Zoe's mother, Charlotte, was nine years younger than her husband, the daughter of a wealthy family whose business was in the ceramics industry. Her interests included fine arts and antiques. Her first marriage to an army officer had ended abruptly when he was killed in a riding accident. Her second husband, Zoe's father, had been an acquaintance for many years.

Zoe was attending St Cecilia's convent school as a day girl. From what we could ascertain from the court papers, Zoe had returned home from an access visit and had told her mother that she did not want to go again because 'Daddy tickles my bottom and puts his finger in it.' Much to her family's consternation, Charlotte had impulsively telephoned the local police station and reported the matter; the police and social services department had made a visit. The child had refused to elaborate.

'Damned inconvenient of her, really', the solicitor grinned at me across the desk, '"refusing to elaborate".' Our minds had obviously focused on the same sentence at the same time.

'Joanna, you're a rotten cynic!'

'Mmm. There's a lot of money in child abuse these days. Can't afford to allow our cynicism to take over, though, can we?'

I was beginning to bristle.

'She just may be telling the truth.'

'Who are we talking about now?'

'The little girl – Zoe, isn't it?' – she glanced quickly at the bundle of papers on her desk. 'Mm. But it looks as though it's caused a complete furore. Grandparents are outraged. Family can't live it down. By the look of the affidavits, Grandad's threatening to have a heart attack any minute. Granny wants to cut them off from the family. And that's only Charlotte's parents. Father's psychiatrist says he's mentally sound and probably incapable of such perversion. And I've already had the father's solicitor on the phone to say that they'll produce evidence from the school. Apparently since he left home Zoe has been very distressed, can't concentrate, bullying other children. The headmistress seems to think the mother's the villain of the piece and has put the child up to making these dreadful allegations.'

She looked at me thoughtfully, pursing her lips. I met her gaze.

'But she's only ever said one sentence by the looks of things.'

'Yes, but that's dreadful enough in the circumstances, don't you think? Thank God I'm the solicitor acting for the child! Mind you, I could bet on how I'd prepare father's case if I was representing him.'

'A pure-as-the-driven-snow job?'

She laughed openly now.

'I bet you could – you solicitors are a really hateful bunch sometimes. Where's the morality in all of this?'

'Morality, Madge. Come, come, don't talk about morality to me. That's not my province.'

'But you'll prepare Zoe's case properly and well?'

'Mmm...what do you think?'

'Very well indeed.'

I like Joanna. Although I hadn't worked with her before I'd been on the receiving end of her skill as an advocate. She had been a formidable if immodest opponent, and I had written her name in my diary for future use.

I made my way up the tarmac drive towards the family home. It was beautiful. Set back in its own grounds, with views over the surrounding farmland. I began to wish that I had at least taken the car through the car wash – it looked out of place parked squat and dirty in front of the elegant Georgian facade.

A boy of about fifteen answered the door.

'Yes, please do come in.'

I was ushered into the drawing room.

'My mother is upstairs – I'll go and fetch her now.'

He left the room and I heard him bound up the wide wooden staircase, three steps at a time.

I looked around me. A strange mixture of styles. Cream-coloured walls, oak panelling. A regency chaise longue, delicately re-upholstered in pink satin. A wonderful marble fireplace; an arrangement of dried flowers.

I could hear voices from upstairs. A tall, striking woman entered the room, closing the door behind her. Her hair was pulled tight off her face and held firmly with a clasp at the back of her neck. She walked towards me, hand outstretched, smiling slightly. I rose to my feet to greet her, relieved to have left the toybox in the car. Now was not quite the time or place.

'I though you were expecting me today? I'm sorry to have disturbed you.'

'No, no, please. No trouble.'

She fumbled in the pocket of her jacket for some cigarettes, then strode across the room to pick up the brass table lighter. I saw her hand shake. Drink? Tranquilisers? Or maybe simply anxiety?

'I know you've come about this business...'

'Yes.'

'It needs to be settled as quickly as possible, for all concerned.'

'Yes, I understand.'

I could feel myself softening to her. She was working terribly hard to maintain a modicum of decorum in circumstances which patently lacked respectability. I wondered how long we could continue to talk about 'it' in the abstract.

I explained to her how I worked. That I would like to see her daughter on her own. I would audio-tape the sessions with her child. I would use play to communicate and with the aim of attempting to understand what, if anything, lay behind her daughter's comments to her. It might be that I would ask her to be present at a subsequent session, depending on what progress was made. I explained that it might also prove necessary to conduct a play session with her husband present also, although I would seek the court's direction on this matter if necessary.

She nodded slowly. Face empty, close to exhaustion. She drew on her cigarette.

'Yes, thank you. I'll go along with whatever you say.'

'Once I've seen Zoe once or twice, I'd like to sit down both with you and with your husband, separately, and try to understand how you think you've got to be where you are now. What exactly has happened. Please will you try not to grill Zoe, though, about what happens in the play sessions. I think she may be under enough pressure as it is...'

'Oh, I haven't spoken to her since, about what she said...if that's what you mean. I haven't quite known...how...well, how to broach it, really. I can't bring myself to question her about it again.'

I smiled at her.

'Strange, though, she's been asking lately about how babies get made. Asks persistently. I think she's too young, you know, for that sort of thing, so I've told her I'll tell her when she's older... I know she does seem confused about it all, but how much can one tell her at her age, without taking away from her innocence?'

'Any other unusual behaviour you've noticed?'

'Well, it's terribly strange', she bent forward, pushing a wisp of hair back into the clasp at the nape of her neck, 'but she does seem to have been sleeping badly recently. Wakes up terrified. Ingrid goes to her; (she's the au pair). But I've moved her into the bedroom next to mine, so that I can hear her.

'Then there's the spiders. She's become hysterical at the sight of spiders. And babies too! Crosses the road if she sees a pram coming. Flatly refused to come into the room when my friend and her husband brought their new baby to see us.'

There were tears in the corners of her eyes. Her voice was desperate.

'And then there's school. She's been affected terribly by the divorce, but the worst... I mean...we used to be so close...she's the most important thing in my life...you have to believe I...'

Small, sobbing, choking noises.

'I...love her so much. But...but she won't come near me now. She won't let me touch her hardly...so independent suddenly...wants to bathe alone, wash her own hair – or wants Ingrid to do it. Maybe she's punishing me for Adrian leaving...but...is it natural? Do you find this with children?'

Not hesitating for a reply, she continued,

'So up until all this happened I've insisted she sees him and that he keeps to his visits. I think she needs to see her father. I wanted her to keep in touch with him... Rupert, my son...he's never had that chance...So...'

Her train of thought interrupted itself...

'And now... Oh, goodness...this! It's all too terrible. I simply can't believe it of Adrian. Not his own daughter. I'd be terribly relieved if it isn't true. I know I can hardly believe it. I don't want to believe it. You haven't met my husband yet, have you? I know he'd never be convinced of this, but I pray, I pray, I pray constantly that you will find it's not true. You see, Zoe's suffering terribly – but she won't let me near her. I can't bear it. If he would come back now I'd rather have it. I'd rather put up with the women and his unfaithfulness, but not this. I'd do anything. I look at her sometimes when she's asleep and I think, it must all be a dream. Maybe I didn't hear her correctly. Maybe I over-reacted. My mother thinks I did. She's terribly distressed. And Adrian's father – he's absolutely furious with me.'

'Mrs Govier, can we talk about all this once I've seen Zoe? I know it's very vital, but right now I've come to spend some time with Zoe and I wanted just to ask you about what changes you've noted in her behaviour generally. I want to try to be as scrupulous about this as possible. Would you mind if we discussed this after I've spent time with Zoe, please.'

'Oh, yes, of course. I'm sorry. My head feels as though it has an elastic band round it at the moment. I can't even think properly.'

Her voice tailed off as there was a knock at the door. Ingrid entered with a tray of china tea cups and what looked like handmade biscuits.

'Thank you, Ingrid. No, please leave us. Thank you.'

She grappled for familiar control. Earl Grey tea. The biscuits were delicious. Almond with fondant icing.

A taxi drew up outside. We watched as a sturdy little dark-haired child climbed out of the taxi, straw boater in one hand, satchel in the other, and walked purposefully across to the front door. Her mother laid down her cup and went to the door to greet her.

'Hello, darling. Had a good day at school? Look, we have a visitor in the drawing room, poppet.'

Zoe stood in the doorway, eyeing me curiously. I turned towards her, remaining seated.

'Hello, Zoe. My name's Madge Bray.'

'Hello', she said politely.

Her mother had returned to her seat:

'Come here, darling. I want to talk to you.'

I watched the child's body stiffen as her mother pulled her on to her knee. The gold-brown school uniform fitted her body tightly. She sat bolt upright, ramrod stiff.

'Zoe', her mother continued. 'This lady has come from the court...you know...where Daddy and I have to go to talk about the divorce and...and...', she was fumbling now, 'and the rest of this business. So she will want to ask you some questions.'

I waited until she was finished. The urge to interrupt had been strong. I didn't want Zoe to feel pressured by my presence before our relationship began.

'Mmm, well. That's part of what I do...but I don't ask children to sit down and then ask them questions. What I like to do is bring my toybox, and we get down on the floor and play together. Some children have lots of muddles in their heads and sometimes we can get to the bottom of the muddles. Sometimes my job is to help the grown-ups to understand what children's muddles are about.'

The child was watching me carefully. Sallow skin – large brown almond-shaped eyes – a front tooth missing.

'Sometimes, though, I have very special jobs to do, you know, and this time I have been asked to help the judge. Do you know what a judge is?'

Zoe stared at me, fingers in her mouth. Her mother removed the fingers.

'Like Charles' Daddy?'

'Oh yes, darling, Charles' Daddy is a barrister actually, but that is not a judge...'

'Shall I show you what a judge is like? I keep a pretend one in a bag so that I can explain to children.'

I took the model judge out of his TESCO carrier bag and stood him on the table. The little girl moved off her mother's lap and came across towards me to examine him. We looked at his glasses, his wig, and his black cloak.

Zoe's mother had begun to relax slightly.

'You know, a judge who is a bit like this person wrote to me. He knows I spend a lot of time with children. He said "Madge, I know you spend a lot of time with children and I know you have a toybox and sometimes you are good at getting to the bottom of muddles...well, pretty soon I'm going to be doing some deciding about a little girl called Zoe".'

'And what did you say?' She was already absorbed.

'I said, "Well, certainly. I'd like to help."

'He said, "Oh, good! It's pretty hard work deciding and deciding all day, and I think I need a bit of help. So can you go and see Zoe, please, and talk to her Mum and her Dad, because I know they don't live together any more, and can you ask Zoe to help us, please?"

'I said, "I certainly will try." And do you know what he said?'

Zoe was on her knees, eyes and ears alert, holding the judge in one hand, balancing her straw boater on his head.

'He said, "You know, I think she might have some muddles about touching, or being touched, so can you find out about that, please. Do you think she'll help us?" I said, "I think she might".'

Slowly and decisively Zoe nodded. Her long black ponytail bobbed across her shoulders. Fair and square she met my eyes.

'Well...anyway', she said, 'she will.'

'Oh good! "Oh, well, Mr Judge, Your Honour, she says she will." Shall we get the toybox in from the car now, then? Can you help me?'

Zoe's mother stood up quickly, 'Please, if you wish, you can use Zoe's playroom...'

'And see my Wendy house and my Barbie dolls.'

The little girl remained strangely composed, although her voice carried anticipation and excitement.

'Thank you. What do you think? Zoe, can you help me unload the toys?'

The child ran eagerly to the door – then stopped as if a sudden thought had entered her head...

'Mummy, I shan't have time to change – but I won't get my clothes dirty, I promise.'

The situation had gained an impetus all of its own. An urgency even. There was no time to waste changing into play clothes.

'Very well, darling, if you must – but only this once.'

Zoe ran across the hall, feet clumping on the parquet floor, and pulled the door open with both hands. I struggled to keep up with her. Together we unloaded the box and lugged its contents, with Ingrid's help, up to the playroom, which lay almost at the top of the house.

Breathless, we deposited the boxes on the ground and I made my way to the door to close it behind me and set up the tape machine.

Before I had time to recover my breath, it seemed, the game began. Zoe picked up the green plastic telephone and dialled urgently:

'Hello, hello. Is that the lady?'

'Yes, this is the lady.'

'Well, the little girl has a problem – a very serious problem.'

'Oh, dear.'

'She has the Spider Disease.'

'The Spider Disease? Oh, I see.'

'Yes, OK. Bye now.'

'Bye...'

She watched me carefully. I rummaged in the other toybox for the red phone. Thinking time...important just to go with her.

'Brr-Brr. Brr-Brr.'

'Hello, yes, this is the lady again.'

'Well, this is getting more seriouser every day. More seriouser. You've got to help this little girl. She has the Spider Disease. And there are poisonous spiders in her tummy. And it's full of, full of, poisonous spiders and soon her tummy's going to burst open and the poisonous spiders will fly out everywhere and poison every human in the land...'

Silence, while the lady at the other end grappled for equilibrium at news of such magnitude.

'This sounds very serious', she answered lamely.

'Well, can you help her?'

'I think so – it sounds a very serious problem.'

'Well, you must help the children.'

'I certainly must. How did the poisonous spiders get in there, then? Into the little girl's tummy?'

She gestured to me silently, and to the phone. I picked up the phone again and dialled.

Ring Ring Ring Ring

'Is that the little girl with the Spider Disease?'

'Yes, it is.'

'Well, can you ask her if she can tell the lady how the poisonous spiders got into her tummy?'

Silence on the line, and then:

'They came in a hole in her mouth and in her tummy and the naughty man put them in there with the white stuff.'

'The naughty man put them there with the white stuff?'

'Yes – and he's disgusting pooey stink. Very, very naughty.'

'Naughty, disgusting pooey stink?'

Suddenly she was marching round the playroom, chanting the chant:

'Pooey stink, pooey stink. Naughty, naughty pooey stink.'

The green telephone lay discarded among the toys. Her eyes fell on the anatomical dolls. She picked up the male doll, and grasping him by the leg, swung him upside down against the side of the Wendy house.

'He's going in the dungeon.'

The toybox, emptied of its contents, was placed neatly over the prostrate doll. And now she clapped her hands in glee, jumping up and down. She banged the top of the box with her fist.

'Are you scared in there, pooey stink?'

I inched my way slowly, although the resistance was minimal. This little girl had urgent news to impart.

'What have you been doing, you pooey stink man?', I asked. Lying horizontally, I knocked on the side of the dungeon. 'Can you hear me in there?'

She ran round to the other side, to face me.

'He can. Ask him what he's been doing.'

'What have you been doing, you naughty man?'

She shook her head.

'He says "You don't know anything – useless bitch." And he won't tell you. It's a secret.'

'Oh.'

'But you're not really a useless bitch. Pretend you're not really. Daddy says Mummy is.'

'Well, no. I don't think I am. I think we have to find a way to ask him what he's been doing.'

'Well, he won't tell. And the little girl can't tell you, because she's naughty too…'

'Poor little girl. But I'm sure there must be a way to help her. I'm sure we could both try to help her.'

'Yes, and this little girl is getting very, very, very, very worried.'

'So we must find a way.'

'Ask him why he does it. Say, "Why do you do it, you naughty man?"'

I did as I was bid, but the man in the dungeon remained silent. The little girl stood, hands on hips, kicking the man…

'Now do you realise you are being silly, really silly. You're behaving terribly badly – pooey stink man. Now come out here. If you don't behave again you're going straight into the hot fire and you will fry to death. That's all there is to it.'

We racked our brains in shared frustration. The pooey stink man's reluctance to come clean was becoming tedious. We stared at each other in perplexity. Finally the little girl had an idea. Fiddling with the toys, she had located the cooker timer.

'I know!' she explained excitedly. 'I know. You have to ask him questions and I have to ring a noise if it's "yes".'

'Oh, I see. Well, maybe you could help me with the questions. You could whisper the questions in my ear and then I could ask him and see what he says.'

'And if he says "yes", I can make the bell ring.'

'Yes. That would be a good way to get him to tell us.'

We were entering into a three-way dialogue here – but it was likely she would be unable to answer direct questions put to her. She wasn't ready for that yet. And there were more ways to skin a cat than one...

'So, OK. Are you ready?'

She sat, poised. Inside the dungeon the naughty man awaited his fate.

'What shall I ask first, then?'

She crawled across the room and whispered a sentence in my ear, grinning conspiratorially – eyes shining.

'Wait, wait.' She was winding the cooker timer. 'Now ask him.'

'Have you wee-weed in the little girl's mouth?'

Brrrrrrr! The cooker timer sounded, harshly raucous. She nodded earnestly, 'He has! He has! And...' More whispering. 'Ask him, then.'

'And have you put your tail in her front bottom, and wee-weed on her legs?' Brrrrrrr! She nodded authoritatively again.

'Yes, he has!' – high-pitched, gleeful.

The whispering in my ear continued earnestly. I caught only parts of the sentence. Slowly she repeated the sentence again.

'And did you marry her with your tail a long time?'

Brrrrrrr! Emphatic nodding.

'You ask him now. He's a very naughty Daddy', she gestured to me.

'OK. "Man, did you say anything would happen if the little girl talked to anyone about this?"'

Brrrrrrr!

'Yes, he did. He said we're the special people and don't tell Mummy because…because…if you tell Mummy…if you tell Mummy…then she won't love you…because she…', she was stumbling now, the words difficult to say. I ached to help her.

'Because she…?'

'Because you're a dirty girl who does it.'

'So if Mummy knew about the dirty girl, she wouldn't love her?'

'Sssh! Sssh!', she glanced round quickly, momentarily frantic. We listened carefully. We were not being overhead. Mummy was downstairs.

'Has this Daddy got a name?'

'Mmmm. Adrian Daddy. But don't tell Mummy, OK?'

'Can you show me with the dolls what else Adrian Daddy does?'

She got up and collected the doll family, and removed the clothes from the male adult who had gained temporary reprieve from the dungeon. She then removed the clothes the little girl doll.

'Look. Like this.'

Demonstrating with the dolls, she laid the male doll on top of the little girl doll. 'Look, the front bottom. He puts the tail in the front bottom.'

'Can you point to the front bottom?'

'In there, silly.'

She poked her finger between the girl doll's legs.

'And how does marrying happen?'

She moved the dolls up and down in a rhythmic motion.

'And then he does this, see. He wee-wees in the little girl's mouth.'

'Does he? And what does it taste like?'

'Ugh! Yugh!' Utter distaste registered in her face. 'Like compost!'

'Like compost?'

'And… And…what place does this happen in?'

'In her bedroom. And in Daddy's car.'

'Oh, I see.'

'And it's a very very very serious problem, because now the little girl has the Spider Disease. And soon her tummy will burst open and all the frogs will catch it and the robins and all the little creatures that are very precious – precious to God. And they'll go dead.'

'Well, this is a very serious problem.'

'And that…is the end of the story.'

We sat in silence for what seemed like a long time. This was new territory.

'What an important story! I know that the judge will want to hear it very much.'

She picked up the judge doll and placed him ceremoniously on top of the dungeon.

'Maybe next time I come back we can find a way to help this little girl.'

'And make her better?'

'Yes. And make her better.'

She helped me tidy the toys away, self-possessed and careful. Dutiful almost. The play had reached a natural end. We had been in the room for over two hours. I had forgotten to turn over the cassette in the tape-recorder. Suddenly preoccupied, I felt sick. What if the important bits were not recorded!

She stood dressing the little girl doll, stroking her hair lovingly. For a moment I was preoccupied elsewhere, mind on the tape. How much of it would be intact?

'You've got bird earrings on.'

'Mmmm.'

'Haven't you? Bird earrings?'

'What, sweetie? Oh, yes. Bird earrings. You can look if you want to.'

I removed one from my ear and handed it to her. She whispered softly to the earring and held out her hand to return it to me. I knelt beside her.

'Zoe, I know we can find a way to help the little girl. I'd like to think about it and come back to see you again.'

I parked the car in a layby and played the tape. It had recorded as far as 'You ask him now – he's a very naughty daddy.' I added my recollection of what had happened next while it was fresh in my mind. Pity about the 'Adrian Daddy' part not being on the tape, but sure as hell in this world you can't win 'em all! And to have interrupted to change the tape over might have stopped the flow at a crucial point.

There were times when I longed for high-quality radio equipment, and a two-way mirror, and a technician. Collecting information this way seemed so haphazard. But on the other hand, Zoe's playroom had been the right place. A safe, familiar place. And it would be in that place that the little girl would find the key to her healing.

The enormity of the Spider Disease was beginning to register. What an appalling position for a little girl to be in! Whatever had happened with Daddy Adrian, and I had no reason to doubt her account, an inevitable consequence of it was that she was forced to distance herself from the one source of protection she had left, and to profoundly doubt her mother's love for her. How could she risk it? How could she possibly risk her mother discovering her dirtiness? Better to keep a distance, to bear the burden alone. And so she failed at school, couldn't concentrate, vented her pain and frustration on other children. Nobody would believe it anyway. It was all too incredible for words.

And the Spider Disease? What an amazing construction! One had to step into her shoes and imagine it. I wound the car seat back and lay listening to some quiet music – Tchaikovsky's *Pathetique*. Just imagine being four or five. Bright, alert, only child. You know how wee-wees happen. You know how poohs happen. You know where they come from. You have some idea where babies come from. You've seen it maybe on television, and one of your friends at school had a new baby sister and told you it came under Mummy's legs out of her tummy. Suddenly Daddy begins to touch you. To do things to you, to put his penis in your tummy and hurt you, maybe to wee-wee on you and into your mouth. It's dirty, he says. Don't tell Mummy. You're dirty, he says. I do this because you are special. Why doesn't Daddy wee-wee in the toilet? What happens to the compost wee-wee that goes in my mouth? It's dirty, yugh-ey dirty. It's inside your tummy now. It's dirty. Like poison. Creepy dirty... Spider Disease. Don't tell Mummy. Clean yourself or let Ingrid do it if she must. But don't let Mummy come close!

I sat up in the car. Watery evening sunlight streamed through the back window on to the dashboard. Reversing out of the country lane I could see the chimneys of the house in the distance, through the trees. Spider Disease! Poisoning every human in the land! But somehow it was not completely new. I struggled to remember where I had come across similar images before... Places, events, times, thoughts, reflections.

Crazy Maggie, for one, in the psychiatric long stay ward. Spider Disease, the advanced stages of twenty years gestation. Grown in a culture of family disfunction – parents divorced, poor relationship with her mother. Drugs and ECT. What proportion of the Crazy Maggies of this world had been filled as little children with such distortions, and struggled against an insane reality ever since? Zoe's current experience certainly begged that question.

It was three days before I managed to contact Joanna, the child's solicitor, from a training engagement in London.

'Joanna, it's Madge. I'm in London.'

'Have you been yet? How did you get on?'

'Yes. Well, OK, I think.'

'What do you mean, "OK"?'

'Well, she's got Spider Disease.'

'She's got what?'

'Spider Disease.'

'Who has?'

'The little girl, Zoe.'

'What's that?'

'Well it comes in a hole in your mouth and in your tummy and the naughty Daddy Adrian puts it in there with the white stuff...'

Silence.

'Joanna, I think we should get a psychiatrist.'

'Who for?'

'Oh, come off it! I think we should go back to the court for leave to seek a psychiatric opinion on what this child is revealing and the way in which she's talking about it.'

'Madge, a thought just occurred to me...'

'Yes?'

'Do you have spiders in the toybox?'

'Yes.'

'And what did she do with them?'

'Nothing. I don't think she even noticed them. She certainly didn't pick one up.'

She was considering the possibility that I could inadvertently have implanted such ideas in the child's mind. Her thought processes were beginning to make sense.

'Oh, Joanna, how on earth could I have put her up to this? I mean, where would I get the imagination to put this in her mind?'

'No – I suppose not. I'd certainly try it, though.'

'Try what?'

'Cross-examine you on it, if I were acting for the father.'

'Well, you're not.'

Frustration and anger were beginning to creep in. I told her that if she didn't want these instructions there were plenty of other solicitors who would.

'Oh, come on Madge. I was thinking out loud. I'll get a request for a psychiatrist before the judge as soon as I can. May well get it agreed with the other solicitors anyway. Can you give me the names of three suitable children's psychiatrists we can approach? I think you're right – an independent psychiatric oversight of your work with the child may be a useful precaution.'

The following week the court gave leave for an independent psychiatrist to the appointed. Legal Aid agreed to fund professional fees.

Ten days after my first visit I went to Zoe's home again. I had set aside a large portion of the day, first to talk to her mother, continue the session with the child and follow it up perhaps with some more time with the mother.

This time the atmosphere was charged. Charlotte Govier showed me into the drawing room in clipped, formal tones. She was angry.

'I have to say, Miss – Mrs is it? – Bray, that Zoe's behaviour has been dreadful since your last visit. I quite simply do not know what to do with her. She's become quite defiant. I think all this with the toys has been affecting her terribly. Must you continue with your work? Can't you just ask her the necessary questions and be done with it?'

I felt terribly sad for her. But this had to be handled with care.

'Mrs Govier, I can't. It simply doesn't work like that. She's been asked lots of questions before and nobody got very far, did they? Please bear with me a bit. I'd like to set it up so that you can observe today, and hear for yourself what she has to say.'

'You mean she told you something?'

'Yes, she did – in her own way. But I'd like you to hear it directly from her if we can manage to do that.'

In the meantime I clarified with her what precisely Zoe had been up to since we last met.

One bout of hysterical screaming on the toilet:

'She was constipated, you see. And she screamed and screamed, "Mummy, I'm going to have a baby!"'

One spider's web construction made out of knitting wool in her bedroom, '"To catch naughty people", she said.'

Two severe tellings-off at school, and one major crisis the day after my visit, when she was poked in the bottom by another child who had sustained a cut eye in the ensuing fracas. Hardly convent school behaviour, without a doubt.

'You see, I'm desperate about her, Mrs Bray, quite desperate. Adrian has filed another affidavit – have you seen it? – He says I'm an unfit mother. He wants custody of her now.'

'Would you mind if we dispensed with the formality? My first name is Madge, perhaps I can call you Charlotte?'

She nodded, 'Of course.'

I tried to be gentle, but firm.

'Now, look. I can see how much pain this is causing you. I can see how much you love Zoe and I know that as her mother there isn't much you wouldn't do to try to help her sort this out.'

She glanced quickly at me – the angry veneer had disappeared. She blew her nose, nodding amidst her sobs.

'Zoe will be home in an hour. Oh, dear. I am in a mess. Do you mind if I pour myself a gin? Frightfully bad manners, this. I'm so sorry. I should have offered you. Obviously you don't drink on duty.'

A tiny smile played on her lips. She turned to face me. The mascara had run. She left the room ostensibly to bring some ice. Soon she returned, slightly more composed – the smudges gone.

'What would you like me to do, then?'

I asked her to sit in the armchair in the corner of the playroom, and to busy herself taking notes of the proceedings. I asked her not to interrupt, to let her tears come freely, and above all not to leave if and when the going got tough. She was to concentrate on listening carefully and writing an account of what happened. We would call her in after I had had a talk to Zoe.

'She's expecting you today, actually. She talks incessantly about your earrings. I think she's looking forward to it. I'm sorry I was so angry with you. I can see you're only – only doing your job.'

She took a deep breath and pulled her shoulders back.

'I must try to be strong, for her.'

My heart went out to her.

'I know you can do it.'

The taxi pulled up in exactly the same spot as it had done before. Scarcely waiting for it to stop Zoe was out, bounding up the stone steps to the front door – hair loose, flying behind her. We walked round into the hall to greet her. The door flew open. She ran up to me, stopping inches short of my toes.

'Hello, sweetie.' I knelt down to say hello. 'It's lovely to see you.'

Suddenly coyness overcame her for a moment. She covered her face with her hand and looked at me from behind splayed fingers.

'Have you brought the toybox?'

'Yes, it's in the boot.'

'Can we play Spider Disease Part II?'

'Certainly can...but first, after we carry the toybox up...a little bit of talking. Just you and me.'

The grandfather clock chimed. Zoe's mother stood behind me. The child made no attempt to approach her. She maintained a distance. Like a watch with a broken mechanism the cogs were failing to engage.

We deposited the toys in the playroom for the second time. I explained again that we needed to do a bit of talking before Spider Disease Part II, and suggested we could do it while Zoe changed into her play clothes. Did I have play clothes? No, I didn't have play clothes.

'Because grown-ups can play in any clothes they want to', she sighed deeply.

'Yes, I suppose you're right.'

'Well, it isn't fair...'

I sat on the bed while she changed into green tracksuit, clothes folded neatly as she had been taught. No, she didn't want any help, thank you... I had thought out plan A on the train one day. I hoped it would work, because I didn't have a plan B. I thought carefully; very, very carefully. Slowly does it...

'Zoe. You know our game – the Spider Disease game?'

She nodded, struggling to smooth out a pair of long white socks.

'Well, I think I know a way to help the little girl.'

'How, then?'

'I think we need to have a Mummy in the Spider Disease Game.'

'No, we don't.' She was quite emphatic.

I held my ground.

'Mmm. Yes, I think we do. I think we need to make the Mummy do just what we want her to do. She could sit in the corner and write, in the armchair. And we could pretend she was at the cinema, watching a film. She could just look. She wouldn't say anything.'

'Or in the theatre?'

'Yes. Or in the theatre.'

'Well, she wouldn't be *her* Mummy – the girl in the game's Mummy?'
She frowned a little, scratching her ear. It was a complex puzzle.
'No, it wouldn't be *her* Mummy. It needs to be a real Mummy.'
'My Mummy... Charlotte?'
'Mmm. There aren't any other real Mummies in this house, are
there?'
'No.'
'Shall I ask her, then?'
'That's a good idea.'
We walked along the oak-panelled corridor. We stopped at the
bottom of the stairs up to the third floor playroom. Zoe was making
the necessary preparations in her mind. We sat down on the top step
to think a bit more.
'We have to whisper if it's a horrible part of the game', she said,
'and then she won't hear it.'
'Oh, OK, then. We can do that.'
'And she might be sad.'
'So we could give her a box of tissues in case she wants to cry.'
'Yes. I can get them.' She ran back to her bedroom, and returned
brandishing a box of blue tissues.
'And a pen and some paper, because she has to write, remember?'
'When she comes in, you say: "This is a pretend game about a little
girl with a very serious problem. She is called Barbara Ann." And then
say "This is the story of the Spider Disease and the Child – Part II."'
Spider Disease Part II proceeded as planned. Charlotte sat in the
armchair, clutching a tissue in one hand and a pen in the other. Zoe
glanced anxiously at her mother from time to time as she busied herself
preparing the remainder of the ground. Toys tipped out in a heap. Male
doll back in the dungeon again. The toy telephones.
Brr Brr. Brr Brr. She picked up the green telephone.
'Yes?'
'Is that the lady? Well, help! Help! Come quickly. The pooey stink
daddy has broken out of the dungeon and he's doing it to all the boys
and girls. It's very serious.'
'What is he doing to all the boys and girls?'
'Giving them Spider Disease – with his penis.'
Zoe ran around the box, foraging for all the female figures, down
to the tiniest finger puppets. She placed them in a pile behind my body.

Then she retrieved the animal images, hedgehog puppets, frogs, bears, and placed them in a separate pile.

'We have to keep them safe while we make the girl better. We have to make the girl better now', she said emphatically.

'Oh, yes, we have to make her better. Well, how can we do that?'

I had been pondering the subject since I last saw her, to no avail.

'You have to ring a very, very, very clever doctor.' She handed me the stethoscope. 'Pretend you're a doctor.'

The phone rang again.

'Hello.'

'Hello.' She pushed her hair off her face. 'Hello. Are you a clever doctor in Japan?'

'Yes, I am.'

'Do you know about Spider Disease. Have you heard of it?'

'No, I actually don't think I have.'

She replaced the receiver quickly. 'He's not clever.' Wrinkling her nose. 'Stupid, he is.'

Charlotte smiled as she wrote.

Brr Brr. Brr Brr.

'Is that another doctor in Shepherd's Bush?'

'Yes, this is the Shepherd's Bush doctor.'

'Well, the little girl has a Spider Disease.'

'Oh, dear, that's very serious. How did that get there?'

'Well, they came in a hole in her tummy. And the naughty man wee-weed in her mouth.'

'That's very serious.'

'Well, do you know how to make her better?'

'Yes, I do have some pills. Special medicine.'

'No, thank you. She's had aspirin and tablets and banana medicine and they're not dead. Bye.'

'Bye.'

Frowning, she surveyed the scene. Special medicine was not the answer. The room was silent. She seemed to be aware again of her mother's presence. Quickly she walked over to me and whispered in my ear.

'Don't tell the Mummy about it, because she would be sad and she might cry.'

'OK.'

'Now. I know! Pretend you're the doctor. You have to do an operation. You have to cut her tummy and take out all the poisonous spiders.'

She picked up the little girl doll from the pile behind me. On her way past, she punched the dungeon with her fists.

'Pooey stink Daddy. Stay there. He's in there. You'll stay in there for eight days because you've been so naughty. Just look what you've done. And now we have to make her better, don't we?'

The little girl doll lay naked, carefully and lovingly placed in front of me on a cot blanket.

'No, pretend you've got a scissors. Now cut her tummy – she's sleeping now – and get the poisonous spiders out. You have to pull them out.'

I followed the instructions to the letter.

'Wait! Wait!'

She ran across the room to the kitchen corner of the beautifully laid out playroom. Soon she was back with a toy jug and a plate.

'Now, put the spiders in there.'

I pulled more and more spiders from the little girl's tummy and placed them in the jug. But still there were more. Zoe bent over, peering at the stomach.

'You have to wipe the blood now.'

Her eyes darted around the room. She grabbed the tissue box from her mother's lap and brought them to me. I wiped away the blood.

'Oh, wait, wait! Stop! Stop!'

Her voice was urgent.

'The heart! The heart! we must take the heart out. It might get poisoned with the spiders!'

A cup was produced from the kitchen corner.

'Put the heart in there.'

With great care, I managed to manoeuvre the heart into the plastic cup.

'Then the heart can be safe.'

'Of course, we must take good care of her.'

'Will she die?' Zoe was concentrating hard on the operation. 'There's a lot of blood.'

'No, she won't die.'

'But if children tell about naughty things, they might die.'

'Might they?'

'Yes', her voice dropped to a whisper, 'and the Mummies don't know, and they don't love them any more.'

I continued to pull more and more poisonous spiders out of the tummy. The conversation resumed.

'But, say in this game the Mummy found out what the naughty Daddy had been doing – would she be cross?'

Panic crossed her face. She glanced swiftly at her mother. Their eyes met. Charlotte was crying. She shook her head, and moved in her seat. I could see she wanted to move across the room to pick her little girl up. To cuddle her. But now was not the time. I frowned a little and gestured with my eyes. Not yet, not yet, Charlotte.

'Perhaps we could ask this Mummy what *she* would do if a naughty Daddy gave her little girl a Spider Disease? Mummy, would *you* be cross?'

Zoe sat transfixed. In my head I begged her not to bolt from the room, but she stayed put.

'I'd… I'd be very c-c-c-cross…with the man.'

'What about the little girl?'

'I would…just love her…'

Charlotte's voice broke. She wept openly. Zoe looked up at her mother, ran across the room, and without a word handed her the tissue box. I continued with the operation. Zoe returned swiftly, to supervise the proceedings closely.

'Are they all out now?'

'No, not yet. There's quite a lot, you know.'

We had settled down again into the game. Eventually it was time to sew the little girl up. Zoe couldn't see any more spiders in there. Meticulously we replaced the heart and then sewed the little girl doll up again. Zoe shook her head to wake her up, gently, very gently, and replace her clothes. She stood up slowly, raising the doll above her head.

'I know, pretend she's light now and we can throw her like thistledown. You have to throw her gently. And she's so light she can float now.'

Zoe threw the doll into the air. She landed in my arms.

'Throw her back. She's so light. She can't fall.'

Her foot caught the edge of the cup. She stopped stock still in her tracks, and gasped, 'Oh! Goodness me! We have to put a lid on the jug, or the poisonous spiders may escape. I know…'

With great purpose she strode across to the dungeon and tipped the contents of the jug in beside the man. Strong, resourceful, purposeful little girl. I grinned at her.

'Throw the girl back to me, then,' she said.

'Can Mummy catch her too?'

She turned to face her mother. Charlotte stood up and gestured with her arms, ready to catch the doll. I looked towards Zoe for permission from her eyes.

'OK. Mummy, you catch her.'

A three-way, pass the post-operative parcel ensued.

'Mummy,' I said. 'Guess what? This little girl doll in the game used to think she was terribly dirty because she had the Spider Disease. And do you know what else? She used to think that she mustn't go near her Mummy because maybe the Mummy wouldn't love her if she knew about the things the little girl had done with the Daddy.'

Charlotte's lips trembled. She clutched the doll tightly, cradling it in her arms.

'What do you want to say to the little girl doll, Mummy?'

Come on, Charlotte. I willed her on. The moments seemed endless.

'I… I want to tell her… I want to tell her I love her. Mummy loves her little girl more than anything in the whole world… And… And…', she hesitated. 'And she's very, very angry with the naughty man in the dungeon. He… He won't… He won't ever, ever do that again.'

I sensed Zoe's presence beside me. She was watching her mother breathlessly. She slipped her hand into mine:

'I want to whisper…'

I knelt down. She placed both her hands round my right ear; I winced as the hot air rushed into it.

'Don't tell Mummy it's *my* Daddy.'

I smiled at her. She was amazing, simply amazing.

'I think you are super duper amazing!'

'I can talk to Mummy about the game after, can't I?'

'Yes – it's Barbara Ann's Daddy, remember.'

'OK. Would you like a cup of tea and some biscuits now?'

I glanced at Charlotte:

'We'd love some, wouldn't we, Mummy?'

'Just pretend?'

'How about both pretend and real?'

'Shall I ask Ingrid if we can have some?'

'Yes, that would be lovely, thank you.'

Zoe left the room. I could hear her shout excitedly down the stairs to Ingrid, 'We had the Spider Disease game and the little girl had an operation…and…', her voice tapered off in the distance.

Charlotte slumped in her chair, ashen-faced. Still clutching the doll. Her hands shaking.

The interview with Charlotte lasted well into the evening. We explained that Mummy wanted some time with me now. Zoe accepted the explanation without question. My heart went out to the woman. She wept openly now. Numb. For a time we sat in silence, alone in our separate worlds. Eventually she registered my presence.

'He's been…been…having oral…oral sex with her…hasn't he?'

'Sounds like it', I said gently.

'And the penis in her tummy… Does that mean she's…she's…', she looked down again, 'she's…not a virgin?'

'Possibly, but he may have used the tops of the legs as a channel – intracrural intercourse, it's called.'

She began to retch, body shuddering. She clutched her hands to her mouth. I looked urgently around the room for a receptacle. She was sick in the log basket. I moved over to sit beside her. It was going to take time – time to assimilate.

'I can't believe it. I can't believe it. Not Adrian! Maybe she's imagining it. Don't you think she could be?' She grappled for reassurance.

'What do you think?'

'But how could she know about oral sex? And the white stuff?' She spoke in a whisper now.

'I don't… You tell me.'

'Well, she couldn't, could she? It's impossible.'

'She knows what it tastes like too.'

'Why, what did she say…?'

'Like compost.'

For a moment I thought she was going to be sick again.

A knock came at the door. I rose and went to it. Ingrid passed me a tray of tea and biscuits. It was better that she did not enter. The plate of biscuits lay, beautifully arranged on a white lace doyley. The legacy of Charlotte's upbringing held fast.

'Please…please let me help you.'

She rose in a flurry. Her handkerchief fell on the floor; there were tiny flecks of vomit on her green silk blouse. Sharply incongruous, now, in her surroundings. Suddenly she stopped – self-conscious.

'Ooh, goodness! Look at me. Will you excuse me? I must use the toilet.'

I had almost finished the first cup of tea by the time she returned, having changed her blouse.

Thoughts raced and tumbled through her mind. Now was not the time to take a history from her for my report. I decided to abandon that plan.

'Will… Will she…will she ever recover from this now?'

'I'm sure she will. But that depends upon how it's handled from here on in.'

'How? How…what…is there anything I should do?'

'Well,…love her, but don't push it on her yet. Let her come to you. I think she will, now. Try not to probe. Don't hide your pain from her – she knows anyway, but she needs to know how sad you are about what's happened to her.'

'But how could I have been so stupid – not to see it for so long. All the time he was having access. It wasn't until she said herself about "Daddy tickling my bottom" – she seemed so clear about it I panicked and called the police. I didn't suspect anything before, you see. Nothing. I feel so guilty. I must be a disastrous mother. Maybe I… Maybe Adrian is right. I'm an…unfit mother.'

The grandfather clock chimed again in the hall. I laid my teacup down.

'Charlotte, I know you want to punish yourself for this. But you didn't do anything to her. Just remember that. And I think you would have been the last to find out, anyway.'

'Why?'

'Because I think what was said to her was that, if you were to find out, you'd know what a dirty little girl she was and you wouldn't love her.'

Her mouth gaped open in incredulity.

'Masterful, eh?'

'But that would be why… I mean, it could account for it, couldn't it?'

'What?'

'Well," she examined the buttons on her cuff, folding back the sleeve of her blouse, 'she won't let me cuddle her, will she?'

I nodded.

'I think so. Would you, if you were in her shoes?'

'No. I suppose not.'

It was time for me to leave.

'Charlotte – there is something you could do to make things better. Talk to her about the facts of life.'

'But she's far too young, isn't she? Most children don't need to know about that yet, do they?'

'Charlotte. Zoe isn't "most children". Don't you think she may already be quite experienced in that area?'

'Oh. I see what you mean.'

'And she does keep asking, doesn't she? Maybe you could buy some books written for children about the facts of life, and read them with her. Safest to wait until all the investigations have been completed, though, because it may be that the court will require her to be spoken to again about this.

'And, Charlotte. Be kind to yourself. You will get through this. I know you will.'

On the way out, I popped into the kitchen to say goodbye to Zoe. Ready for bed, she perched on a stool in a corner, eating her supper while Ingrid programmed the dishwasher. I bent over to talk to her. She put her hand up to grasp one of my earrings.

'Can I look?'

I took the earring off and handed it to her – a small wooden squirrel.

'Why do your wear big earrings?'

'Because I like them, I suppose.'

'Mummy said you see lots of children. Do they like them?'

'Yes, I think they do.'

'Well, I like them.'

'I know.'

I stood up and swung my bag on to my shoulder. In a sudden movement, she put her arms around my waist and hung on tightly. Her arms were tight and tense. I kissed the top of her head.

'The Spider Disease girl was very lonely for a long time, without any hugs or cuddles, wasn't she?'

The arms relaxed slightly. We stood together, swaying gently. Zoe raised her head – there were tears in her eyes. I picked her up – a solidly-built little lady. She was quite a weight.

'Zoe', I whispered softly, 'Zoe, we can tell the little girl that things will get better now, can't we? Because she's such a brave, clever little girl. And her heart is full of love, isn't it? It didn't get hurt because none of the poisonous spiders got in there, did they?'

She shook her head. Her body began to relax in my arms. I carried her through to the drawing-room and we knocked on the door. Charlotte opened it.

'Charlotte, we have a sad little girl here, who…'

She held out her arms. The words tailed off – superfluous.

Darkness was beginning to fall as I loaded the toys back into the car. The drawing-room curtains were not yet closed. The log fire burned brightly, lighting up the room. As I closed the boot I could see a little girl, cradled in her mother's arms. A glance was enough. To wave goodnight would have been an intrusion.

I met Adrian by arrangement at a subsidiary office. A secretary showed me in. Adrian was on the telephone as I entered. He ushered me with his eyes to be seated in front of his desk. Sensing immediately the power dynamic between us, I tucked my legs under the chair and located the pen and writing pad in my bag. A small cigar lay in the ashtray. He leaned over the telephone, one hand stroking his temple, the other writing. An attractive man, rugby build, hair greying slightly, rounded fresh face. Eyes like his daughter. The telephone conversation ended. The secretary brought coffee.

Indeed, he understood the purpose of my visit to him. His solicitor had explained my role. He would, of course, do whatever he could to assist me with my enquiries in what must certainly be a difficult task. He was devastated to find himself in this position. The reaction of his parents and friends had been one of disbelief and horror. He could not and would not allow his wife to sully his name like this. Didn't I know – yes, of course he thought I must if I had done my homework (and I looked to him like someone who would undertake my work thoroughly), that Charlotte had a history of depression which had once necessitated psychiatric care? That she should stoop to inventing such fabrications to punish him for leaving her was almost unbelievable to him.

Faced with it, though, he would fight her tooth and nail. He had already engaged a QC. He simply could not afford to have his reputation tarnished in this way. Truth in the allegations? Of course there was no truth in the allegations. They were at best a figment of Charlotte's deranged imagination and at worst a malicious and culpable attempt to destroy him. He would now be forced to teach her a lesson in court which she would not forget in a hurry.

Questions about his early childhood? Well, he would certainly answer any questions I had, although frankly he wasn't convinced of their relevance. He had had a very happy childhood. Eldest of three sons. Very close family relationships. His father was an upstanding member of society. Had I read of that in the affidavits?

Towards the end of the conversation, I brought up the subject of Zoe. Didn't I think she was a wonderful child? Marvellous imagination. That would, of course, be why she was so susceptible to Charlotte's attempts to discredit him. But to have concocted this! It was evil, thoroughly evil. And in light of it he certainly could not entertain the possibility of his child being brought up by such a woman. Originally he would have been satisfied with monthly access, but now he could only do the right thing for Zoe and apply for custody of her.

Arrangements for her upbringing? He had, of course, given this a great deal of consideration. He would enroll her in a preparatory school near his address on a day basis, and would employ a nanny at least until she could attend boarding school full-time. His mother would wish to play a part in her upbringing.

And what of me? He understood from his solicitor that I had quite a reputation in this field. Didn't I know a friend of his, a psychiatrist? Dr So-and-so? He had heard of me. Indeed, this man had offered to attend court on his behalf.

All this had caused him a great deal of distress and he would be very glad when it was all over. Now that the police had investigated and found nothing, he was anxious that the case should be heard quickly. His solicitor anticipated that it would not take more than a day. Was that my experience?

He was very glad to have met me. Please would I not hesitate to contact him again should I wish to do so. How long would it be before my report was ready? He would be flying to Germany on business next week for ten days, but any time after that...

It was a month before I saw Zoe again. The psychiatrist had requested as part of his assessment that he observe a further play session between Zoe and myself. He did not believe it would be right for him to attempt to forge a relationship with the child himself. Rather he wished to observe her with me and form an opinion on the basis of that interaction and his other enquiries.

He followed me to the house in his car. Charlotte stood at the door nervously, touching the delicate gold necklace around her neck. I introduced them and left them to move into the house together while I unloaded the boot. We had arranged to interview Charlotte together prior to Zoe's return from school.

It proved a tense, anxious, interview. Charlotte was again close to tears.

Troubled early life, poor relationship with her mother, although close to her father. Married before; devastated by the death of her young husband. Her son Rupert had never accepted Adrian. Adrian had offered stability; he was interesting, fun, witty. She had enjoyed his company greatly. They shared artistic interests. Zoe's birth was difficult and necessitated a Caesarean section.

Their intimate life together? Their sexual relationship? She hesitated, gasped slightly, braced herself. She would prefer not the discuss these things at the moment. Her eyes searched mine, begging understanding. I heard myself talk gently to her.

'Some things are too hard even to think about?'

She nodded quickly and rose to her feet hurriedly. Such intense pain. I could sense it. Poor lady. The doctor cleared his throat. I glanced quickly at him. We did not pursue it.

The child was in the room before I realised she was home. Absorbed as we were in Charlotte, neither of us had heard her entry. She opened the door and ran headlong across the room, stopping with a careless flourish by the coffee table. No trepidation.

Spontaneous. Alive. Grinning from ear to ear. Obediently she stood as Charlotte removed her coat. Like a fervent puppy straining at the leash.

I introduced the Clever Doctor, who understood about Spider Disease.

'Zoe, this is Dr David Benson and I asked him to come and talk to us today.'

Nodding, she eyed him, still grinning.

'Have you got the toybox?' she asked.

'I certainly have', I said.

'What's happening with the spiders today?' I continued, 'Are we going to play another game?'

'No, well', eyeing the doctor carefully, 'most of them have gone.'

'Oh, well I'm glad to hear that – most of them have gone?'

'But there's two left', she added stoically.

'Two left?'

'Yes, and then they get more.'

'Oh.'

My mind whizzed frantically. I had no answer. How do we make the final two spiders go away?

'If we played a game with the little girl, would they go away in the game?'

'No, they can't, because they're magic.'

'Oh.'

I exchanged glances with Charlotte, who sat smiling benignly now. Suddenly the Clever Doctor spoke.

'I think I know a way to make them disappear.'

'What way?', the little girl pressed him, eagerly, turning to look up into his face.

'Well', he measured his worded, 'you have to love them and love them and love them and love them and then they disappear altogether.'

I was impressed with this doctor. We held our breath. He went on:

'But it's a special kind of loving that they need. The kind of loving that only Mummies can give. And they only need a tiny spoonful of it because it's so strong…'

Zoe's eyes opened wide. Tears ran down her mother's face. The little girl moved on the settee and cuddled into her mother. A spontaneous flowing of love. A moment in time.

I grinned in admiration at the Clever Doctor. What a Clever Doctor! He winked.

We sat in silence for many moments.

The little girl then scrambled down and approached the doctor, this time quite closely.

'Have you got any paper?', she asked politely.

Slightly bemused, he reached in his brief case.

'Do you need crayons as well?'

She nodded. I gave her some from the toybox.

She carried her acquisitions across to the table and sat down to draw, quietly absorbed.

Charlotte smiled.

'She's been like this since you left last time. I can't tell you how relieved I am. It's as if…'

The little girl slid off the high, adult-sized dining chair and walked towards me.

'That's a picture…for you… Madge…' Open-faced and smiling.

I sensed a lump in my throat. She climbed on to my knee.

'Thank you, sweetie. That's a lovely, lovely picture.'

'Can you tell me what's happening in the picture?'

'Well', pointing to the top right-hand corner, 'That's the sun, and', further down, 'that's a rainbow and a door.'

'Mmm.'

'And on the other side of the door is… Madge.'

The lump in my throat blocked sound. No words came. She put her arms around me and hugged me.

'I love you', she said.

'I know.'

'Feels like it's OK for me to go now…'

She was playing with my necklace.

'Yes, but you can help other children.'

'Zoe, I can use your picture to help other children and grown-ups understand. Would you like that?'

'Yes. You can.'

Some weeks later, the High Court hearing took place. Acrimonious and bitter, it lasted five days. After considering the reports, hearing the tape and evidence from Dr Benson and the Consultant Psychiatrist employed by Mr Govier's solicitor, the Judge ordered custody to mother. No access to father.

The following week I received a letter from Charlotte, containing a number of other pictures from Zoe 'to help other children'.

Afterword

The interactions with Zoe, a bright articulate little six year old girl, were almost exactly as they occurred. The dialogue remains largely intact. The adults reactions and responses were as described, although for reasons of confidentiality their actual family context has been altered. In my experience children victimised in this way often use whatever means available to them, including their creative imagination to make sense of such distressing events in their lives. Sometimes these are viewed as children's fantasies.

I am still in touch with Zoe. She is a remarkable young person with a wisdom and depth of understanding far beyond her years.

BECKY

'This has been going on ever since she came. We've been fostering her nearly four months now. She'd do it all day long if you let her. So we decided to ration it a bit – we let her have about an hour every afternoon now.'

'Oh... I see...what about the music...is that her choice?'

I could hear the blast of music through the wall.

'Yes...strange isn't it? I mean, you would think she'd prefer nursery rhymes, but the 1812 Overture has always been her favourite. I think she gets lost in it...'

We sat in the green and pink sitting room with grey co-ordinating carpet and ruched, patterned curtains.

'I tell Gareth to pay no attention to her – he's used to it by now, so he goes out on his bike and ignores her most of the time, I'm afraid. He's embarrassed by her. Especially her language. More coffee, Mrs Bray? You're not cold, are you? I tend not to put the heating on until evening – it's a large house to heat and what with the mortgage rate going up and everything...we do like to go skiing, you see...' She laughed nervously, a neat, auburn-haired young woman, in a Laura Ashley blouse.

'We adopted Gareth as a baby – he's eight now. We did want another. We wanted a little girl actually. But...well...' she tapped the china coffee cup comfortingly, '...we know Becky will never fit in. We can't help her. I've told the social worker.'

She looked close to tears.

'I...I...I mean it's impossible. We can't go out as a family with her... Ian...my husband is...well...too embarrassed. When we're in church she can't sit still. I tell her Mummy's in heaven, you see. So we go to church to see Mummy in God's house. I have to sit and hold on to her hand or she'd do it there...I mean...'

'Do what?'

'Well...rub herself,' she hesitated, flushing hot with embarrassment. Gulping her coffee quickly. 'I've told her God doesn't like little girls who do that. I've told her it's dirty and she mustn't do it. It's rude. But she still carries on. And...well...she tries... I mean she tries to get me to rub her between her legs... And her kisses... Ian won't pick her up any more. We both feel so...well, so guilty. Anyway,' she shifted her position defensively, 'the social worker said you could offer her therapeutic help. I hope you can do something for her. We saw your documentary on the television actually...'

My turn to feel embarrassed. Tchaikovsky's cannons boomed through the wall. Missiles rained. Napoleon was retreating from the city.

'Can I see her now?'

I followed Mrs Newnes up the hallway. Through the dining room door I could see her. Jumping. Jumping. Jumping. Eyes fixed straight ahead, lips taut, fists clenched. Bearing down with her arms as her feet returned to the floor. Skipping with an invisible rope. Curls bobbing strangely out of rhythm with the rest of her body. The music reached its crescendo. The rhythmic movements remained constant. Thud. Thud. Thud, as her feet made contact with the parquet floor.

'What happens when the music stops?' I whispered slowly.

'Oh, it turns itself over.'

With that the cassette reached its conclusion. Silence.

The little girl continued her dance...no pause...no relief...the music began again. White knee length socks, black patent shoes, a blue striped dress with red buttons on. Red bow in her hair. Her face turned away from us.

I made myself visible in the doorway for the first time. The scene had a faintly voyeuristic feel to it. Stark and discomforting. Moments passed. Music softer now, Napoleon was on the move again.

'What's that up there?' I whispered, noticing a toy perched on the table by the window.

'Oh, that's a Rebecca doll. We bought it for her soon after she came. She talks to her all the time: whispers, mostly. She puts it on the table when she dances.'

Suddenly aware of our presence now, the little girl grimaced.

Screwing her eyes – covering her ears with her hands in a sudden movement. Blotting the vision of us from her mind. Her back firmly turned.

For a long time I watched her. Silent, demented little girl. Body taut and tightly wound. No quiet. No peace. Tireless, relentless motion. Without warning, she stopped. And with an aggressive stamp of her foot threw her arm upwards towards the red velvet curtains. Laughing distractedly, she studied the curtain rail for a moment, eyes darting along the rail. One corner to the other. Hands on hips. Pose defiant.

'Ha...slag...slag...slag... Mummy...ha ha ha,' she chortled. Voice contemptuous, derisory...

'That's another thing she does – thinks her mother's in the curtains,' whispered Mrs Newnes, as we moved away from the door. 'Don't you think they'd want to change her – the next family who have her...?'

I shrugged my shoulders. Another imponderable.

The jumping, dancing child continued. Far away. Lost. Out of sight. Out of hearing. Out of reach.

'We're trying to collect more information – we don't really know too much about her history.' The social worker opened a thin buff-coloured file. 'She was being cared for by a distant maternal aunt. We know her mother died about eighteen months ago, when Becky would have been about five. Apparently the child witnessed the death. It appears that the man she was living with – she calls him Daddy but someone else's name's on the birth certificate – anyway, he got people in from the CB radio to look after her. A series of different people, by the look of things. Then he upped and left. We think maybe he's in prison, but we can't trace him.

'The distant aunt had her for about three weeks over Christmas then brought her here. Said her behaviour was too difficult and she "wasn't the full shilling". It seems she did attend school for a time – but I'm having to dig for more information. Somewhere back on the file it says that her mother was known to this department when she was about fifteen. Looks as if she was pregnant with Becky by the time she was sixteen. The aunt reckons she was refused an abortion but...it's hard to tell really, the details are so scanty.

'Think we believe she should eventually go for adoption. We'll have to find another temporary placement for her in the meantime. She can't stay where she is much longer And well,...she does have some, er...behaviourial difficulties.'

Our eyes met...she grinned sheepishly.

'I suppose that's an understatement really, isn't it – when you look at the behaviourial difficulties, they're pretty gross. She's destructive; she wets the bed; hysterical and high most of the time; can't concentrate; doesn't sleep; eats like an animal; giggles and cackles at imaginary things on the ceiling; pokes her finger into every orifice she can find; whispers all day long to that doll of hers; tries to seduce adults and children alike; masturbates publicly; and the language she has is choice; she's at least two years behind where she should be and any school which takes her will have to have ancillary help... And the dancing – well that's something else...!'

'Certainly not most people's idea of an ideal adoptive daughter, then?'

'Well, not as she is at the moment. I mean, we really want to do something for her – my team leader reckons I can make this a priority. I'll try to give you as much back up as you need. I'm going to comb the blinkin' country for relatives. I expect we'll end up having to advertise for adopters for her eventually.

'Oh, go on, Madge... Take it on. Please.'

I made my way up the narrow bumpy farm track and parked by the back door. Suddenly I was surrounded by barking collie dogs. The door opened – a voice shouted across the yard.

'I told her you were coming, but I don't think it meant anything. Come in, love. Managed to find us OK?'

'I came on my own. The social worker is off sick.'

'That's it...bring that box into the front room.'

Foster mother number three held the door open for me. A tall, ruddy-faced woman, wisps of grey in her hair. She smiled.

'She's out in the cowshed, love. Singing probably. Or maybe doin' her dancin' in the field with Becky doll.'

There was something about Brindley Farm. The feel was right. The mood was open, unflustered.

'How's she doin', did you say? Well, it's early days yet. She's just settlin' in, so to speak. Never a dull moment. I've heard more about dickies and winkies this last two weeks than I have in the whole of my life, that's for sure.' Stella Maddox laughed. 'I said, Becky if it's winkies and dickies you're after, we've plenty of 'em here; the animals have all got 'em; but don't you go messin' with them. Floss has already bitten her once, so she'll soon learn her lesson. And the cats give her a wide berth, I can tell you, since I caught her with the pencils. Funny little mite, isn't she? When the social worker brought her here, we was both waitin' to welcome her, Fred and me. She leapt up on me, looked me straight in the eye and you know what she said? Could have knocked me down with a feather. She said, "I shag your face?"'

'And what did you say?'

'Well, I just said "No, I don't think I'll bother today, thanks all the same. That's not how we show people we love them in our house, is it Fred?" I said "This is how we do it," and I stroked her head and gave her a squeeze and a kiss on the cheek.

'Fred and Colin, that's our youngest son – he's twenty-one next birthday – they've both had it to put up with, like. I told them, I said, "You'll have to look after your own dickies while Becky's around." We have a laugh about it. Mind you, they both do it now without thinking. When she climbs on to Fred's knee, he says, "Has Becky learned to sit on Uncle Fred's knee yet, like we do it in our house?" If she's rubbing at his crotch, he just lifts her off gently and sits her beside him with his arm round her. He says she can sit on his knee when she's learned how to do it the Brindley Farm way. She'll learn.

'She'll be out in the cowshed now, I expect, dancin' with the cow. Colin's rigged up the music in there for her – just an old cassette recorder. She dances all day. And talks to the cows. Mabel cow she talks to most, I think. Never without that doll of hers, though. I reckon she's got plenty of dancin' to do till all of it's out of her system. She's a very clean little thing, though. Always washing herself. I've never seen her dirty yet.'

'Can I go and see her?'

'Yes. She should be in the building on the corner, past the corrugated iron shed there.' She gestured through the window.

I banged the door deliberately on my way into the byre. I had no wish to frighten her. Becky was jumping still. No music this time. A strange hum interspersed by gasps filled the cowshed. Two large brown and white cows looked on placidly, unconcerned, munching slowly.

She was out of breath. Hair loosely held back, some of it fell over her face. She turned slightly and still humming surveyed me with her eyes. Shaking her hair back. Self-absorbed. But I knew she had registered my presence.

I sat myself down on a hay bale. Rebecca Doll monitored the scene. A bastion of defence. The humming became more silent. A whispered hum. Then, without a word she walked across to the dusty cassette recorder in the corner, pressing the button deftly with concentration. Kenny Ball's Jazzmen. Petulant. Challenging.

'Hello, Becky. My name's Madge. Is it OK if I sit...' Before I could finish the sentence, Kenny Ball's Jazzmen echoed off the rafters. Top volume. Small index finger on the volume control switch. The cows looked up, startled. Casting a glance at me again, she moved away behind the animals this time and continued her dance alone.

The noise was deafening. I felt the muscles on my forehead contract into a wince. Momentary struggle with the urgency of the moment. Ears implore brain to take instant action – action legs – march across – switch off racket. But the noise belonged to Becky. It was her noise. Her territory. We worked on her terms. Get on with listening or get out. I got up, placing the little musical doll from the toybox which I had brought with me on the hay bale and, hands over ears, began to dance.

Scoo bee dooo, I wanna be like yooo hoo hoo. I wanna walk like you, talk like you...doobee doobee scoobee doobeee doobee. Not an elegant dance. More a shuffle, really. Fred Maddox's borrowed size nine green wellies precluded anything too adventurous. But before long the primitive emerged and, scoobee dooing in time to the noise, the dance took over. Swirling, twisting, shuffling, arms flailing 'I'm the king of the swingers – the jungle VIP,' I sang, momentarily back in my student days. Moments passed. Three pairs of eyes viewed the scene. Self-consciously I stopped. The small body moved back again behind the cow's tail. Mabel cow moved obligingly. Becky stood hand over her mouth, smiling.

'Do it again.' She ran across to the cassette, and silently rewound the tape. Rubbing her hands with glee – pointing to the ceiling, laughing again hysterically. 'Do it again! Dance! Dance! Jump!'

Together we danced. I shuffled. She jumped. Eyes sparkling, face flushed and pink. Suddenly she stopped and grinned at me, peering curiously at my face. Giggling. I held out my hands. Roughly she snatched them, and jumped higher, levering herself up on my arms. I was beginning to feel exhausted. Limply I gasped for breath and moved backwards, letting go of her hands, slumping wearily on to the hay bale. The music stopped. Silence. I put my hands over my ears in anticipation of the next blast of noise. It came almost instantaneously.

Becky had noticed the little musical doll.

'What's her?' she shouted over the music.

'Sorry, can't hear you very well…?' She turned on her heel and ran purposefully to the cassette recorder. Suddenly there was silence.

'What's her?' she demanded again, pointing to the doll.

'Oh, that's the little girl doll…'

I picked the doll up and wound the key in her back.

'She has so many muddles in her mind, her head goes round and round.'

The doll's musical head turned slowly round and round. Becky clasped her hands to her mouth delightedly. Then, snatching the doll from my hand, 'Gimme! Mine. Slag. Drop on yer 'ead.'

'No, not yours, sweetie. She lives in a toybox in my car.'

Hysterical laughter again.

'The rest of the toys are in the house. Maybe we could go and look.'

'No…mine!' Thrusting the doll behind her back.

'OK, yours for now, but when I go, she must come back with me. Poor little girl…she has lots of muddles.'

Becky put the doll to her mouth. Whispering. Whispering. The musical doll's head continued to revolve.

'Becky, she says she wants to go back now. She'll come back here another day. I'll bring her back. The toybox is her house. Can you let her come back now; she wants to…'

'I bring Rebecca doll…' Both question and answer in her statement.

'Yes.' I moved towards the door.

She followed me out of the cowshed clutching both dolls, pausing at the door to stick her tongue slowly out and in, out and in, at the clumsy, uncomprehending animals, pushing the creaking door forward with the tip of her index finger.

'Dirty door,' she muttered, 'dirty door. Rude. Slag!'

Frantic giggling.

The next time we went together, the social worker and myself. She wanted to observe and to take notes. As soon as we arrived, Becky scuttled upstairs, giggling, chattering incoherently to herself.

'Oh, she'll be hiding. Does that a lot. She'll be up there for a while, then we have to go and look for her. You'll have to excuse me. I've just come back from feeding the chickens.'

Stella washed her hands at the tap.

'How's she been? Well, quirky little thing, isn't she?' She grinned.

'Thought we'd seen it all before, until we met Becky. We're seeing all the messing about you warned us about, but there are a few things I wanted to mention. I've written them down, like you asked. She's terrified of sick. One of the cats was sick on the path and she went hysterical. Took me ages to calm her down. And all this washing – there must be a reason for it. I mean, she won't have a drop of mud on her – disgusts her, it does. Trust her to land up on a farm, eh?

'Then there's the nightmares. Terrors, I'd call them really. I was up to her twice on Tuesday night. Fred and I had to take her into our bed in the finish, but I'm not happy doing that. It's just not a comfortable thing to do with her. I did it with my own when they were little, but not with Becky. I'm sure she's been used, you know. Her body's been used for sex. She has that way about her. It's not natural. She's been on about slag a lot. God slag. God bitch. Rude bitch.

'Sometimes I hear her whispering to the doll. That's what she's saying. And, oh yes – she's been at the cats again. No, she doesn't mess with Fred and Colin now; Fred lets her sit on his knee now. Such an affectionate little mite she can be. I'm sure she's bright enough. And "Shag your face". She still says that a lot.

'Yes, go on up. She's upstairs. She's been on about that doll you had with…muddles, was it?'

We sat on the landing with the toybox. Becky played a hide and seek game. Eventually she appeared through the bathroom door, ran towards the box and grabbed the muddle doll. I followed her into the bedroom with the box; she stood facing me, the muddle doll clutched to her chest. Defiance in her eyes.

'Mine,' she said babyishly, backing towards the sideboard. And laying the doll carefully by her brush and comb she issued her command: 'Don't touch. OK?'

Then the handstands began. Displaying herself. Handstand after handstand. I got down on my hands and knees and knelt on the floor.

'Becky, you can play or do whatever you want to do, and I'll just be with you. Cathy's going to write.'

Becky ignored me. Handstand after handstand again. Balancing her bare legs against the wall. Knickers on display. Then suddenly, 'You lay me?'

'No, Becky, I don't lay children.'

'Bitch! Slag!'

Hysteria again. Then, enticingly, she moved round the room. Hips thrust forwards. Pulling down her tights and knickers she thrust her groin in my face. Hard to stomach. Hard not to show the revulsion welling within me.

'I like you, Becky, but I don't lay children, and I don't shag their faces. That's not how I show children I like them…'

'Slag! Drop on yer 'ead…'

She paraded round the bedroom, one hand between her legs rubbing herself. The other covering her face, giggling profusely…

'Rude. Rude.'

She was almost hoarse now, waving her arms, bellowing distract-edly. Shouting into my face.

'God bitch. You are. God bitch…'

Suddenly she halted in her tracks, eyes focusing on the doll perched on the sideboard.

'Aaaw, little baby, little baby. You got them muddles. Muddle. Muddle. I sing a song. I sing a song. No. You sit,' she commanded, gesturing towards me. 'Sit there.'

I did as I was bid, cross-legged on the pink flowered quilt.

'You clap. Clapa Clapa Clap. No, not like that. Like this.' She clapped a rhythmical motion. Clapa Clapa Clap. I echoed her. She sat on the chair opposite, muddle doll in hand. Knickers round her ankles. Eyes closed.

'Clap, then: I said Clap…' exasperation in her voice. 'Now Becky sing…'

She wiggled her bottom from side to side to settle into a comfortable position. I lifted my arms poised.

'No-o-o…not like that.'

I retracted my arms, closer in to my body.

'Yep… All right. Now I sing. Listen Rebecca Doll, listen; an' muddle doll, listen, now:'

> I can sing a song of you
> You can do a Toshva
> You can do a song of me
> In the clouds – a big cloud
> I marry a daddy a daddy
> By daddy pooey in the bath
> An I am a good good
> Good Good Good Good

> Goody like the girlies
> Not a shag your face
> Naughty say naughty slag
> I do poke a Flossie Poka Sam Poka Toshva
> A big sticky pokey Pokey Stick a slag...

She opened her eyes slightly – watching me intently – eyes searching, inviting a response.

I quickened the clap to applause. Wrong cue.

'No... Not that... No-o-o. Slaggy! No. I sing more.'

> I you dance a song
> Lovely song. You be a slaggy girl
> I can sing a song. Naughty Pauline
> Licky big a naughty boy. A dick.

I listened intently – straining to make it all out. Pauline was Mummy's name, but Toshva and Sam were new to me.

'Finish now.' She grinned at me openly now.

I smiled. 'Cor, what a song!'

'Clap, then.'

I clapped rapturously. She beamed.

'You sing now.'

She smiled triumphantly. Hastily I marshalled my thoughts.

'I clap now. Come on... Come on...' importantly. 'Sing!' she said, voice imperious, commanding. I searched frantically for a tune... 'Let it Be'.

> Well, once upon a time there was
> A little girl called Melanie
> An she had lots of muddles
> In her head.

> For she had lived in lots of houses
> Lots of people she had seen
> Sometimes grown-ups weren't
> Very kind.

> She had muddles about touching
> She had muddles about rude
> And she had some muddles
> About God.

> Grown-ups went away and left her
> And she never saw them again
> And I think...

'No... Shut up. Slag! Bitch!'

In a sudden movement her hand's clutched her ears, face contorting in pain. She leapt off the chest of drawers and landed in a heap. Hysterical, she picked herself up only to fall again as her knickers round her ankles curtailed her exit. Screaming. Battering the floor with her fists in frustration. Punching her ears. The social worker got up, startled. Catching her eye, I shook my head. To touch her now would have been yet another insensitivity.

Becky left the room on all fours, kicking the door as she left. Still mouthing obscenities. I knew in my heart I had gone too fast...too fast. Her pain was raw and I had moved the edge of the sticking plaster. Let it be. We looked at each other, despondently.

For three consecutive Tuesdays we arrived at Brindley Farm. The same routine every time. Park the car. Open the boot. Lift out the toybox and make our way towards the porch. And for three consecutive Tuesdays Becky made herself scarce. On the first occasion she ran from the house like a scalded cat, screeching, and ran off down the fields, disappearing completely through the hedge. But I sensed we had made contact. The bridge was there. She knew it, and I knew it. And it was only right that she should be allowed time for prevarication, time to breathe, to summon her courage, before placing one tiny foot on to the planks to test their endurance. It was a journey towards wholeness that her intuition demanded of her. But the direction and the pace had to be hers.

We used the second Tuesday to take stock. The social worker had assembled some more information. It seemed that Becky's mother had never taken to the child and had left her in various different places throughout her short life. In a bid to quieten her she had fed her Phenergan, a child sedative, three tablespoonfuls at a time. Becky had been in a semi-permanent daze. The health visitor reported concern at her failure to gain weight. Emotional abuse, it seemed, had also featured. A neighbour had been interviewed. She reported how verbally abusive her mother had been, calling the child names such as 'slut', 'slag' and 'little bitch'. She had apparently joked to neighbours that Becky took after her dad – wasn't the full shilling – thought the nurses had dropped her on her head at birth.

Eventually, it seems, she had gone to school, although only very irregularly. The school could remember her; a dirty, smelly little girl, constantly hungry, demanding of adult attention. Disruptive in class. They recalled her mother's death. Died of an accidental overdose of paracetamol, when she'd been drinking. Apparently she had vomited a lot and had finally been admitted to hospital, choked on her own vomit. It appeared that Becky had witnessed the scene.

The man Becky called Daddy had given her her mother's ring to wear immediately after her death. He made her promise not to lose it, although it had disappeared down a drain on the way to school. No one had explained to her that her mother was dead. It seemed she had heard it from one of the dinner ladies.

There was also some suspicion that she was the product of an incestuous relationship between mother and grandfather, but no real evidence. In fact, the family were well known in the neighbourhood as 'one of those families'. Mother's twin brother had been convicted of sexual assault on a niece. Efforts to trace the man Becky knew as Daddy continued to prove fruitless.

We planned a meeting with Fred and Stella, Colin, the social worker and myself, to discuss strategy. Becky was to receive consistent messages about herself from all quarters whenever possible, messages such as 'good girl', 'well done', 'Becky has a beautiful body; we need to take care of it'. Words such as 'dirty' and 'naughty' were to be temporarily deleted from the vocabulary as far as reference to her was concerned. Becky was lovable and capable. In all sexual matters, firm boundaries. 'Rude' to be used as a reprimand for sexually based misdemeanours, poking cats' bottoms, shagging faces etc. This word Becky already knew in that context. 'Bad manners' was to be used for all other breaches of etiquette such as banging, pushing, inappropriate interruption of adult conversations. And she was to be patiently taught the message that Becky doesn't exist to be used by grown-ups.

In the context of animal behaviour on the farm, Fred would make sense of the facts of life to her, as and when appropriate. Loving touches to be encouraged, sexual touches discouraged in the context of 'Becky hasn't learned how we do things here, yet.' Hysteria and silliness to be tolerated although not necessarily in the same room. Becky was to be asked to take Miss Loud Silly outside until she could be a little bit quieter, then she could return.

And Brindley Farm was to be a haven where Becky could stay – a haven while some of her muddles were sorted out and she began to be ready to move one last time, to a family who wanted a little girl very much who would be in their lives for ever. Delicate business this.

'Good, that, eh Madge? Theory's good anyway, you can say that... And Madge's magic box'll take care of the rest.'

Fred grinned at me benignly. I liked Fred – he was a realist.

The breakthrough came the following week. I left the toybox by the porch this time and went into the farmhouse to collect a mug of tea. Muddle doll was perched on the grey flagstone step. On my return I sensed Becky's presence somewhere in the yard. Hidden. Alert. Watchful. I wound the little doll. The head began to revolve. The tune began. Biting into a mouthful of scone, I shared my dilemma with the little doll, talking out loud.

'Well, it was like this, you see. I'm a lady who knows quite a lot about children's muddles – because children teach me about their muddles and how to get to the bottom of them...and...well... I was playing with the toybox at Brindley Farm with a little girl called, ah... Becky, I think her name is, and...oh...well she was singing a song to me and I was clapping. Like this, it was, see...and then I sang a song... But there were words in my song that were too hard for Becky to hear and she had to put her hands over her ears...because her brain doesn't want to think about some of these words yet, and it made her frightened... Yes... I know it was silly... And...yes, well Becky was angry. Very angry. And she's still angry with me now. What did you say?... Will I say I'm sorry?... Yes, I will...of course I will... But I can't...you see Becky isn't here. She runs away every time I come now, and...'

'Say it, then.'

A small figure in a blue tracksuit emerged from behind one of the sheds.

'Becky, I'm sorry.

'What does she say?' Gesturing to the muddle doll.

'She says she thinks I was silly... She says it was too soon for the little girl to hear a song like that...'

Becky nodded. She held out her hand, gesturing.

'Gimme. I want her.'

I placed her in the child's arms. 'Shall we take the toybox inside?'
Becky led the way.

'I carry your cup,' she said.

Phew! Back in touch again!

'Cathie's going to come too, OK? She's going to do some writing…'
No resistance.

She knelt down and rummaged through the box. Furry puppets,
tummy balloons, hiding dogs, baby feeding bottles, heaped in disarray.

'What's this?'

'You want to know what that is?'

'Open it.'

I did as I was bid. It was an anatomical jigsaw, the lid tied round
with a pair of yellow tights. A four-layered jigsaw – outline of male
and female body, top layer clothes, second layer skin, third layer inner
organs, fourth layer skeleton. Becky tipped it out and proceeded to try
to put the pieces back. Her concentration was poor. The complexity of
the task beyond her.

'You do it.'

'OK. I do it.'

I handed her a piece and pointed to its location on the board.

'What's this? It's a brain. Say "Brain". Say "Braaayne".'

'Braaiyne' (explosions of laughter). 'Say "Drop on yer 'ead…bitch."'

'Drop on yer 'ead, bitch.'

More hysteria.

Suddenly she stopped, got up and moved towards the toybox.

'Mummy says "Drop on yer 'ead, bitch."' She grinned, tentative,
searching.

'You're telling me Mummy says that.'

She picked up the female anatomical doll. Stuck her tongue out
towards it, and threw it on the floor. In a lightning movement it was
in her hand again. Hurled down with great force.

'Drop on yer 'ead. Drop on yer 'ead. No brain. No brain. Mummy
Bitch!'

'You're very very angry with the mummy.'

'Cor, Slag, Shit!' She was jumping on the doll's head. 'Yeah, bitch.'
She spat out the words, breathless, determined.

'Tell 'er. Tell 'er.' She gestured to me. 'Tell 'er a story. Come on.'

'Well…this is a story about a mummy who didn't know much about
how to be a mummy, and do you know what, she wasn't kind to her

little baby. She wasn't kind at all. And she used to shout at her little baby…'

'What did she shout, then… "Bitch"?'

I nodded.

'An' "Slag"?'

'Yes.'

'An' "Drop on yer 'ead"?'

'Mphm.'

'Well, she's just not a kind mummy, and I put her in the jail.'

She thrust the female doll under the bed.

'Dead now,' she said at last in triumph.

'You reckon she's dead now?'

Suddenly the impact of my words reached her. A look of horror passed across her face.

'No! No!' Her voice was anguished now, her screams louder. On her hands and knees scrambling under the bed. 'Not die, Mummy, not die. Mummy… Mummy…' She retrieved the mummy doll. Clinging to me, mummy doll squashed between us, she sobbed loudly now.

'You don't want Mummy to die?' I whispered, holding her quivering body close. 'You're angry with Mummy but you don't want her to die?'

'No,' she murmured, 'not…not die, Mummy.'

'Becky,' I whispered gently, rocking her. 'You didn't kill Mummy. Her body was sick and couldn't work any more.'

For half an hour she sat locked in her thoughts while I hummed tunes to her.

As the weeks moved on into months, Becky would await our arrival eagerly. Sometimes swinging on the gate into the yard. Other times absorbed in a task with Auntie Stella. Occasionally dancing in the cowshed. Colour in her cheeks.

We dealt with each obstacle as we came to it. Becky would present it and together we would grapple with it. Each monster, each nightmare, one by one. Sometimes monsters would rear their heads in sessions with me, only to be laid to rest finally by Fred in the cowshed or on the back of the tractor in the early morning. Becky's speech was improving all the time. Her hysteria diminishing. We walked together in unison. The child led the way.

'Naughty mummies' took us a number of sessions. The mummy who didn't know much about looking after children, and who shouted at her baby and hit her because really she didn't understand what a special little girl she had, poor lady; this was played out again and again. Baby dolls were dropped on their heads. Mummy dolls were punished and locked in dungeons, boiled in pans, dropped on their heads and miraculously brought back to life. Just pretend.

We practised on the doll babies. Giving them loves, talking nicely to them, soothing them when they cried. Feeding them gently. No shouting. No violence. Feeding, nurturing, tending; meticulous, loving.

Fred and Becky would watch the animals feed their young. She would practice on the baby calves, without shouting at them and scaring them. Fred reckoned that words like 'shit' and 'slag' weren't words the calves like to hear much. Put them off their dinner. Becky would nod seriously. Clutching the feeding bucket in her small hands. Competent. Responsible. Deserving of praise.

'Dead' emerged naturally from the naughty mummy play. We discovered that dead people didn't all live in ambulances now. Or hospitals, either, come to that. Their bodies weren't much good any more, because the life had gone from them. She found a dead pigeon by the gable end one day. Together she and Stella buried it in a shoe box under the kitchen window. Becky had dug it up twice, but as yet it hadn't come alive again.

They studied electric light bulbs carefully.

'Colin's idea,' said Stella proudly.

Becky ran to the drawer to show me.

'We kept it for you, Madge. See,' she said shaking the spent light bulb vigorously, 'once it's gone it's gone, an' you can't make it come on again.'

'Yes, well the element's broken, see,' Stella reassured me by way of explanation. 'Tell Madge where the light goes.' She smiled.

'Goes into the light in the sky. All everywhere,' Becky said seriously, eyes moving round the room in childish wonderment.

Not that it was all plain sailing. There were eruptions from time to time, like the occasion when she gave Mabel's calf a swipe on the eye with the milk pail.

'Jealous, she was,' said Fred. 'Plain jealous. Mabel was paying her calf too much attention. We had to get the vet up here, the beast's eye was badly cut. Becky was in disgrace.'

'And what a few days we had, Fred, remember?'

The mere thought of it brought a frown to Stella's face.

'Tantrums at bedtime. Screaming fits before school. And we had the language again. I tell you, Madge, if you'd not have been across in Norway that week I'd have sent her back with you. We'd had enough of it.'

'Yes, love, but I suppose it's when we have weeks like that we remember what she was like when she first came... Makes you remember how she's come on. An' she was in trouble at school that week as well. Sickin' up an' hysterics. An nickin' the ring. She does that still. Hoards them in behind her shoes in the wardrobe.'

The months went by, progress would plateau. Then we would break through again. Becky would be ready to tackle another demon. The rings had been a problem for some time. Altercations at school. She would borrow rings from other children and refuse to return them at the end of the day. And a ring belonging to Colin's girlfriend had gone missing. Stella had bought Becky two rings of her own to keep, but to no avail. Becky's preoccupation continued.

Rebecca Doll seldom left her bed now. Becky went on her travels on the farm unaccompanied as a rule. Occasionally the little girl doll with the muddles would be wound up and perched on the sideboard to watch the proceedings. Becky was playing with the baby doll, feeding it gently, a repetitive theme this, especially since the calf incident. Suddenly she noticed my ring.

'Is that a special ring?' she asked quietly, eyes eager in anticipation.

'You want to know if that's a special ring?'

'Yes, is it special?'

'Well...quite special.'

'Can I wear it?'

[Think this one through, Madge; careful now...my mind fumbled for direction.]

Hands between her legs – rubbing...twisting her dress excitedly.

'I want to...'

'Becky, of course, I could let you put my ring on your finger. But it's a ring which fits my finger. And I'm a big lady, not a little girl. My ring's far, far too big for a little girl's finger.'

'Come on!' she demanded. 'I want it.'

'Well, I can't let you wear it unless...'

'But why?' Her voice was frustrated now. 'I want it.'

'I know you want it, but it would be very silly of me just to give it to you and let you wear it, because it's far too big for your little finger, and it might fall off...'

'And I might lose it?'

'Yes, and you might lose it. And... And it wouldn't be a little girl's fault if she lost a ring which a grown-up gave her, if it was far too big for her finger.'

'But I won't lost it... Oh, please...'

'OK, Becky, but I'd like you to stand over there, please.'

'I stand on the chair?' she volunteered, clambering up on top of the chair by the bed.

With studied concentration she held out her arm; forehead crimpling into a frown, she watched as I took the ring from my own finger.

'On there,' she whispered, waving the fourth finger of her left hand.

With great care I placed the opal and diamond ring on her outstretched finger. She stood in silence, deeply absorbed, rigidly at attention, ring dangling on her finger, other hand cupped underneath. Gently she blew on her hand – the ring swayed slightly. Her lips moved again in silent self-instruction. Suddenly she looked up. Our eyes met. I smiled at her triumph.

'I not lose it,' she said, shaking her head emphatically.

'No, Becky, I won't let you lose it. If a grown-up gave a little girl a ring that was far too big, and the little girl lost it, it wouldn't be her fault, would it? Because the grown-up should be more sensible than that, eh?'

'Not silly bitch?'

'Not silly bitch.'

With the same meticulous care she took the ring from her own finger and placed it in the palm of my hand.

'I wear it again? Another day?'

'Yes, of course you can, but only if I'm here with you, OK?'

She nodded again, lips moving, muttering softly to herself, 'Not silly bitch daddy – not silly bitch.'

The next time I saw her she beckoned me into the bathroom.

'Leave it,' she commanded as I began to negotiate the toybox through the bathroom door, 'just you.' Door ajar, the social worker sat on the stairs.

Immediately, she pointed to the ring. 'I wear it again?'

'Well, you know the rule. I have to be with you.'

She clambered into the bath and held her hand out again with great concentration, the other hand cupped underneath – an extra insurance. I placed the ring on her finger.

Again rigid, poised, she gazed at the ring on her finger, blowing slightly on it, moving it gently up and down. The ring swayed gently on her finger. Gradually she lifted her eyes, peered at me for a moment, just checking, and laid her eyes to rest back on her left hand again. Very gradually she allowed her cupped right hand to move down by her side, ring still poised on her finger. Then she moved her left arm right and left, casting triumphant glances in my direction as with each new arm movement the ring stayed precariously in place. More confident now, she took the ring off, placed it between her index finger and thumb and, bending down on her hands and knees in the bath, pulled out the plug, leaving it to dangle on its metal chain. My heart skipped a beat. The tension grew. Red faced, the child concentrated, slowly moving down, down towards the gaping hole.

'You're holding on to the ring very carefully,' I said, surprised at the apparent calm in my own voice, 'and you're making sure you don't lose it.'

No acknowledgement. Deep absorption in the task.

'And now you're holding the ring between your finger and your thumb and it's dancing round the edge of the hole. And you're holding it very tight, and I'm watching you.'

My heart beat wildly now. Throat dry. The risk was overwhelming. And yet somehow it was right. It had to be done. The seconds dragged. The ring bobbed up and down, up and down, perilously close to the abyss. My body poised to lunge forward.

Suddenly it was all over and, the process ended, she moved backwards, plopping on the bottom of the bath. I held out my palm and, beaming delightedly, she placed the ring again in the palm of my hand.

'An' I never even lost it...,' she said.

'Go on, then.'

'Go on, then, what?'

'Go on, then. Say like Uncle Fred, like this: "You'm a clever little Miss Muffet"', voice gruff, a perfect imitation.

I felt the laughter rise in my throat as she held up her arms to be lifted out over the rim of the bath. And as it turned out, the ensuing months were to see the preoccupation with rings pale into insignificance as an issue in her life.

There were weeks when nothing of note occurred – nothing of note to me, it seemed, although Becky strode firmly on, pausing sometimes to rest, to survey the route. On these days we spent the precious time meandering round the chicken run or counting berries on the rowan trees by the side of the gate to the yard. On these days, too, she would keep me in check, refusing to move, sensing my frustration at her prevarications, but moving only in her own time. Many children had taught me this lesson over again in countless guises, and still I could not know it. But Becky did. And in these moments unspoken between us, Becky would call me to heel.

'How many o' them berries are there?' she would demand, pointing to the rowan tree.

'I don't know.'

'Well, you don't know much if you don't know that,' came the acid response. 'Come on.'

It took a long time for the plate game to offer up its meaning to me. It followed the same ritual each time. There were thirteen plastic plates in the toybox, each with a different face. Angry, sly, smug, sad, enraged, withdrawn – the expressions varied. These plates would be liberally coloured over with navy-blue felt tip pen, with some force, until their expressions were obliterated. The dirty, dark blue pile was then carried through ceremoniously to the bathroom, together with muddle doll.

'Talk to 'er, then. Put her up there and talk to 'er. Tell 'er, then!'

The stool was dragged to the sink, the sink filled with water and copious bubbles of soap. Great care taken to test the water. Not too hot and not too cold.

'Talk to 'er, then. Say it. What you say…'

'OK, and now Becky's sitting by the sink and she's rolled her sleeves up tight and now she's picked up the first plate with the dirty blue covered up face and now she's wiping it very gently, very carefully with the sponge and lots of soap, and gently, gently, round and round she's rubbing it. And now it's very clean and all the bluey stuff has been washed off. And now… Oh, now she's giving it a kiss and she's stroking it gently and giving it to me… Thank you.'

'Dry it now.'

'Oh, OK. And now she's telling me to dry it now.'

One by one the plates were lovingly tended, dirty mess washed off, tended, cared for, kissed with great care and lovingly handed to me to be dried. A protracted operation.

Suddenly she leapt back from the chair, swearing, 'Oooh, no – no!' (Hysteria mounting in her voice.) 'It's them horribles. Get the horribles off now. Now!'

Some of the dark ink had inadvertently splashed on to her cardigan. Quickly we splashed some water on it and rubbed until the faint muddy splashes disappeared from the fabric. Then, after close examination, she proceeded again.

'Becky's not a dirty girl,' she said, studying my face.

'No, Becky's a clean girl; not a dirty girl.'

Nodding emphatically at me, 'She is. Say she is.'

'Becky's not a dirty girl, she's a clean girl.'

The nodding approval continued.

'Not "dirty bitch"?' Shaking her head, her eyes searched my face beseechingly.

'Not dirty bitch, Becky.' I knelt down to face her. 'Beautiful girl.'

Her eyebrows furrowed in uncertainty.

'And nice?'

'Yes, and nice,' I answered her question.

'You're a nice lady.'

An unexpected gift – 'Thank you, Becky.'

'Nice lady and nice me, isn't it? Not slaggy girl?'

'Not slaggy girl.'

For three consecutive weeks we washed and dried the plates and put them on the 'clean girl' pile.

Within the cocoon of Brindley Farm, Becky continued to flourish. Friendships with children of her own age, though, proved hard to sustain. Becky's behaviour was overbearing. She snatched, demanded, couldn't share. Social visits outside were also strained because Becky was as yet unable to tolerate the insecurity of any prolonged disruption of her daily routine. Her confusion would express itself in antisocial and aggressive defiance.

Altercations with adults continued, some more dangerous than others.

I arrived one frosty day in January to find Becky banished to her room. She was to stay there every day after school for a week. No pocket money for a week. No tractor on Tuesday with Uncle Fred. Something very serious had happened. Stella needed to talk it through. Hastily she filled the kettle.

'Becky doesn't know you're here yet. She's upstairs. I just want to have a word. Fred says...well...hang on.'

She cut a slab of lemon curd tart and placed it on the table in front of me.

'Now, well...we were doing the shopping – yesterday, it was. And we were stopped at the check-out in the queue. Becky had been upset at school for some reason. I haven't got to the bottom of that. She was a bit mopey though, when I picked her up. But she loves coming round the supermarket with me. She counts the cans of cat food for me, usually, and gets them off the shelf. Well, anyway, what was I saying? Oh, yes, we were at the check-out and she was eating a bar of chocolate I'd bought her. I think she might have been bored waiting. Suddenly she noticed a little lad propped in front of a trolley, no more than two, he must have been, eating an ice cream cone. She asked me if she could have one like it, and I said, "No, Becky, you've had chocolate." Then she started to whinge a bit, and then I said "Look, Becky, I don't want to hear that noise, you've had your chocolate, now be quiet."

'I could hear her whispering under her breath. I should know, you know, by this time to look out when the whispers start. The next thing I knew she must have marched over to the little lad, grabbed his ice cream and started to eat it. Well, you can imagine! He started to howl. I wheeled round to see what was going on. I was furious. "Becky," I said, "come here this minute." That was it. She stood, eyes glaring at me, and started to shout these awful words we used to hear when she first came: "Cunting bitch! Slag! Drop on yer 'ead." I was mortified – see I'm not so used to it now. Everybody looked and then she threw the ice cream at me, kicked his trolley, and before anyone could grab her she took off.

'I flew after her, like, but she was too quick, and she dived off over the road, not a bit of regard for the traffic or anything – a lorry had to skid to miss her. A couple on the other pavement could see what had happened, and he made a lunge at her and managed to grab her, but she bit him. The language was awful. I was just beside myself, too, with fear. I mean she could have been killed easily.

'When I finally got hold of her I was livid. She was struggling with this man, see, but, well...it was the look in her eyes, and the way she held her body. It was as if she expected me to beat the living daylights out of her, shaking all over, she was. Surely she knows by now that I don't hit her. Fred and me have never hit our kids. You don't have to hit 'em, do you? That don't teach them respect.'

Stella was holding back tears – she was shaken, afraid. This incident had tested her faith in herself, her ability as a mother. She had been questioning her actions ever since.

'Fred said if I'd have smacked her bottom it might have all been over with. I'm still angry with her even now. It was such a shock, Madge. I mean, what if an accident had happened, and something awful happened to her. I'd never forgive myself. And now she's talking to that Becky doll again. God help us, we haven't seen or heard of her in weeks or months.'

'Stella' I touched her arm. 'Stella, I... I think you're an amazing woman, and a superb mother.'

She looked at me in incredulity. 'Oh, Madge. Cut it out. Don't be daft.'

'Stella, I'm really serious. You and Fred are remarkable people. The progress you've made with her is superb. She's a different little girl. What you're doing is healing her. Most of the population wouldn't have a clue about what you're doing, let alone contemplate doing it. You know that...'

She turned on me angrily.

'Well, I'm not most of the bloomin' population, and I've made a mess of this!' Then wearily, 'Sorry, love...'

'Stella, I know how much you've been through with her, and I know how brilliant you and Fred have been, and I can see the results. Whatever you do and however you do it, the chemistry works.'

My voice was earnest, uncompromising.

'And now we've had an explosion in the chemistry lab, eh?'

'Yes, a small, controlled explosion.'

'A small...controlled...explosion! So that's what it was, then? Like they say in the news "A small controlled explosion took place..."'

Stella was laughing now.

'Well, when I think of all the little sticks of dynamite that have walked through this door one time or another.' She cradled her head in her hands. 'I get tired, you see, Madge. What with me hot flushes and all that, I run out of patience sometimes.'

'I bet you do!'

When I went upstairs to find her, Becky was sitting on her bed scribbling fiercely on a colouring book. Tiny pieces of paper littered the floor. She looked up at me, sadness and resignation in her eyes.

'Where's the toybox?'

'Toybox? Not right now, Becky. Later, maybe. Talking today, OK? Talking today with Becky and Auntie Stella. No shouting at Becky. Just talking.'

She followed me without a murmur, clutching Rebecca Doll, into the kitchen. Stella was on her hands and knees stoking the coal fire.

'I said to Becky that we had some talking to do today. A big muddle happened yesterday...'

Stella held out her hand to Becky. Trembling she moved closer, eyes guarded, tentative.

'Tell Madge what happened yesterday, Becky, can you?'

Becky shook her head.

'Well, maybe I could help a bit,' said Stella hurriedly. 'You see, Madge, we were doing the shopping, weren't we, in Tesco's, and Becky was helping me with the tins, ever such a clever girl she is now, Madge, looks after the cat food all by herself. And then we had a bit of a disaster, didn't we, love? She wanted an ice cream and I said "No", so she snatched a cone from a little boy who was waiting with his mummy.'

'Oh, dear,' I said, 'that was a pretty silly thing to do, wasn't it, because the ice cream belonged to the little boy, didn't it?'

Becky nodded.

'Was he crying?' I ventured.

Becky nodded again.

'Yes, he was,' Stella continued. 'He was crying all right. So I turned round to tell Becky off, and do you know, Madge, an even more awful thing happened then.'

'Oh, dear!'

'Yes, she shouted those words at me, you know, the rude ones that we don't use at Brindley Farm and threw the ice cream at me.'

'Well, that was very, very silly. Very, very bad manners.'

'Yes, it was. I was very cross and just as I was about to catch hold of her, well she shot off out the door and across the road...'

'An' not looking,' said Becky considering carefully.

'*And* not looking?' I echoed her words, with fitting solemnity. 'Oh, my goodness, what a very, very serious muddle! Well, Stella, were you cross?'

'I certainly was!'

'And were you very worried?'

'I was worried.'

'And did you think little Becky might get killed?'

'I did. I thought we'd lost her. I was just about in tears, I was. I couldn't bear to think of her getting hurt by a big lorry.'

'So what did you do then?'

'Well, a man had got hold of her because she was running away...'

'Was she?'

Becky was listening intently, nodding quietly, remembering.

'And I grabbed her. I got hold of her and...'

'Madge, an' she never hit me. She never even smacked me one bit!' Stella gasped.

'She never smacked you one bit?'

'So you don't do smacking and shouting and belting, Stella?'

I stayed with it.

'No, I don't.' Stella had regained her composure.

'An' lock in the coalshed, an' punch in the mouth, and the 'orrible medicine?' Becky said quickly.

'The 'orrible medicine? What's that?' I asked.

'I think that's what she used to get to make her sleep,' Stella said.

'No,' Becky shook her head. 'No...'

'When you're a naughty girl you get it?'

'Four spoons.'

Stella and I exchanged glances, minds momentarily confronted with the same appalling mental picture.

'Well, we don't have none of that here, do we, love?' she said softly, cradling the child on her knee.

'Becky,' I said gently, 'Becky, can you remember yesterday? Did anything horrid happen at school?'

She nodded, tears welling in her eyes.

'Becky, what happened, love, tell Stella,' stroking her hair gently.

The child sat, head moving from side to side, eyes closed, fists clenched. Whatever it was, it was terrible.

'Becky, tell Auntie Stella, lovey. Come on, let's have it, sweetheart.'

The child's face contorted, hands frantically clutching her ears, her mouth. Body convulsing. Stella held on, hastily moving the flailing legs out of range of the fire. I knelt by them. Not interfering. The child was distracted, screaming, now wriggling, hysterical.

'Sick…aagh…' covering her mouth with her hands. Sobbing, 'No-o-o, Peter be sick… No-o-o, horrible… Get away… Get away!'

Stella held on grimly. Instinctively, she knew. The flailing subsided. The body relaxed. This horror had run its course. The child cried now, sobbed quietly, nose buried on Stella's shoulder. Moments passed. Eventually Stella turned her face slightly.

'Becky sits next to a little boy called Peter. I think he must have been sick yesterday…'

We sat in silence, thinking.

'On my shirt,' a tiny whispered voice.

'Oh, on your shirt, lovie. Oh, dear!'

'And did Miss Anderson clean it up?'

Nod.

'And wiped your shirt?'

More nods.

'Peter won't die, Becky,' Stella said slowly. 'Lots of people get sick, but they don't die. And Becky, you had sick on your shirt, but that doesn't mean you're going to die either.'

She turned to me.

'Sick is such a problem for Becky, isn't it, darling. She's so scared of it. But remember, you've seen the cats be sick and they're not dead, are they?'

Becky looked up; flushed red little face; energy gone.

'Can I have the hedgehog puppet?' she asked, gesturing to the toybox.

I handed her the wise hedgehog puppet.

'He hasn't seen you cry before,' I ventured smiling.

'She's only cried once before, all the time she's been here, haven't you, precious?'

Becky nodded, burying her face in the hedgehog's fur.

A car drew up outside. It was Colin, back from buying some baling wire. A big jovial lad he was, round faced and strong.

'Do us a favour, love, can you?' Stella called through to the porch. 'Becky wants to sit here for a bit with me. Just give the Johnsons a ring and see how little Peter is. Seems he wasn't well yesterday at school.'

Colin did as he was asked. Becky watched intently.

'Yeah, fine now, Mum. Something he ate didn't agree with him. He'll be back to school tomorrow. Ann says thanks for askin', and she'll see you on Thursday.'

The judge who decides about children came to a decision about Becky. He listened very carefully to what everyone had to say. Stella and Fred went to talk to him – so did everyone else. Becky's stepfather was traced to a lodging house in Bradford, but he said he wouldn't be able to care for her. The judge decided that the social workers should find an adoptive home for her with a family who wanted a little girl very much and that my work with her should continue well into her new placement until it was no longer necessary. The local authority would advertise for a suitable home for the child. Then there would be introductions.

Stella rang me at home one evening. Unusual. Very unusual.

'Madge.' She talked in a low voice. 'Next time you come, do you think you could have a word with Fred. He's getting a bit steamed up about Becky going and... I'll keep her in town next Tuesday for a while. That'll let you have some time. He wants to see you. 'E's been layin' down the law with the social workers again. I don't know what to do with him when he gets like this.'

When I arrived Fred was sitting by the fire in the kitchen. He got up, awkwardly.

'Stella's left us out some cake. I'll just make the tea.'

He walked past me into the scullery, to fill the kettle.

'Stella's told you I'm fed up, then?'

'Yes, she rang me on Tuesday night.'

I sat down by the table at the window. A jug of daffodils and red flowering currant sat on the windowsill. I felt the delicate petals between my fingers, absent-mindedly. It took Fred little time to come to the point.

'Madge, I'm bloody fed up, I am, I'll say. I mean we've had that little mite here now well on a year, 'aven't we? An' just look at the state she was in when she came.'

I nodded.

Fred continued, 'An' over my dead body is she bein' messed about any more, I'll tell you. Them social workers advertisin' her like she's a bit of car number plate out o' *Exchange & Mart*. Bloody ridiculous. She's a human bein', Good God, not some bit of filth to be swept one way or another. That little un's been through enough an' we've been through enough with her. Many's a night we haven't slept for lyin' listenin' to her whimperin' and her nightmares. But she's a real little lady, Madge. I mean, surely to God they can't just advertise her like a second-hand car!'

I opened my mouth to reply.

'No, don't say nothin'. I haven't finished. An' they keep bringin' us papers of different couples as want to adopt her. An' none of them looks bloody worth it on paper anyway. Bloomin' insurance salesman the last one was. Some of them, soon as they hear "sexual problems", "behavioural difficulties" they're off. I wouldn't give 'em houseroom. None o' them's good enough for her. I'll tell you that and I've told that social services boss man. I've told him, she's not leaving my door until I *know* she's going to be looked after proper an' loved. It's the very least she deserves.'

Fred stopped suddenly, for breath. Big chapped brown hands clumsily clutching his teacup, banging it back on the saucer.

'So, there. I've said it. I don't want you to say nothing. I just wanted to say it an' that's it.'

'OK, Fred, I get the message. Becky's worth the very best.'

'Too bloody right, she is.'

'And we're not settling for less? Let's shake on it, then Fred.'

We shook hands. He looked at me for the first time, across the table. His eyes had changed. More gentle now. Genial.

'I misjudged you, Madge. When you first came here I thought, "Toybox? Therapy? What the hell next?" I thought you was one of them brainy folks all bloomin words between yer ears and no common sense. But you've worked wonders with 'er, too. We couldn't have done it without you…'

Then his thoughts took him on a different path.

'You know, Madge, it's a case of knowin', isn't it? You learn about nature and the flow of things, and you look at the sky an' you can tell the rain's on its way, an' the field o' barley knows it too, like. It's hard to explain. An' the animals know when their time has come, an' they tell you with their eyes. An it's a knowin' that you get with the seasons and the elements an' you share it with the earth – am I makin' sense?' pondering carefully.

'I think so.'

'An' you mustn't interfere with nature. All this interfering we do, it's goin' to find us in ruin… Look at little Becky. That was interferin' with nature. Her parents not bloody fit to be parents at all. Poor little blighter. Why? I ask myself.'

'I ask myself that question too.'

'Aye, lass, an' I bet you don't get the answer neither. Here, have another bit o' cake.'

'Fred, you and Stella are going to find the parting very hard.'

'We always do, lass, but you have to be tough with yourself. Stella and me, we're gettin' on now. Both pushin' fifty. We've had ours. Life's been good to us, Madge, all in all. You feel you can put something back, doin' this.'

'I'm only doin' it if it's right, mind. I'm warnin' you. I've told them! She's only goin' if it's right!' Fred raised his voice again.

'I think we'll know, if it's right…'

He smiled at me for the first time.

'Aye, likely we will; likely we will.'

Fred was relaxed now, his handling of Becky was intuitive – he wasn't asking me for guidance, rather exploring his experience with me. It was no effort to him to see the world through her eyes.

A car door banged somewhere.

'That must be them back.' He craned his neck round the daffodils, pulling aside the orange floral curtains.

'Cor! Will you take a look at this.'

I moved beside him to the window. Becky had seen my car, and Tuesday was toybox day.

'Right little ragbag she is now, that's for sure.' Fred laughed. 'None o' yer Miss Prim.'

Hair tousled, white knee socks round her ankles, grey school cardigan hanging off one shoulder, she made her way quickly down the path and bounded through the door, grinning from ear to ear.

'How are you doin', then, Muffet? Had a good day?'

'Mphm.'

'Miss Anderson is ever so pleased with her, Madge. She's turnin' out so clever we can hardly keep up with her.'

Becky came closer to me and held out her hand.

'Ooh, Madge, you're to have a present, I see,' Fred chuckled. He got up. 'I'll just go and give Stella a hand in with the shoppin'.'

I accepted the present gracefully. Four grubby, bedraggled, over-clutched violets.

'I picked 'em for yer.'

'Oh, thank you, Becky. Tell you what, I'll put them in here until it's time for me to go.'

Becky nodded approval as I plopped each tiny flower in the daffodil jug. She ran out again to help with the carrying of the shopping, and returned carrying a large box of cornflakes, Fred and Stella close behind.

'She's been pesterin' all the way home in the car for Fred to take you down to see the lambs. Is that all right with you?' Stella was breathless.

'I'd love to.'

We stood together at the side of the pen. Becky ducked deftly underneath the wooden strut and with great assurance approached the two ewes and their lambs. One of the lambs was feeding, guzzling voraciously at its mother's teat.

'Tell Madge about these, Becky. Our special lambs, we call them.' Fred stood, knee resting on the side of the pen. 'Mind, now, Becky. Don't pull her away. The ewe won't like it.'

The little girl put the lamb down again – did as she was bid. Changed days.

'Well,' she said, brushing her hair back. 'See this one 'ere, this is a mummy, right?' (Pointing to the ewe.) 'An' her baby died inside 'er tummy. An' she was cryin'. And,' she continued, 'an' see this baby lamb? See, its mummy died. An' that one there,' pointing to the other lamb, 'her mummy wasn't kind to 'er. So Uncle Fred had to take her away.'

'An' what did we have to do then?' Fred drew on his pipe.

I stood rapt, arms folded on the side of the pen, chin balanced Marvelling at the simplicity of it all. Becky continued the lecture.

'Well, we had to find them two babies a mummy.'

'An' before we could do that, what did we have to do?'

'We had to make the lambs a lovin' jacket to keep 'em safe.'

'That's it, Becky. You've got it. We had to make the lambs a loving jacket to keep them safe in, because sometimes the new mummy who's been cryin' for a baby all this time takes a bit o' findin'. We have to look long and hard, don't we, darlin', to find the right ewe to fit to the lamb. An' then what happens after that – can you remember?'

'She loves it like it was her own, and they're happy together.'

'You got it.'

She was down on her hands and knees now, watching the lambs feed.

Fred moved closer to me, and whispered out of the corner of his mouth: 'I 'ave to skin 'em, love. Take the skin off the dead lamb, see, else the ewes would never take to 'em see. Smells wrong.'

We had been preparing Becky for moving now for some time – the concept was well fixed in her mind. It was difficult to focus her, though, until a suitable family were finally selected.

I contacted the social worker on my return from holiday. Events had moved fast in my absence.

'I think we've come up with the family, Madge. Fred and Stella think it's the one, anyway. Fred says to tell you he knows. They've two lads already of eighteen and fourteen; been longing for a little girl but can't have any more. He keeps a market garden and she's a teacher at a special school. Lovely couple. Hobbies: kite flying, rambling, conservation, and they both dance with the local morris dancing team.'

I was beginning to imagine the match. Looked good so far.

By the time I saw Becky again, she was on the brink of her new life. Apprehensive pensiveness interspersed with high giggly behaviour. Fred and Stella had already met the Jamesons and approved. Introductions were to begin to Becky the following week. Although she had never been allowed to entertain the illusion that Brindley Farm was to remain a permanent home, nevertheless she understandably wanted to stay. For the next two weeks her play was flat, silent mostly. She laid a number of white china houses out – some with black windows, some with lighter ones, and moved backwards and forwards with the toy car between the two of them. Slow, repetitive movements. My heart went out to her. Change was in the wind. The agony of not knowing weighed heavily. I longed for her to meet them. Tantrums here and there, nightmares and wet beds came into profile again. Soon it would be time. The local authority's adoption panel approved the placement. The way was clear. Fred and Stella, having met the family, could talk to her about them with authority. The special Mummy and Daddy, up until now a figment of imagination, had become real.

I think I liked them as much as she did. The introductions, carefully planned, became more intensive now. Becky had found a family who more than anything else wanted a little girl to love. Wanted her. And seeing the lie of the land, she strode on with confidence and a new self-assurance I had hitherto seen only in glimpses.

'God, Madge, it's as if she knows they're for her. It's as if she's known them all her life!'

Fred was bemused by the certainty of it all.

'She didn't want to come back here last weekend, after she'd been over there. An' all that worryin' we've been doin', me and Stella!'

Fred was feeling redundant.

We had been out with the camera, taking photographs of all the nooks and crannies on the farm, the lambs, Mabel Cow and the tractor shed. The pigeon's grave. The red flowering currant bush. This was to be Becky's last week at Brindley Farm and we wanted to gather it together in a Life Story Book for her – for future reference. There was a new air about her, a serenity, hard to put into words, but it was as if she had come to rest.

When our last time together at Brindley was over, Becky disappeared upstairs to change into her slippers. There was a sadness in the air which took the edge off the joy and relief which all of us shared.

'Feel as if I should be wearin' me bloomin' demob suit,' Fred muttered. Stella had made me a cake to take home for the freezer.

'Keep you goin', Madge. An' there's plenty more, any time you're passin, you will call in...?'

There was a polite knock at the door, the handle twisting this way and that as a small hand rumbled with the round brass knob. Becky walked across to us, waiting politely for a break in the conversation.

Stella anticipated her move: 'You know, Madge, Becky's such a polite little girl now, such good manners she has, an' she tries so hard...'

Becky had waited long enough.

'Madge, look.' She placed a small white plastic box in my hand. 'Open it an' look. You have to. Look what Uncle Fred gave me.'

Inside the box was a small silver heart-shaped locket. Fred and Stella looked on, smiling.

'Come on. Open it. Open it.'

She was dancing from side to side. I did as I was bid. The locket was empty.

'I can't see anything in there, but it's a beautiful little locket.'

'Well, there is. You can't see it, but it's there.'

'What's there?'

Becky looked at Fred, smiling, eyes wide.

'Shall we tell 'er, Becky?' Fred shifted in his seat with embarrassment.

'Well, it's just a bit pretend – a little bit pretend. I whisper to you.'

She moved across to my ear and whispered softly. Then giggling loudly.

'Say it then! Say it then! What I told you.'

'It's a little piece of Uncle Fred's heart.'

She stood close to me – a coy, beaming, delighted little girl.

'That's it,' said Fred. 'A little bit of Fred's heart. Cos you're my special Miss Muffet aren't you, darlin'. Always will be, that's for sure.'

He stroked her hair.

'Come on, now, then.' He stood up abruptly. 'We've work to do.'

'We got two. Another one for the Jamesons to keep, just in case she loses it,' whispered Stella, as the farmer's apprentice looked for her wellington boots.

I felt a lump in my throat. An exquisite moment. Ordinary people. Yet patently extraordinary. A privilege to be in their presence.

Becky's adoption was granted about nine months later. The Jamesons take her back to Brindley Farm now and again just to visit, and next summer holidays she will spend a week there. Stella found Rebecca Doll wedged down behind the wardrobe in her bedroom and sent it on by post. It was quickly returned with a note and a beautiful card. 'Hope it's OK. Becky says can you keep Rebecca Doll. She left her for you to find.'

At Christmas I had a cryptic card from Stella.

'With love and best wishes from all at Brindley.

PS Fred says to tell you we've got a couple more lambs some ewe didn't want. Lads this time – eight and six. He's having a helluva job getting the jackets to stay on. Blighters keep pulling them off. Any suggestions?'

Afterword

Becky exists very much as described. I was referred her case by the police, via the Social Services Department, when a number of attempts at interviewing her as a suspected victim of child sexual abuse had failed, resulting in hysteria. She is now adopted. Her social worker describes her placement as 'brilliant'. Fred and Stella exist too. Their portrayal represents a composite of two very remarkable foster families whom I have met in the course of my work. In this story I have taken limited fictional licence with two incidents: the meeting in the cowshed and the incident in the supermarket. In relation to the latter, Becky's life was peppered with such events, too many and varied to portray as they happened. Becky's good fortune was to come up against a couple with the wisdom and common sense which Fred and Stella provided. Many other children whose needs are overwhelming are placed in families who eventually find the continued emotional demands of caring for them impossible to sustain. For some of those families, at times naive and ill-prepared, the 'fostering experience' ends tragically in failure and recriminations for the adults and another rejection for the child.

JESSICA

'But Uncle Bob says I can't talk about me bottom – so I can't say nothing. I mean, I can't, can I? I'm not allowed.'

She was pacing up and down the room, puzzling, puzzling. I shifted my position on the grey leather settee, mind grappling for answers. Distractedly she paced, eyes flickering, trance-like, sometimes stooping gracefully to rearrange an ashtray on the coffee table on her way past, other times halting suddenly in her journey, fingers twisting the strands of her hair round and round, fists clenched.

'You think Uncle Bob doesn't want you to talk about your bottom?' I whispered gently.

'No, he doesn't. I think it's naughty and he's not allowed.'

'Jess,' gently. I got up and moved towards her.

'Jess. Can you look at me? Can you take my hands? Now, we're going to breathe slowly together. That's it. Deep, deep breath – in…and out…in…hold it…and out…in…and out…' Slowly she began to focus on me '…Slowly…now Jess…slowly… Calm… Jess…calm. Soothing…soothing… Jess…' For the first time today her body began to relax.

'Jess, come and sit down, sweetie.'

Gradually she let me lead her to the settee, body brittle still, but focusing now, focusing slowly.

'So many muddles, Jess. So many muddles for a little girl, eh?'

I picked up the furry rabbit puppet. She watched as I placed it in her hand, gently unclenching her fingers with mine, one by one.

'Stroke her, Jess, for a little while. Feel her against your skin. She can't move unless you make her. You're the boss of her.'

Her lips were dry, flaking. Her eyes still wild.

'Let's try again, Jess. Can we? Uncle Bob says you can't talk about your bottom... He says it's naughty to talk about your bottom and you're not allowed to talk about it? Is that what you meant?'

She nodded slowly.

'But why, Madge? I don't know why. Why? Do you not want to tell me why if I'm naughty?'

'Hold on, Jess. Just a minute.'

Another muddle was on its way, and I was losing my own bearings.

'Jess, can we go back to the beginning? This is a very big muddle, isn't it, and it's going to take some sorting out.'

Jess's muddles were like that...before you knew where you were you were hopelessly lost in the mire. Drowning slowly in a morass of muddles.

'Jess, Uncle Bob told you not to talk about your bottom to the taxi man and the lady in the post office, is that right, Jess?'

'But why, Madge? Is it naughty?'

'No, Jess, your bottom isn't naughty and it isn't naughty to talk about it either – but I think you must choose very carefully who you tell about your bottom, and the scissors, and the blood and yukky stuff and the other things that happened...'

'But why?' Her eyes turned to me, searching, searching.

'Well...because some people don't really want to hear about it, and they might find it very hard to listen to and feel sad and surprised that such a little girl knows about some of the things you want to tell them about. Uncle Bob and Auntie Ruth are your foster parents and they don't think it's a good idea for you to talk to everyone about it... It isn't naughty, it's just not a very good idea.'

'But why?'

'Because not all grown-ups want to hear about it.'

'No,' she suddenly exploded, grabbing my arm...pinching her fingers into my flesh. 'No! No! No! Why? Why? Why did he do it? Why did he do it, Madge?'

Eyes open now; flashing, defiant gaze fixed on me.

'Jess, it's hard for grown-ups to explain to you. Some questions have no answers.'

I was floundering now in my own sea of muddles.

'Well, why? Come on. Why? I want to know. Tell me. Come on, tell me why. Come on.'

Furious and demanding.

'Well, probably because he wanted to do it and you happened to be there,' I ventured apologetically.

'You make me sick. Bitch. Why do you come here? Why do you come here if you don't know why?'

She punched me full on the arm. The rabbit puppet left her hand and sailed across the room. I sat in silence watching her pace…up and down…up and down. Puzzling…puzzling.

'Oh, Madge, I'm sorry. Sorry… I'm naughty aren't I? I love you, Madge. You like me?'

She was caressing my face now, stroking my leg with her fingers. Sexual caresses. I moved my leg away instinctively.

'Jess.' I lifted her on to my lap. 'Jess, I'd like to give you a cuddle now, like Mummies give cuddles to their little ones. Not sexing cuddles. Just a cuddle… OK?'

Her body was taut and brittle.

'Jess, you're not a naughty girl, honest. Just a muddled girl. I think maybe I need to write a story for you so that you can understand. We could call it "Jessica's Story", and maybe we could put it on to a tape so that you could play it when you want to. Would you like that?'

Jessica sat bolt upright on my knee.

'Jess, I'd like to give you a cuddle but it's quite difficult to hug you. Can you put one arm over my shoulder and turn sideways a little. Then I'll be able to put my arms round you. If you would like a cuddle, can you do that?'

Slowly and reluctantly the arm jerked round my neck. The other hand held my chin and turned it to face her.

'Do you want to write? Do you like to write me a story?'

'Yes, I do.'

'But how will you know it's me?'

'I'll try to get it as close to you as I can.'

Jessica nodded pensively.

'I don't cry, do I, Madge? Will I cry in my story? I haven't cried, ever.'

'No, then probably you won't cry in your story.'

'Have I got any in my head?'

'Any what?'

'Any crying. You know. Tears?'

'Lots and lots and lots and lots.'

'How do you know?'

'I just know.'

'Have I got more than you?'

'Probably.'

'Why?'

'Well, because I've cried some of mine.'

'Well, I haven't.'

'I know.'

Jessica's Story

Once upon a time there lived a little girl. The little girl was called Jessica Anne. She was seven years old. Jessica Anne had milky, grey/green eyes with long eyelashes and thick, wispy clouds of brown hair tumbled over her neck and onto her shoulders. She lived with her Mummy Catherine, and her Daddy Joseph, and her little brother James in a red brick house with a grey front door near the racetrack. Jessica's house looked quite like all the other houses in the street but her house wasn't a very happy house. Jessica's Mummy and Daddy didn't get on well together and they argued and shouted and it didn't seem to Jessica that they loved each other very much. Sometimes it didn't seem to Jessica that they loved her very much either. Often Jessica's Mummy wasn't kind to her, and what made things worse was that her Daddy used to touch her body with his penis and kick her bottom with it. He used to do this lots and lots of times to Jessica and because she was only little she just had to put up with it. She didn't know why he did it. Jessica's Daddy got it very wrong, though, because he knew that what he was doing was wrong and that it was against the law. What was even more awful was that it used to hurt Jessica and she was often in pain. When she went to the toilet it hurt a lot, too, because he also used to put other things like scissors inside her which made her insides bleed, and he made her shout rude words like 'Fuck' and 'Shit' when he got excited and his face got red. This was her big monster secret.

Jessica's mind was very wise and she thought about it all the time. She used to wonder why her Mummy didn't help her and make her Daddy stop, because her Mummy knew about it. Sometimes her Mummy was even in the room when he was doing it to Jessica. Often Mummy wasn't there at all, though, because she got a job in a bar in the evenings. Jessica heard her telling someone once that it was to get her out of the house because the kids got on her nerves. Some nights Daddy put Jessica and James to bed on his own, and Mummy didn't come home till very late. Then there would be loud bangs and shouting downstairs and Jessica's Mummy would come and sleep in Jessica's bed with her. Jessica got very angry with her Mummy because she didn't seem to care for her like she wanted her to, and often she thought her Mummy liked to pretend everything was nice and nothing bad was happening. In fact, Jessica's life was a bit like one of those nasty dreams you have when you can't sleep very well.

Jessica didn't sleep much. She began to worry and worry and her mind began to work very fast. Sometimes she couldn't think very well, and often, when she spoke, her words came out a bit jumbly. She didn't have much space left in her mind to think about learning things in school because the big monster secret about what was happening to her used to clutter up her whole head. Sometimes she did funny things and people who didn't understand used to think she was odd. She didn't really play much with the other children at school and didn't have any friends although she did talk to her little brother James quite a lot. James knew, because Daddy had started touching his bottom too. Daddy said he was 'over the moon' when James was born. He had always wanted a little boy, he said. Jessica's Mummy didn't help much, in fact she didn't help at all because she used to say funny things, and Jessica used to hear her pretending to other people that Jessica was a bit mad and that you couldn't believe her. Sometimes it felt as though the big monster secret was the boss of her life.

Jessica wasn't learning much at school at all, and her teachers thought that maybe it was because she wasn't very clever. You see, they didn't know about the monster secret, so they arranged for her to go to another special school for children who don't learn very fast. Actually, they got it wrong too, because Jessica is a very wise little girl and her mind works very fast. Sometimes it works like a grown-up's mind and that's because her Daddy, and sometimes her Mummy too, used to treat her like a grown-up person. Her Daddy used to pretend to himself that her body was a grown-up's body and that she liked him to put his penis inside her, even when it hurt her a lot and she cried and screamed and said 'No'. Sometimes he used to be kind to her too, and sometimes when he was being kind to her she would wish that the warm cosy feelings could go on for ever and that the monster wouldn't come back. But the monster came back. It always did.

Jessica's monster secret wouldn't go away. She wanted to tell people about it. She tried to tell her teacher and she tried to tell Pam who was a friend of her Mum's, but the words came out jumbly and quite often big people don't listen to children, do they? Angelina, an Italian lady, was another friend of her Mum's. She was an especially kind and smiley lady and Jessica knew that she cared lots about children because she had seen her be kind to other children often and her house was full of stray animals that didn't have a home. Sometimes Jessica thought that big people would guess if she scratched her bottom again and again and complained about it being sore and drew pictures of bodies at school, but nobody seemed to pay much attention and even the doctor didn't notice because he didn't look at her bottom properly like he should have done. You see, they didn't tell him about children who have monster secrets when he was learning to be a doctor.

Jessica's headmistress, Mrs Banks, and her teacher Mrs Collinson were very wise ladies and they cared about Jessica. Mrs Banks used to look out of the window and see Jessica in the playground. Often she would be standing on her own just thinking and thinking very fast, and sometimes her mind could pretend that she was in a safe place far away where there were no monster secrets and the worries were little ones, like 'I forgot to clean my teeth last night' or 'will Mrs Collinson be cross with me for taking two biscuits?' When Jessica's mind took her to a safe place she would dance and sing to herself, because every one who knows Jessica knows she has a very beautiful voice. Some people even think she could be a pop star or even an opera singer because she knows how to perform, too. When Jessica was performing she liked to be just on her own and she didn't like other children to come anywhere near her. She learned that they would go away if she stared at them without blinking and with a kind of 'nothing' look on her face and wished very hard that they would go away. It worked every time, and it even worked with big people. Maybe that was why some people thought Jessica was odd or funny but she wasn't really. It was just that Jessica liked to know that she could make people go away by just looking. That made her feel big and strong and brave. Maybe we could call it giving them spooks. You see Jessica hasn't really told anyone what she calls it, so we have to guess.

Mrs Banks and Mrs Collinson used to worry about Jessica because often they could see her chewing her lips until they bled and they could see that a big, big something was weighing her down and down and down. They began to guess something was wrong although they didn't know about the monster secret, and they asked the lady doctor to come and see Jessica at school. But this doctor really didn't understand about children who have monster secrets and she went away again and didn't help.

One day Jessica's bottom was hurting lots and lots, and blood and yukky stuff was making a sticky wet patch between her legs. When she went to the toilet and did a pooh it came out in very big pieces and she thought she must have a great big hole in her bottom. Sometimes she wondered if the whole of the insides of her tummy would tumble out of the hole in her bottom, and it hurt to sit down. We mustn't forget, though, that this story is about a very wise and very brave little girl whose mind works very well indeed, even though sometimes it gets jumbled. Jessica decided what to do. She would tell Angelina. She knew Angelina was going to come and see her Mummy in the afternoon and she would just have to stamp and push and pester Angelina and make her take a look at her sore bottom. She knew what a big risk it was going to be, and that her Mummy and Daddy would get very, very angry with her and hit her around the head like they sometimes did, but she decided that anything was bound to be better than keeping the monster secret one day longer.

When Angelina came to the house Jessica's heart began to beat very fast and she began to get very frightened, but she took big breaths and acted as though she were as brave as a lion. She went up to Angelina and put her face right in front of her eyes and held on to her ears.

'Angelina,' she said, 'I want to show you my bottom. I want you to come with me into the toilet. I have got blood and yukky stuff in my bottom and I want you to look.'

Her Daddy's face began to get very angry and her Mummy went very red and she knew she was in trouble. Angelina looked at her Mummy and Daddy and then at Jessica. For a moment Jessica felt so frightened that she wrinkled her face up and closed her eyes, but Angelina did come with her and Jessica showed her her sore bottom and told her the monster secret. Angelina looked very shocked and sad and gave her a big hug and a kiss and promised to get her some help. She made Jessica promise to tell the police her secret too, because Angelina knew that she had to tell the police. Because, of course, Angelina knew hurting children like that is against the law.

Outside the toilet Jessica's Daddy was getting very, very angry and was pacing up and down. Her Mummy's face was even redder, and she shouted, 'Come on, Jessica, what are you doing in there?'

Angelina and Jessica came out and very soon Angelina went away. Jessica knew she would come back with help although by this time she was shaking and her legs didn't seem to be holding her up very well. For a while Jessica made her mind pretend it was somewhere else. She can do that sometimes when all the worries pile up so much that it feels as though they're going to eat her up altogether.

But Angelina came back, and soon both Jessica and James and Angelina and Mummy were at the police station. Jessica didn't want to let Angelina out of her sight, but nobody quite understood. The police people wanted to ask her lots of questions and wanted her to tell them lots of things about Daddy and what he did to her. Jessica's Mummy sat and glared at her and Jessica's mind was working very, very, very fast because the worries were piling up so much that everything came out jumbled. Her mind kept pretending she wasn't there like it used to do when Daddy was hurting her and the police lady asked her to make sure she was telling the truth.

You see, the police lady had to make sure she was telling the truth and wanted Jessica to tell her what had happened. The trouble was Jessica really didn't know which bit she wanted to know about because her Daddy had been hurting Jessica for a very, very long time, since she was little, and the police lady wanted her to talk about just one time, and Jessica didn't know which of the times the lady wanted to talk about, and all the time her Mummy was watching her and making angry faces at her and it was all jumbling and tumbling in her mind, but she wanted to tell the lady and she wanted not to make her cross. The lady asked her when it had happened, and Jessica didn't know which 'when' she wanted to hear about, because there were lots of 'whens', so she told her about last Thursday the 14th, but Thursday wasn't the 14th it was the 27th and the police lady didn't look pleased. It was very late at night then – about midnight.

Then they took her into an empty green room with a hospital smell and a sort of a bed in the corner, and told her to lie on the bed and put her legs apart. A man came in and began to put his fingers in her bottom. Jessica already knew about men who put their fingers in her bottom. She closed her eyes and waited for his penis to go into her bottom too. Jessica's bottom was hurting and her mind was jumbling and by this time there was no braveness left inside her. She screamed and screamed and screamed.

Soon after that big changes happened in Jessica's life, but things happened so quickly that the big worries in her head bounced and whizzed round with the little ones like dodgem cars, until sometimes she didn't know if she was standing on the ground or spinning or floating. The next day she found herself in a strange house in a strange bed with James, and she woke up and she had to go to another house to stay with a lady who called herself Auntie Marilyn.

Now we all know how hard it is to live in a new, strange place, but it was even harder for Jessica. You see she didn't know whether this was a safe place or whether new monster secrets lived in this house too. And we know, because we have already heard about Jessica's very wise mind, that this little girl can be very brave too and can decide what's best to do. Her wise mind told her to stay in her bedroom and not go anywhere, so that's just what she did. Auntie Marilyn didn't like that very much and made her come down. You see, she didn't understand about children really, and didn't seem to like Jessica very much. She liked James a bit better, though. Jessica didn't like Uncle Laurence very much either, because he had a very, very loud voice and any minute she thought he might come upstairs and tell her to keep another monster secret too. Maybe he might go and tell her Daddy to tell her off or even send her home to her Daddy, so she gave Auntie Marilyn and Uncle Laurence plenty of spooks and kept away. She listened and watched all the time very, very carefully and she wished and wished that she could go back to live with her Mummy just on her own, just Jessica and Mummy.

By this time Jessica and James had a social worker who came to see them. Her name was Suzanne. She had black hair and seemed to like Jessica and James. She could see that Jessica wasn't happy living with Auntie Marilyn and decided to find a family who could care for Jessica and James and keep them safe for a while until some wise people called a court could decide what was best for them. Suzanne was very good at helping children. She tried very hard to find a family which she could trust to take care of them. And that is how Jessica and James came to live with Auntie Ruth and Uncle Bob. They are called foster parents. They are a very different kind of family from her own family. They have three big children. Auntie Ruth is a soft gentle lady who has a lovely calm voice, and when she laughs her face goes all flushed and pink. Uncle Bob is very different from Daddy. He's a big man with a loud voice. Even when he's just talking it sounds as though he's shouting a bit and he likes to laugh and tease. He's a very big man who sometimes looks a bit like Tarzan and it sometimes seems as though he could make anyone do exactly what he wanted them to do just by opening his mouth. People who know Uncle Bob well know that he was a warm, fuzzy heart and that he cares very, very much. One of the nicest things about Uncle Bob is that he can sit little girls on his knee and talk to them gently so that the muddle in their minds slows down and down and down and they feel very, very safe, and for a little while all the muddles and the little monsters stop juggling and jingling around and the big monster secrets go away almost out of sight.

But Jessica didn't know these things when she came to stay at 27 Princess Road which is Auntie Ruth and Uncle Bob's house, and her mind was tumbling and jumbling again because there were lots of new Worries piling on top of the old ones. Sometimes she thought her head was going to burst and that there wasn't going to be enough room for another single, weeny worry and then another one came and pushed itself in. New ones came and knocked on the door to get in. The biggest new one was whether this big man called Uncle Bob might hurt her body and put a monster penis in her bottom. Jessica was very frightened. She managed to say a few words when she got there at first, but her voice came out all dry and croaky and her lips were all cracked because she chewed them so much. She took a deep breath and said, 'My name is Jessica and this is my brother James.'

James just stood and smiled and pretended to be happy. Everybody thought James was a very handsome little boy. Jessica didn't feel very pretty or happy. Sometimes she felt like an old lady, not a little girl. Some people said she looked elegant, but that wasn't a little girl's word, was it?

Jessica went into the living room and she saw the television, and she went into the kitchen where the big microwave is and Uncle Bob's wine brews in big glass bottles with corks on the top and glass loops which bubble.

Jessica's mind was still bubbling too, and soon she was performing her dancing and her singing all on her own and giving spooks to everyone in the room. You see, we know that that's what Jessica's wise mind tells her to do when the worries and the monsters are juggling about in her head, but of course Uncle Bob and Auntie Ruth didn't know that, did they? So they just watched her and smiled and looked a bit surprised and wondered what it would be like to have a new dancing and singing girl in their house.

After a while Uncle Bob went out into the shed to sort out some of his fishing rods. Jessica sat in the kitchen watching the lady called Auntie Ruth who was making some curry for tea. Jessica thought and wondered and wondered and thought very hard. She looked at Auntie Ruth very carefully and said, 'Will I be a special little girl in your house?'

Auntie Ruth was chopping onions and her eyes looked red and watery. She turned round and wiped her eyes with a tea towel.

'All the little girls in our house are special,' she said.

She wiped her hands and gave Jessica a chocolate biscuit, but Jessica wasn't hungry. She was just wondering, and her mouth was so dry she couldn't swallow. She wondered and wondered and wondered and nibbled on the biscuit.

When evening came it was time for the children to have a bath and go to bed. Jessica and James were allowed to bath together. Auntie Ruth ran the bath and poured some raspberry bubble bath into the water. Jessica watched very, very carefully. Auntie Ruth washed James first with the sponge all over his body. Jessica washed herself very carefully. She said, 'I can wash myself, honest,' and scrubbed very hard at her dirty bits in between her legs. Her bottom was soaking in the warm, soapy water.

Soon it was time to go upstairs to bed. Jessica had the bottom bunk. Auntie Ruth knelt down and gave her a kiss. Then she leaned across to switch off the bedside lamp.

'Auntie Ruth,' she said quickly, 'Auntie Ruth. When is it going to be light? Is it going to be light at six o'clock or seven o'clock? Is it going to be light soon? When is it going to be light? The dark won't last a long time, will it?'

Days went by and Jessica began to get used to 27 Princess Road. She slept in new bunk beds with James; she also had some new clothes to wear. Everyone told her how nice she looked in her new blue frock, but she didn't feel very nice. In fact Jessica would often go and put on her old dirty clothes because they felt as though they suited her better. Often she felt old and dirty anyway. Sometimes the muddles in her mind told her to look as old and dirty as she possibly could so that no big monster secret would ever ever come her way again. Sometimes the muddles told her that she was so ugly and so old and so dirty that nobody could possibly like her.

On some days Jessica's mind told her to listen very, very carefully to everyone talking so that she could find out what was going to happen and whether the monster secret was going to come back or whether she was going to have to go back home and live with it again in Daddy's house. So she would sit in the toilet for hours and listen to what people were saying in the living room, and whenever anyone came to the door she would run down and listen and listen and listen to see whether they had any news about what was going to happen. Uncle Bob thought she was just being nosey and told her off.

Uncle Bob's tellings off weren't big tellings off. He just made his voice a bit louder and looked angry, but they made the worry box in Jessica's mind spin and jingle again. Often she wouldn't hear the words because in her mind she was dancing and singing and she was on the stage. If he got very cross Uncle Bob would send her to bed and that didn't matter because when she was in bed she could spend lots of time being somewhere else in her head. She told Uncle Bob once that she didn't mind being sent to bed at all when he got cross, but that seemed to make him even crosser. You see, Uncle Bob thought that sending little girls to bed when they were naughty was much better than smacking them, and of course he was right, wasn't he? But he didn't know much about little girls who had worries and monster secrets like Jessica had, because he'd probably never had any monster secrets of his own to keep when he was a little boy.

Uncle Bob and Auntie Ruth would sit and talk after the children went to bed and wonder how best to help Jessica and James be happy. They did things together like going on trips, going shopping and one day they pressed lots of apples into a big lot of mushy juice with a cider press, and Jessica and James worked hard and got covered in slushy, mushy apple juice. Jessica loved to do things like that because she could forget about all the worries and just be a little girl. Another time big Anna, Auntie Ruth's daughter, rolled her up in the snow and that was lovely too. She was screeching and shouting and flapping her arms and the cold snow on her face was making it tingle, and afterwards she giggled and giggled and giggled. Then she had a big warm bath and Auntie Ruth would wrap her in a big towel and she would feel very warm and loved and very safe. Auntie Ruth and Uncle Bob, you see, were getting very, very fond of Jessica and sometimes they wished she and James could be in their family for a long time. But they knew, too, that they would have to wait and see what the wise people were deciding in court. They decided to ask the wise people if Jessica and James could stay for a long time.

The cosy, fuzzy bathtowel feelings sometimes stayed for a little while, but soon they were gone again and the worries came back. They started like wiggly niggles and grew bigger and bigger and bigger. There was one special wiggly niggle which crept into her mind when she sat near Uncle Bob, for she used to watch and watch and watch his face to see if his cheek dropped a little and his eyes turned to her. You see, she knew from when she lived with Daddy that you could know when the monster secret would be on its way, from the look on big men's faces. Or sometimes she would try to please Uncle Bob by stroking his chest and giving him sloppy kisses on the lips and inside his mouth with her tongue, and sometimes she even thought about touching his monster, which she could just see the shape of under his trousers. But Uncle Bob didn't like that, and she could see that it didn't make Uncle pleased at all, so she tried to see if it made Uncle Bob's son Paul pleased; but kissing him like that just made him look squirmy, so she gave him a bit of spook with her eyes. In fact, Auntie Ruth and Uncle Bob started to teach her a different kind of kissing which you do with your mouth closed on people's cheeks before you go to bed. She thought that that was a bit silly, but she did it just to please them. In fact, Jessica would do almost anything to please any big person, especially if it was a man, just in case they might have a monster secret.

Now you may be wondering what has happened to Jessica's Mummy, Catherine, and you know it's pretty certain that if you were to ask Jessica, Jessica would probably tell you that one of the biggest worries which are jangling in her head is that she doesn't really know what is happening in her Mummy's life. Because, you see, Jessica hasn't lived with Mummy since just after she went to the police station. She lives in a new house now, but Jessica hasn't seen it. But she does see her Mummy twice every week when she comes to see her at 27 Princess Road. She knows her Mummy has moved into a new house on her own, and that Daddy still lives in the old house on his own. Jessica's Mummy has a new man who spends every day with her. She doesn't seem so cross with Jessica as she was in the police station, but maybe that's because she doesn't have to live with Daddy any more. Sometimes Jessica wants her Mum to cuddle her and love her because a big part of her loves her Mum very much, but then some of the big angries climb out of her tummy into her throat and she doesn't even want to look at her Mummy ever again. So she gives her big, big spooks and then goes into the place in her mind where nobody can reach her, and Jessica's Mummy says, 'What's the matter with you, Jessica? Give Mummy a kiss.'

When Jessica's Mummy comes to see her she says that everything is going to be just fine and that she wants both Jessica and James to come back and live with her. She promises to take very good care of Jessica and James when they come to live with her in her new house, and says she's very angry with Daddy and she's never, ever going to live with him again.

There are some times when she looks very sad when she comes, but most of the time she looks much better than she did when she lived with Daddy. In fact she's had her hair done and sometimes wears new clothes when she comes. She seems to want to put the monster secret to the back of her mind. And not only that, but she's still getting some of it wrong for sure, because she's still telling people she didn't know anything about Jessica's monster secret. Often after she sees her Mum and her mind box is jangling and leaping off into the safer place we talked about before, the muddles tell her that it's all Jessica's fault anyway, because if Jessica hadn't told Angelina then none of this would have happened. Then another niggle tells her that maybe Mummy is right and nothing happened to her at all. Maybe it's all in her head. And then Jessica's worries and jangles and wiggly niggles and big monsters threaten to eat her up altogether, and before she knows it her lips are cutting themselves and bleeding and her old clothes come out of the laundry basket and it seems as though she's been singing and dancing and laughing 'ha ha ha' for hundreds of years, and Jessica's life still seems a bit like one of those bad dreams we talked about before.

And what made it even worse was that Jessica heard that the police people had gone to see her Daddy and asked him to come down to the police station. They asked him about Jessica's bottom and, do you know, he said he didn't know anything about it! The other man who put his fingers in her bottom in the police station was a doctor. When he told Daddy that Jessica's bottom was hurting and sore and that he knew someone had hurt her bottom, Daddy just said it must have been somebody else.

Some people might say that Daddy was wicked and horrid to tell lies like that, and other people feel very cross with him, but we know because we know about Jessica's story that Daddy is just Daddy and that's how it is. And we know that he has been doing very silly things for quite a long time. If he wasn't a bit silly he wouldn't have hurt Jessica and James, would he? And anybody can understand why Jessica has such a lot of angries in her tummy when she thinks about him and that she doesn't want to see him.

You see, we mustn't forget that everybody else in her family is still holding on to big bits of monster secret and trying not to let anybody know. We know that Jessica's Daddy says he thinks it was somebody else, and Jessica's Mummy says she didn't know anything about it, and little James gets churny tummies about it, and smiles happy smiles even though he is sad, and doesn't say anything about it to other people. (James has got his own story which we can write about when we understand about James.) So really the only person who's told anybody is Jessica, you see, and it still comes out a little jumbley, although even the jumbles which come out of her mouth are truth jumbles.

Mummy carried on coming twice a week, though, and sometimes Suzanne came with her. Sometimes Suzanne tried to teach her Mummy new things to do with her children so that they could all be happier if the children went to live at home. Suzanne didn't know, you see, that most of the monster secret was still being kept, and everybody thought for a while that Jessica's Mummy really didn't know anything about it at all.

All this time the wise people who decide about children were scratching their heads and wondering what to do. Sometimes their heads got a bit like muddle pots too, because it's quite hard when you have to decide and decide and decide and try to get it right every time. But the wise people knew that Jessica and James were very important little people and the wise people had heard about monster secrets before, because they happen in other families too. So they asked a lady called Madge to go to see everybody and try to help them to get things absolutely right for Jessica.

Madge has another name which is called a Guardian ad Litem, but she isn't called Madge Guardian ad Litem; her name is Madge Bray.

One day she came to see Jessica at 27 Princess Road and sat down with her and tried to understand about her monster secret and her wiggly niggles and muddles and her giving spooks and singing and dancing and all the other things which are part of Jessica. Jessica liked Madge because she was big and round and cuddly and she always wore bright clothes and earrings, and Madge always tried to explain things and sort out the muddles a bit. At first she thought Jessica was a very pretty little girl, and it took just a little while for her to realise what a very special little girl Jessica was, and how lucky she was that Jessica had come into her life. For Jessica had many things to teach Madge about being brave like a lion and strong like an elephant and wise like an owl, and she was very, very glad she had met Jessica because Jessica could also help her understand about how to help other little girls who had monster secrets in their lives. Madge has a toybox in the back of her car with lots of things in it which help children to talk about monster secrets.

One day Madge brought her toybox in and asked Jessica if she would like to play. Inside the box there were many different toys. Dolls with happy and sad faces, wiggly worms, monster spiders, frogs which sat on each other's backs and jumped along, magic pencils which drew secrets, tummy balloons, a wise hedgehog puppet and a not-very-clever rabbit which you put on your hand. But Jessica didn't want to play with any of them. In fact she was much too grown up to play with toys. She sat on the settee, folded her arms, crossed her legs and said, 'I'm not a little girl; I'm nearly eight.'

'Oh, I see,' Madge said. 'Does your wise mind want to say anything?'

'Yes, it does, but it's singing; dancing; crying; it's nice; it's beautiful; it's copilashon; copilashon; it's balldrey; it's beautiful; it's calm; and nice; nice; very handsome; and colderey ta; it's a colderation; and rum tee tum tee tum a lovely girl; it's an old lady; I'm an old lady; I'm a lovely girl; I'm an old lady; I'm a lovely girl; and friends and friends and friends,' she sang and sang and sang and sang and Madge listened and listened and beat time to Jessica's tune.

One of the things which Madge did was to ask Andy Carter to help her understand about Jessica. Andy is a gentle sort of man who talks very slowly and softly and sits on the floor when he talks to people. He also happens to be a doctor, so really he is called Dr Andy Carter. He has a very wise mind which knows lots about children with monster secrets and jingle jangle dodgems and worry piles in their heads. Jessica showed him, with a doll which was like a real person, what Daddy had done to her bottom, and James even managed to let him know a little bit about what had happened to him too. Then Angelina Massocchi came to join them as well, and it was a lovely surprise to see her again, although Jessica did wonder afterwards why she had come. And then Mummy came and Jessica told Andy, while Mummy was there, that

Mummy had been there sometimes when Daddy had hurt her bottom with his penis, but Mummy said she hadn't at all. Dr Carter believed Jessica, and not her Mummy. Uncle Bob and Auntie Ruth came in too, and it was the first time they really understood about what had happened to Jessica, and just how brave she had been.

Before that, you see, Madge had spoken to Andy Carter on the phone, because we know how Jessica's mind works very fast sometimes and Madge wondered if her body was working a little bit too fast too, but she wasn't sure. So Dr Carter told Madge that he thought Jessica's body was growing just fine and maybe just a little bit fast, but that it would be quite a good idea to ask another doctor who knew about fast bodies, since he really knew more about fast minds and monster secrets.

Now Madge has to go back and see what the wise people at the court say and talk to them about Jessica and about how we can get it right for Jessica and James and, oops, we forgot to say that that's another of Jessica's wiggly niggles which is making all the others jingle and crunch in her head, because she thinks and wonders and thinks and wonders about what's going to happen, and you might be wondering what Madge is going to suggest that the wise people do. One, two, three, go...

1. Madge is going to ask the wise people to make sure Jessica and James are kept safe and that no more monster secrets are going to come into their lives. That's very important.

2. Madge is going to suggest to the wise people that it wouldn't be right to force Jessica to see her Daddy even though he wants to see her, because she doesn't want to, and it wouldn't be the right thing to happen, would it? (Unless, of course, he was going to say a very, very big 'sorry' to Jessica for all the hurt he has given her in her body and in her mind.)

3. And she is also going to tell them that she believed both Jessica and James when they told her that Mummy knew all the time. Because of that it wouldn't be right at the moment anyway for Jessica and James to live with Mummy, because nobody can be sure that she will be able to keep the children safe, and every time she comes to see them she tries to make Jessica pretend nothing has happened.

4. Madge is also going to tell them how Uncle Bob and Auntie Ruth have begun to love Jessica and James and would like to live with them at 27 Princess Road for a long time, at least until the muddles go away a bit.

5. Madge is also going to ask the court and Suzanne if Mummy coming to see Jessica can stop, at least for a little while, because Jessica seeing Mum makes the jingles and jangles worse, and the fizzles and the dodgem's clank and explode in her head.

Madge knows that Jessica's mind will slow down and get quieter as the worries lie still, and only little tiny, tiny niggles, like 'What shall I have for my tea?' and 'Have I got enough pocket money left – I want to buy some sweets?' will want to come into her mind. You see, Jessica isn't ever going to forget the monster secret altogether because he is part of her life, but she can wave him bye-bye because he is going to wizzle and rizzle and shrink in her mind and become a tiny speck, and he certainly won't ever be the boss of her life again. And pretty soon, when her mind is calm and only teeny weeny wiggly niggles can get in, she won't even need to chew her lips or give people spooks or fly away into another singing, dancing world. And one of the nicest things about this story is that Jessica's mind is going to have such a lot of space left that she will be able to learn to read and draw and to go places and to choose lovely clothes and to have snowball fights and to press apples and to watch telly, and do lots of other things that little girls do. Auntie Ruth and Uncle Bob want to take care of her and love her, just like they loved Anna when she was a little girl, and she grew up without any monster secrets at all. And, guess what – this isn't the end of the story because inside Jessica another little part is going to come and live with the brave lion and the strong elephant and the wise owl, and it's going to be called 'the beautiful swan', and it's going to grow and grow and grow more calm and white and sparkling and beautiful.

Madge wrote this story for Jessica. Maybe it's a bit like giving her a present like an oak tree. And maybe when the monsters and the wiggles and the jangles and dodgems and the wiggly niggles come back, which they might for a little while, she can curl up in its cosy branches and lean her back against its strong brown bark and think about the next part of her life, with the new beautiful swan in her tummy, and the wise owl and the brave lion and the strong elephant who will be with her for ever and ever. But that's another story.

Jessica listened intently, index finger moving along each line slowly as I read, guided by my hand. She did not interrupt. At the conclusion she took the pages from me and spent some time stooped, frowning – poring over the lines of typescript again with her finger.

'Did you know it was me?'

'Well...' I hesitated.

'Well, how did you know it was me?'

'I had to try and think in my mind, what it would be like to be you.'

'How does your mind know, then?' she persisted.

'I don't know... I suppose I understand a bit about children's minds.'

Jessica nodded.

'Well, it is me...and you knew it was me, didn't you?'

'Mmm, I think so...'

'And you couldn't make me cry either...'

Afterword

I have often written stories for children which paralleled their own life experience in order to help them make sense of distortion in their lives. Jessica's story is an example of one of these. Jessica exists. Her story is largely real. I have changed only small details of her family structure and context. In real life this is only part of Jessica's story. Details of her mother's acts of barbarous physical and sexual cruelty upon her have only recently come to light. The sexual abuse of children by women is often mistakenly seen as a freak occurrence. In some quarters its very existence is subject to hot debate and it remains a can of worms which we are apparently particularly hesitant to open. Jessica now lives in a therapeutic community. Her future is uncertain.

POSTSCRIPT

Much heart searching has gone into the writing of this book. Although great care has been taken to disguise the identities of the children whose lives have been portrayed here, this book has been written unbeknown to some of them and without their consent. The decision to present the information in this way was tempered by the almost certain knowledge that for some, the motivation to read such a book would arise out of a desire, conscious or unconscious, for sexual titillation.

On reflection, there have been many times in the past when I have asked for permission from children and adults to share part of their stories to teach others, and without reservation it has been given. Children have often, unsolicited, drawn me pictures, written poems and stories 'to help other children, Madge', and 'to help grown-ups understand'. Adults, too, have sometimes, at great personal cost, written their accounts and shared conference platforms in order that their experiences could be used to further public and professional awareness. The challenge in writing has been to do justice to them, portraying them clearly and accurately with minimal use of artistic licence, for they already live their lives with misrepresentation and distortion.

Tracey, Michael, George, Zoe, Becky and Jessica: by the turn of the century these will be yesterday's children. They will have reached or be reaching adulthood, legally afforded the right to vote, and they will be expected to be capable of bearing adult responsibilities. They may even be parents themselves of the next generation of children. In broad terms their stories may have provided partial answers to an array of questions:

'Are the newspaper accounts true? Does this really happen?'
'Yes, it does.'
'Does it only happen in poorer families?'
'No, it doesn't. It happens in all social classes.'

'Is it usually men who abuse little girls?'

'Often, but by no means exclusively.'

'You mean, women do 'it' too?'

'Yes.'

'In many cases?'

'Yes.'

'Really? What about boys?'

'They are victims too.'

'Who is most likely to abuse?'

'Someone close to the child.'

'Do children lie about abuse?'

'Yes, often – they say it hasn't happened when it has.'

'But what I meant was, do they make stories up and say it has happened when it hasn't?'

'I think I've come across that twice. It's difficult for children to make up lies with information outside their experience.'

'How many of these children have you seen?'

'Our agency has seen hundreds, possibly thousands.'

'Do they ever get over 'it'?'

'Some do, some don't.'

'What does that depend on?'

'Many factors, but often on how the important adults in the child's life behave.'

'How old was the youngest child you have come across?'

'Days old.'

'Days?'

'Yes, days.'

'Is this a new problem, or has it been happening for centuries?'

'I think it's been happening for a very long time.'

'Why do we suddenly hear so much about it now, then?'

'I suppose because only in the last decade have we begun to understand the scale of the problem and the devastation it wreaks on many human lives.'

The questions go on and on. I have had conversations like this on training seminars, in airport lounges, school staff rooms, Women's Institute coffee mornings, witness boxes, tyre-fitting bays, old people's homes.

This is a perpetuating problem. It has woven itself into social fabric. We are only beginning to acknowledge the existence of the knots it creates. If indeed we do accept, and many do not, that these knots need to be unravelled, we are still a long way from discovering a formula which will even begin the process on a broad scale. We make the problem manageable by isolating and individualising it. In doing so we prevent the development of expertise and resources necessary to make significant progress.

Could it be that at the centre of the knot lie our own sexual prejudices – a fearful forbidden zone? We titter, we blush, we covertly buy pornographic videos, and visit prostitutes. Often the message our children receive is that sex is a private affair, a taboo subject, not quite nice perhaps, certainly seldom something we talk about openly. On one of SACCS training courses we ask participants to work in pairs and discuss a recent sexual experience. What most discover within themselves is the difficulty of the task, the sheer embarrassment, the shame, the fear that the information may go further. For some the task is an impossible one. Few find it easy. If we are patently unable as adults to share aspects relating to our own sexuality, how can we possibly begin properly to address the issues surrounding children and the powerful emotions involved in our responses to them? For they too are creatures with powerful sexual feelings.

In a sense maybe it is hardly surprising our current approach is either to ignore the problem or to provide crassly simplistic solutions. While senior politicians publicly castigate child abusers, the reality is that at present only a tiny proportion of those convicted of sexual crimes receive any treatment. There is little if any evidence that simply locking sex offenders up for periods of time without treatment helps them to channel their sexual desires to less destructive ends.

If we look briefly at the six children's stories individually, we can begin to identify some of the confusions in what is an infinitely complex jigsaw.

Tracey's rape had a definite outcome. A man was convicted. The focus of my work with her was to obtain evidence for a criminal case. The child's emotional adjustment to such a serious assault on her body could not be the priority under such circumstances. My services were not requested for the purpose of providing therapeutic help, desperate though the child's need may have been. In the event, it was Tracey's good fortune that the offender pleaded guilty. Had he not done so I could have anticipated a very difficult time in court accounting for the methods used, which in staid courtroom circles would likely have been viewed with circumspection at the very least and, depending upon the defence barrister's stance, with derision.

In law her assailant, until proved guilty by the court, is an innocent man, and any professional interactions with a child victim prior to the court hearing must be undertaken with great care and delicacy.

Over and over again at SACCS we are placed in an impossible position: gross abuse has come to light, the child needs urgent therapeutic help, but until the criminal court process has taken place it is dangerous to provide this help, for fear of prejudicing the case. The needs of the court – and within it the accused's innocence until proved guilty – take precedence over the needs of the child victim. No matter how desperate the child's plight, it is often not possible for therapeutic work to begin until the legal aspects of the matter have been dealt with. Children old enough to recognise their predicament often are forced to conclude that, for them, justice does not exist.

Michael, seemingly, remains beyond our capacity to care. His story highlights the fact that mere suspicion on the part of social workers is not enough. The courts demand proof. Social workers are not infallible people. Their gut instincts, and mine, may possibly have been wrong in respect of Michael. Imagine a scenario, however, where these instincts were not wrong. Michael, not yet four years old. Michael whose currency of life is violence, humiliation, and degradation. The slow, pernicious, daily destruction of a child's life. The vagaries of our legal system and vicissitudes of public opinion are what lie between Michael and a possible lifeline. And in the meantime, what we must ask ourselves is – how many Michaels grit their teeth in silence? And what sort of adults will they become?

What of George, the quick-witted, determined little boy who by the age of eight had learned to inflict his sexuality upon children weaker and more vulnerable than himself, for gratification? George, eroticised by early abuse, had a desperate need of firm boundaries which could teach him how to manage and control adult sexual impulses in a little boy's body. What was there to offer him? What ensued for him was further sexual abuse in a children's home, followed by a period of isolation in an overstretched and under-resourced psychiatric hospital which failed to isolate the cause of his difficulties. Fortunately this was to culminate in a placement with a foster-parent who, despite her ignorance and lack of training, struggled valiantly to care for him.

The burden which children like George place upon ordinary people such as Irene who are asked to care for them is vast. Again and again placements break down. In order to help George to manage his behaviour within acceptable limits Irene would need to question her own fears and prejudices about sexuality. Indeed many of us cannot acknowledge that children, like adults, have sexual feelings and erogenous zones which respond to stimulation. When George 'rubs his willy like Sam done', it feels nice. This phenomenon continues on the whole to be poorly understood. Indeed, for some in the caring professions it is still shrouded in the realms of Freudian Oedipal complexes.

Sex offenders, as a group of people whose sex lives depend on gratification from children, are under no such illusion. They recognise children's sexuality and exploit it for their own ends. Recent American studies of adult sex offenders indicate significantly high proportions were themselves molested as children. We need to know more about how we learn to develop controls and restraints around the sexual impulse and what factors are likely to erode these. There is a clear need for more resources to be directed toward research into this problem and into treating perpetrators.

Sexual abuse of children occurs through all social classes and the potential destructiveness of Zoe's predicament was unlikely to have been ameliorated by the material comfort of her circumstances. What was of fundamental importance was that she was heard and believed, albeit with initial reservation and denial, by her mother who, with help, offered her unconditional love – Zoe's best route to overcoming her difficulties. Zoe had begun a process of creating her own reality in her head – 'Spider Disease' – in an attempt to make sense of her experience. Had this process continued unchecked, it could clearly have been detrimental for her long-term physical and mental health.

Much research still remains to be done into the long-term effects of sexual abuse. However, there now emerges, mostly again from America, ample evidence to link adult psychiatric illness, and indeed some physical illnesses, with childhood abuse. In the present climate we as a nation plough many health resources into a 'shutting the door after the horse has bolted' approach, by the provision of adult psychiatric care. If we understood these issues more clearly, perhaps we could direct some of these resources towards concentrating our efforts into the Zoes of this world. There remains an embarrassing dearth of services in existence which offer effective therapeutic help to children who have suffered sexual abuse, and even for those who have the income to seek private help such skills are at a premium, and in some areas cannot be bought.

Jessica weighs heavily on my own conscience. My attempts to reach her fell short much of the time. Now, four years on, other children have pushed the boundaries of my understanding further forward. I begin to grapple with the knowledge that an innately sensitive and creative little girl, in order to deal with the overwhelming stress in her life, had dissociated her mind from the pain of her existence, creating an infrastructure of personalities in her head whose function it was to deal with aspects of her life which were untenable and threatened to destroy her. Jessica's influence upon me as a human being was profound. I tried everything in my power to reach her and to help her towards healing, but I now know that the level of my understanding at the time limited my capacity to reach her and help her deal with all the aspects of her fragmented personality.

I am not aware of any resource in this country at the present moment which successfully treats children like Jessica. In discussion with colleagues in the United States it becomes clear to me that the term 'childhood multiple personality disorder' could well be applied to her as a diagnosis. As far as I am aware this diagnosis in Britain is seldom, as yet, recognised in child psychiatry. What seems patently clear, however, is that as more cases of bizarre, planned, sadistic, sexual torture of children come to light, more Jessicas will emerge from the wood-work, urgently requiring therapeutic help. If we cannot as yet bring ourselves to accept that these cases exist, how can we possibly develop treatment expertise and resources?

In a sense Becky's story symbolises hope for the future. It outlines what can be achieved given the right setting and blend of skills. But Freds and Stellas and Brindley Farms do not grow on trees. They need careful selection, preparation, nurture and encouragement themselves, to give of their best and provide the quality of care in which children such as Becky are able to blossom. Becky was a child who needed a period of intensive help before an adoptive home could be found for her. Now, as a result, she has regained her strength, and with it a sense of her own power and dignity. She now knows how to give love and to receive it, and that she is worthy of respect rather than exploitation.

As for SACCS: where to from here? Together as a staff team we continue to refine and develop our work. Our aim is to expand the organisation in order that more children may benefit from the services we offer. This will mean further recruitment and training of staff. There are times when the organisation teeters on a financial knife-edge. There are also times when it threatens to consume every part of our lives. As an additional project, however, a decision has been taken to raise the money to develop a residential unit, where we can provide intensive therapeutic help for a small number of grossly abused children under ten years old who courts have decided will never live with their parents again. We will recruit and train prospective adopters for these children and continue ongoing help post-adoption as and when needed.

Each move forward is fraught with difficulty. Mud flies, missiles rain, darkness envelops, exhaustion debilitates. Another inaccurate sensational press headline breaks and editorial columns pontificate. Despite the inevitable toll that all of this takes on many professionals in the field, we can at least take some comfort from the knowledge that by the end of the 1980s we have arrived at a status quo which puts an end to centuries of silence and denial. The pretence that child sexual abuse does not exist has become an untenable position to maintain with credibility. This in itself has been a considerable achievement.

The task confronting us now is to endeavour to create a climate where children in such predicaments are able to come forward in the certain knowledge not only that they will be heard and understood, but that their wounds can and will be treated. So far our response has been dominated by an adult perception of the problem and by an adult-centred hierarchy of priorities. This, compounded by a lack of understanding of the impact of these experiences on the developing child, and the long-term consequences in adult life, has resulted in an overwhelming lack of appropriate resources. Only now is the problem beginning to be addressed.

Day in, day out, in homes across the country, pain and suffering is inflicted upon children within their own families. Children who are not afforded the status of individual human beings with individual human rights. Until we as a society can rid ourselves of the 'happy families' myth and bring ourselves to recognise and appreciate the nature and extent of the problem of child sexual abuse, then we will continue to invest next to nothing in seeking solutions. The challenge to each of us and to society as a whole must surely be to exercise our collective responsibility and act with resolve now, to offer these children an optimum growing environment where they can take root and flourish. For it is upon our current action that the future health of our community will depend.

The project, 'Leaps and Bounds', is now in existence. Our first tiny unit comprising four small children is now full. A second house is now being established.

ADDENDUM

Incest is the most unloving thing that can happen to a child. It's an abuse of power and an abuse of trust on the deepest level. It affects the child sexually, emotionally, intellectually and spiritually and, sometimes, physically. All the values that we as children have been taught are upset, because, as a small child, the world we know, the place we begin to discover who we are and what life is about, is the family we are born into. We trust our parents without question. Our expectation of them is that they will take care of us, feed us, clothe us, and, in all practical and emotional ways, be there when we need them. It never occurs to us that they might wound us. To be smacked for a misdemeanour is experienced as our world being threatened, we, as children, hasten to set it right again, to re-establish ourselves in their favour. So we say 'sorry', and receive the cuddle that holds forgiveness. We know that we are loved again. Our world is once more secure.

When a parent or well-trusted adult sexually abuses us though, things can never be the same again. We learn a whole set of different messages, while being required to live as if the original set of messages – of care and love – were still in force. To anyone else, our world appears the same. Only we know that it is not. Because we are children we don't understand, and cannot put into words, how it is different, but we experience it differently ever after. From the moment of the first instance of abuse, we are internally in chaos, living two lives – one which has familiar ingredients like eating, going to school, doing household chores, loving our parents – and the other secret life which holds pain, terror, shame, anger and great grief. We are confused by the conflicting messages, and overwhelmed with the burden of maintaining two contradictory realities, both of which raise deep feelings. As adults, we would be baffled if a friend sent us flowers and then hit us – it wouldn't make sense. But, as adults, we can choose whether we go on seeing them. For children, there isn't that choice – we are dependent on our parents for our very survival.

For many of us who were sexually abused in childhood, and for whom there was no help at the time, the repeated abuse 'trains' us to be victims. Without realising the consequences of what has happened to us, we move into adolescence and then adulthood unaware that training is affecting our choices and what happens to us. We become victims again and again in other areas and other times in our lives. We have learned early not to protest – sometimes threatened with death should we tell – and we grow up with all the confusion and the unexpressed feelings, not knowing that now we expect to be let down by the people we love, to be hurt by them. And when we are further abused, we don't relate that to the early abuse. We don't even know that there is any other experience of life, or, seeing others who do live differently, come to the conclusion that they are 'normal' and we are 'freaks'. By the time we are adults, there is a heavy build-up of painful feelings – rage and grief and fear – accompanied by extremely low self-value, a profound distrust of other human beings and a despair of life itself.

In exactly the same way that if we keep on pouring cups of milk into a jug, eventually it will overspill, so will the emotions we carry. Rage in overload can turn against ourselves in the form of drug or alcohol abuse, anorexia, psychiatric illnesses, prostitution, self-injury, attempted or actual suicide in the worst cases – or against others, manifesting as crime or emotional, physical or sexual violence against other adults or children. Even in less extreme instances, lack of trust causes difficulty in maintaining friendships, unfulfilling sexual and marriage relationships or a complete inability to form any close ties at all. When we get angry over some incident in our present lives, it can happen that it sparks off the huge pool of accumulated anger we are carrying, and what begins as a minor disagreement suddenly becomes an eruption of rage that is inappropriate to the occasion. Damage is done to the present relationship, and we are left shaken by the force of our apparently irrational rage, ashamed of our loss of control and our hurting of a partner, or friend. We become even more enmeshed in our feeling of inadequacy and 'badness', and don't make the connection between our present feeling and behaviour and our childhood experience of sexual abuse. When, in addition, we don't remember that abuse – loss of memory being one way of coping with such painful experience

— we have no possibility of making that connection, so we despair of ourselves.

Our healing begins when we can acknowledge what has happened to us — first to ourselves and then to someone who will believe us and can hear our pain. As sexual abuse is the most unloving thing that can happen to a child, then love is the key to our healing. Not the romantic or sexual love we mean most commonly by that word, but the love that is acceptance of the people we are. It's someone listening and believing: someone caring, and understanding the complex mix of our emotions: someone accepting all the rage, grief and terror we have concealed for so long: someone helping us to replace the old tape that told us we weren't worth anything, were guilty and dirty, with a true new tape that speaks of our value, our innocence and essential goodness, and of our ability to take control over our own lives, and to trust ourselves and others: someone, too, who will encourage us to play — to catch up on some of the childhood joy we lost. But the person who can enable us in these ways is the companion — we ourselves are the ones who make the journey to recovery and the journey is not easy. But it is possible. We can transform our original traumatic experiences into a new positive perception of ourselves as human beings who are completely lovable and loving, courageous and strong, taking power over our lives with pride, dignity and self-respect.

Constance Nightingale